WASHITA

C&C

CAMPAIGNS & COMMANDERS

GREGORY J. W. URWIN, SERIES EDITOR

CAMPAIGNS AND COMMANDERS

GENERAL EDITOR

Gregory J. W. Urwin, *Temple University, Philadelphia, Pennsylvania*

ADVISORY BOARD

Lawrence E. Babits, *East Carolina University, Greenville*
James C. Bradford, *Texas A&M University, College Station*
Robert M. Epstein, *U.S. Army School of Advanced Military Studies, Fort Leavenworth, Kansas*
David M. Glantz, *Carlisle, Pennsylvania*
Jerome A. Greene, *National Park Service*
Victor Davis Hanson, *California State University, Fresno*
Herman Hattaway, *University of Missouri, Kansas City*
Eugenia C. Kiesling, *U.S. Military Academy, West Point, New York*
Timothy K. Nenninger, *National Archives, Washington, D.C.*
Bruce Vandervort, *Virginia Military Institute, Lexington*

WASHITA
THE U.S. ARMY AND THE
SOUTHERN CHEYENNES, 1867–1869

Jerome A. Greene

UNIVERSITY OF OKLAHOMA PRESS : NORMAN

ALSO BY JEROME A. GREENE

Evidence and the Custer Enigma: A Reconstruction of Indian Military History (Kansas City, 1973)

Slim Buttes: An Episode of the Great Sioux War (Norman, 1982)

Yellowstone Command: Colonel Nelson A. Miles and the Great Sioux War, 1876–1877 (Lincoln, 1991)

Battles and Skirmishes of the Great Sioux War, 1876–1877 (Norman, 1993)

Lakota and Cheyenne: Indian Views of the Great Sioux War, 1876–1877 (Norman, 1994)

Frontier Soldier: An Enlisted Man's Journal of the Sioux and Nez Perce Campaigns (Helena, 1998)

Nez Perce Summer, 1877: The U.S. Army and the Nee-Me-Poo Crisis (Helena, 2000)

Morning Star Dawn: The Powder River Expedition and the Northern Cheyennes, 1876 (Norman, 2003)

This book is published with the generous assistance of The McCasland Foundation, Duncan, Oklahoma.

Library of Congress Cataloging-in-Publication Data

Greene, Jerome A.

   Washita: the U.S. Army and the Southern Cheyennes, 1867–1869 / Jerome A. Greene.
      p. cm.
   Includes bibliographical references and index.
   ISBN 978-0-8061-3551-9 (cloth)
   ISBN 978-0-8061-3885-5 (paper)
      1. Cheyenne Indians—Wars, 1868–1869. 2. Indians of North America—Wars—1868–1869. 3. Sand Creek Massacre, Colo., 1864. 4. Custer, George Armstrong, 1839–1876. 5. Black Kettle, Cheyenne chief, d. 1868. I. Title.
   E83.866 .G75 2004
   973.8'1—dc22

                                                              2003055235

Washita: The U.S. Army and the Southern Cheyennes, 1867–1869, is Volume 3 in the Campaigns and Commanders series.

The paper in this book meets the guidelines for permanence and durability of the Committee on Production Guidelines for Book Longevity of the Council on Library Resources, Inc. ∞

2   3   4   5   6   7   8   9   10

To Robert M. Utley,
For his inspiration and friendship

CONTENTS

Illustrations

MAPS

ACKNOWLEDGMENTS

I wish to thank the staff at Washita Battlefield National Historic Site for their assistance throughout the completion of this study, particularly former superintendent Sarah Craighead and Park Historian Steve Black. Bob Duke, then of the Black Kettle Museum, Cheyenne, Oklahoma, and now at the Oklahoma City National Memorial, also provided many materials for the project. From the Intermountain Region Santa Fe Support Office, I must thank Robert L. Spude, for his continued support of this work, and Alexa Roberts, who provided information about ongoing ethnological projects that benefited this study. Others who provided materials or otherwise helped in the completion of the historic-resource study include the following individuals and institutions: William D. Welge, director, Archives and Manuscripts Division, and Mary Jane Warde, historian, Oklahoma Historical Society, Oklahoma City; Neil Mangum, former superintendent; John Doerner, park historian; and Kitty B. Deernose, museum curator, Little Bighorn Battlefield National Monument, Crow Agency, Montana; Jim Cloud, Oklahoma Historical Society; John D. McDermott, Rapid City, South Dakota; Christine Whitacre and Lysa Wegman-French, National Park Service, Denver; Mort Wegman-French, Boulder, Colorado; Colleen Cometsevah, Concho, Oklahoma; Douglas D. Scott, National Park Service Midwest Archeological Center, Lincoln,

Nebraska; Anita M. Donofrio, Littleton, Colorado; Gordon Chappell, San Francisco, California; David F. Halaas, Colorado Historical Society, Denver; Paul L. Hedren, National Park Service, O'Neill, Nebraska; Paul A. Hutton, University of New Mexico; Lawrence Hart, Clinton, Oklahoma; John R. Lovett, assistant curator, Western History Collections, University of Oklahoma Library, Norman; Richard Sommers, David Keough, and Pamela Cheney, Manuscripts Division, U.S. Army Military History Institute, Carlisle, Pennsylvania; Douglas C. McChristian, National Park Service, Tucson, Arizona; John L. Sipes, Norman, Oklahoma; Margot Liberty, Sheridan, Wyoming; Towana Spivey, director, and Anne H. Davies, archivist, Fort Sill Museum, Fort Sill, Oklahoma; Gregory J. W. Urwin, Temple University, Philadelphia, Pennsylvania; L. Clifford Soubier, Charles Town, West Virginia; Thomas R. Buecker, director, Fort Robinson Museum, Crawford, Nebraska; Sandy Barnard, Terre Haute, Indiana; Paul Fees, Cody, Wyoming; Sam W. Vaughn, National Park Service, Harpers Ferry Center, West Virginia; Robert C. Carriker, Gonzaga University, Spokane, Washington; Loretta Fowler, University of Oklahoma, Norman; Dick Harmon, Lincoln, Nebraska; Jeff Broome, Denver, Colorado; R. Eli Paul, Overland Park, Kansas; Daisy Njoku, National Anthropological Archives, Smithsonian Institution, Washington, D.C.; Michael Meier, Michael Musick, and Michael Pilgrim, National Archives, Washington, D.C.; and Robert G. Pilk, National Park Service, Denver. I would also like to thank the staffs of the following offices for their assistance in the course of my work: U.S. Army Military History Institute; Denver Public Library; Western History Collections, Norlin Library, University of Colorado; Old Army Branch, National Archives, Washington, D.C.; Manuscript Division, Library of Congress, Washington, D.C.; Oklahoma Historical Society, Oklahoma City; Minnie R. Slief Library, Cheyenne, Oklahoma; and the Kansas State Historical Society, Topeka.

Last but not least, I would like to especially acknowledge Bob Rea, site supervisor, Fort Supply Historic Site, Fort Supply, Oklahoma. Throughout my work on this study, Bob went out of his way to ensure its success, contributing his extensive personal knowledge along with information and materials from his office library and his own project research while otherwise keeping me headed in the right direction. Thanks, Bob!

WASHITA

1

HUMAN BEINGS AND SAND CREEK

December 1, 1864, dawned uneasily along Sand Creek in south-eastern Colorado Territory. An anxious, freezing wind whipped across the stark, treeless plain, nudged the buffalo grass as it gusted over low, snow-specked hills and through silent arroyos. It was a wind whose lifelessness mirrored the horrific scene its currents now enveloped in their course. Precisely two days earlier, a village of Southern Cheyenne and Southern Arapaho Indians situated along Sand Creek had been suddenly attacked by mounted soldiers armed with guns, swords, and artillery. The fighting had raged for hours as the tribesmen sought desperately to save themselves. Many managed to get away; those who did not escape had been killed, an inordinate number of them noncombatants—women and children and elderly men—in an indiscriminate slaughter of profound magnitude. Their object secured, the troops marched away, leaving dozens of camp dogs to scavenge the site.

On this day the wind played over a landscape marked by death and destruction of hideous proportion. In a broad southeast-to-northwest swath incorporating Sand Creek and its adjacent lands lay ashes of the village, the hide tipis torn down and burned by the troops along with much of the property they contained. Scattered among the ruins and along their periphery lay some of the bodies—those who had attempted to curb the military assault by approaching the advancing column.

They had been the first ones killed. More of the dead lay in the stream's sandy, mostly waterless, bottom immediately west of the village. But a greater number lay bunched in groups beneath the creek's shallow banks still farther upstream, where the panicked people sought shelter from the guns and swords. There they had hurriedly congregated, frantically scraping out marginally protective pits in the sand to shield them from raining bullets and exploding shells. Amid mounting hopelessness, mothers and fathers fought with guns and with bows and arrows to save their children from the pounding torrent. But there was no way out, and as casualties grew, their resistance gradually waned. Those who managed to escape and flee upstream were surrounded and cut down by the troops in similar fashion, and their bodies lay scattered about for several miles along Sand Creek northwest of the pit area.

The acts of the soldiers following their attack on the Cheyennes compounded the gruesome scene. In several instances tiny children, who had somehow thus far survived, were shot down in cold blood. Then in a seemingly conscienceless, uncontrolled orgy of brutality, many of the troops defiled the bodies of their victims, a process that continued well into the following day. Souvenir hunting certainly inspired some of their actions, yet others presented the worst perpetrations of mutilation imaginable. Most of the dead, including women and children, were scalped. Fingers were cut off hands to get rings, ears taken as trophies, and noses cut off. The genitals of men and women had been removed, those of the former for use by soldiers in making tobacco pouches, those of the latter stretched frivolously over saddle pommels and hats. In some cases women and children were clubbed, their skulls smashed so their brains protruded. Women's bellies had been knifed open—at least one containing an unborn child. Most of the troops went about their business in an extension of the mob mentality that had accompanied the attack. Few officers interfered with the desecration; some took active part in it.

Two days after the carnage and one day after the soldiers departed, the corpses strewn over the frozen ground pretty much told the story of the obscene reality of Sand Creek. The destroyed village had belonged to Black Kettle, the widely recognized peace chief of the Southern Cheyennes. Others in the village included the Cheyenne leaders White Antelope, One Eye, Bear Robe, Yellow Wolf, War Bonnet, Big Man, Bear Man, and Spotted Crow. These nine men, all major peace advocates, lay among the anonymous dead, their remains desecrated along with the rest. Among these chiefs, only Black Kettle had survived, and in the darkness of evening following the slaughter, he managed to return and rescue his wife, wounded nine times. Together that night they stole away from Sand Creek, facing the cold, indifferent wind as well as an ominous future.[1]

The Great Plains, home to the Cheyenne Indians during the late eighteenth century and the entire nineteenth century, lie east of the Rocky Mountains and west of the Mississippi River and stretch north from the Rio Grande into Canada. Geomorphologists have long referred to this region, encompassing the present state of Nebraska, the western two-thirds of Kansas and Oklahoma, eastern Colorado, and the Texas Panhandle, as the central part of the Great Plains Province. This central zone, major portions of which were inhabited by the Cheyennes, is essentially a region of transition between woodlands to the east and desert to the west and is variously characterized by east-to-west rising escarpments that produce an almost interminable flatness but often include dissected terrain, subhumidity and gradually increasing aridity, decreasing forest cover, diverse erosional effects, and short grasses. Elevation ranges from extremes of five thousand to six thousand feet above sea level near the Rockies to fifteen hundred feet at the region's eastern limit. The neighboring Central Lowland Province protrudes diagonally northeast to southwest from eastern Kansas through central and southwest Oklahoma, injecting its characteristic topography of hardwood forests intermixed with rolling prairie. The physiography of the Central Region also includes a provincial subdivision called the High Plains, a broad, mostly treeless plateau less eroded (and thus generally higher) than the surrounding country, which includes eastern Colorado, the Texas Panhandle, and the western parts of Oklahoma, Kansas, and Nebraska.[2]

The surface of the Great Plains is mantled by eons of soil-creating fluvial deposition carried by streams from the mountains and laid upon a geologic marine-rock base as a graded "apron of debris." Several primary watercourses and their tributaries drain the central part of the Great Plains Province. These are, from north to south, the Platte River, one branch of which heads in the Colorado mountains before coursing northeast, then east, through southern Nebraska to ultimately feed into the Missouri River; the Republican River, tracing through eastern Colorado and along the southern fringe of Nebraska before dipping southeast into east-central Kansas, where it joins the Kansas, or Kaw, River, an affluent of the Missouri; the Smoky Hill River and its tributary Solomon and Saline Forks and their own collateral streams, all of which merge into the Kansas; the Arkansas River, knifing east from the Rockies through southern Colorado and Kansas (several of the latter stream's own tributaries—the Cimarron, North Canadian, and South Canadian—variously undulate southeastwardly across southwestern Kansas, western Oklahoma, and northern Texas); and the Red River, which flows east from the Texas Llano Estacado to the Mississippi and today forms the south boundary between Oklahoma and Texas. The region is noted for warm summers and cold winters marked by low precipitation, frequent and strong winds, occasional drought, and rapidly changing temperatures.[3]

Grass is the dominant natural feature of the Great Plains. Beyond the trees and shrubs bordering its water courses, much of the central-plains area is covered by vast carpets of short, shallow-rooted native grasses, known as grama, buffalo, and wire grass, that are nurtured by soils high in alkaline and low in moisture, reflective of the regional climate profile. Depending on specific area and/or moisture conditions, this vegetation is occasionally intermixed with other taller grasses as well as with sagebrush, yucca, small cactus, and other plants. The semiarid character of the region has dictated an adapted ability for many plant species to become dormant over periods of drought, pending renewal with the coming of revitalizing rains in the late summer or fall. Precipitation is a constant determinant of the vitality of grass cover on the plains; the variability of rainfall, shortages of which sometimes threaten endangerment of the sod cover, has historically affected the region.[4]

The presence of grasses, along with their type, determined the species of animals that came to adapt themselves to the Great Plains environment, which in turn influenced the region's initial human habitation. The mammals shared similar attributes grounded in such survival qualities as speed, mobility, stamina, endurance, keen vision and/or smell, and the abilities to masticulate different kinds of forage and to conform their water needs with its inconsistent availability. Creatures such as mice, prairie dogs, jackrabbits, pronghorns, and deer—even grasshoppers—provided ready food sources for coyotes and wolves. But it was the American bison (*bison americanus*), or buffalo, whose presence dominated the plains during historic times. Traveling in herds occasionally numbered in the millions, the beasts were large, ungainly, and slow, with weak vision and little fear of sound. Mostly, they grazed placidly but were capable of summoning great speed and mobility when alarmed. Readily adapted to the plains environment, the buffalo possessed stamina and endurance for climatic extremes of great cold or heat. They consumed grass, and their evolved physiology permitted them to survive long periods without food or water. On the Great Plains of the eighteenth century, they were ubiquitous, and their presence explains one important reason for the ultimate habitation of native peoples during the eighteenth and nineteenth centuries.[5]

Humans occupied the Great Plains for thousands of years before the more recent flourishing of Plains Indian culture in the area. Prehistory witnessed a somewhat intermittent succession of habitation that began as early as 10,000 B.C. and continued into the fifteenth century. The earliest human denizens included big-game hunters who pursued mammoths and other large mammals for subsistence. Following periods of fluctuating temperature and precipitation (5000–2000 B.C.), during which the region was seemingly largely devoid of human presence, hunters and gatherers reentered the region and foraged for smaller game and vegetal foods while also hunting bison. By 250 B.C. to A.D. 1000, more woodland influences reached the Great Plains, transmitted from the Mississippi and Ohio River valleys and mostly located in the eastern parts of the region. These woodland complexes gave way around A.D. 900–1000 to plains village peoples, who hunted, raised corn, and lived relatively sedentary existences in communities along rivers and streams in the eastern edge of the area but who often ventured west to the edge of the high plains to plant corn and seek game. These people manifested cultural traits that set them apart from earlier occupants, such as multifamily earthen dwellings in fixed villages (often protected with ditches and stockades), pottery, and varieties of artifacts fashioned from stone, shell, horn, and other materials. For reasons not altogether understood, but possibly because of drought conditions or enemies, later generations of the village Indians had withdrawn east and, when first encountered by whites in the sixteenth century, were living in fewer but larger communities generally along larger streams. Many of them by this time represented fusions and coalescings of earlier groups. These relatively large-populated agrarian societies, some of which embraced precursors of many of today's native peoples, seem to have peaked in the period between 1500 and 1750.

It was these protohistoric peoples whose cultures were first affected by the presence of horses, initially introduced by Spaniards in the course of their early explorations in the New World. Bearing attributes of strength, mobility, and stamina, together with propensities for eating grass and other vegetation, the animals would modify certain traits already present in these societies and influence a radical change in lifestyle and economy. Many historic village tribes had roots that have been definitely or speculatively traced to the prehistoric occupants of earth- and grass-lodge villages in the eastern plains. Also, white men exploring the southern plains in the sixteenth century encountered semiagricultural pedestrian bison hunters who had likely entered the plains from areas in western Canada. These people seemingly were gone by 1825, perhaps driven out by horse-mounted, buffalo-hunting tribesmen entering the area from the west and east.[6]

Among the incipient peoples who inhabited the prairies east of the Great Plains were a group of Algonquian hunters, fishermen, and agriculturalists who lived in earthen lodges. They called themselves *Tsistsistsas*, meaning "The Human Beings," or "The People," but in time were known as "Cheyennes," a name probably given them by a Siouan-speaking neighboring tribe and meaning "crazy talkers," a reference to their language. This semisedentary people originally lived in the area of the western Great Lakes and upper Mississippi River but had migrated west to occupy the buffalo prairies east of the Missouri River by the middle to late seventeenth century. With their acquisition of horses in the early eighteenth century, along with pressures from neighboring tribes, their migration proceeded. They joined and incorporated with another Algonquian group, the Suhtais, bison hunters who introduced some and helped solidify other religious elements of Cheyenne society, and the combined people thereafter gradually abandoned most of their horticultural lifeways and assumed the cultural characteristics of the classic buffalo-hunting, tipi-dwelling complex that typified the Great Plains Indians by the early nineteenth century. In time the ten bands of the Cheyennes occupied lands beyond the Black Hills as far north as the Yellowstone River and beyond the Platte River to the south. During the period of changing economies and migration, the Cheyennes had developed a strong friendship and relationship with the Arapahos, also Algonquian speakers possibly from the area of northern Minnesota, who themselves had relocated during the 1700s. The Cheyenne-Arapaho alliance, which included intertribal marriage, was founded as much upon mutual enmity toward the various Sioux tribes' regional domination as upon mutual trade proclivities.

In their societal organization, the Cheyennes' basic structure was the band, and it pervaded all aspects of tribal life. Spiritually, the people revered the Four Sacred Medicine Arrows of supernatural origin at the heart of their tribal religious belief. The Sacred Arrows, or *Maahotse*, embodied the Cheyennes' future welfare regarding subsistence and protection. They also exalted the Sacred Buffalo Hat, *Esevone*, which had been introduced by the Suhtais and possessed powers respecting tribal health and well being. These articles, forever in the charge of hereditarily designated keepers, coupled with the sun dance, were together the inspiration of Cheyenne existence. Politically, the Cheyennes were guided by a council of chiefs (Council of Forty-Four), consisting of older and widely respected leaders who deliberated over day-to-day matters affecting the tribe—including such actions as moving the village and determining the start of the annual buffalo hunt—and the assorted soldier societies, whose chiefs promoted tribal discipline besides monitoring hunts, overseeing ceremonies, and providing military leadership against enemies. Each of the ten bands normally contributed four chiefs to the council, while the remaining four were designated Old Man Chiefs, leaders who had previously served with distinction on the council. As band dispersal increased during the mid-nineteenth century, the Old Man Chiefs made decisions for the band that had previously been made by the full chiefs' council on behalf of the entire tribe.

During the early years of the nineteenth century, growing trade prospects connected with the Santa Fe Trail attracted some of the Cheyennes to the area of the Arkansas River valley. One band, the Hevatanuis, moved south from the Black Hills, while the others, including the Suhtai-related Cheyennes, stayed in the north, effectively creating two tribes—the Southern Cheyennes and the Northern Cheyennes—that nonetheless maintained familial, interband, and religious associations while evolving separate and distinct identities. By then too, a third group, consisting of the Dog Soldiers—a sort of hybrid military society that had evolved and expanded to include not only Cheyennes but Lakotas as well—came to occupy a zone midway between the northern and southern tribes. Thereafter, the northern bands took up residence in the area of present north-central Wyoming in the Powder River drainage and cemented enduring relationships with the Teton Sioux and Northern Arapahos, factoring significantly in contests with other

tribes and with Euro-American settlers from the middle of the nineteenth century forward. By the 1830s and 1840s, the Southern Cheyennes, including the Dog Soldiers, had become a dominant force on the
southern plains, horse-riding buffalo hunters with an acquired warrior
complex that challenged the territorial presence of other tribes that had
migrated under similar circumstances between the South Platte and
Arkansas Rivers. In particular, the Cheyennes developed a bitter enmity
with the Pawnees, on the eastern periphery of the plains, and conducted
almost continuous warfare with the Utes to the west and the Kiowas,
Comanches, and Kiowa-Apaches to the south. In 1840 the Southern
Cheyennes and Southern Arapahos (who had also separated from their
northern kin) reached an accord with the latter groups promoting peace
among them and fostering mutually beneficial trade with white Americans and Mexican traders in horses, guns, furs, manufactured merchandise, and whiskey.[7]

During the late 1840s, in the wake of the war between the United States
and Mexico, several events occurred to affect the Southern Cheyennes
and influence their long-term relationship with the United States,
whose own expansive interests were beginning to conflict with those of
the plains tribes. Perhaps most immediate, in 1849 a cholera epidemic
ravaged the plains, decimating tribes and killing as many as one-half
of the Southern Cheyennes; one entire band disappeared, its few survivors assimilated into those remaining. That disaster coincided with
the inception and acceleration of travel west by whites crossing the
plains on the overland trails to Oregon and California, a route that cut
through the Indians' hunting grounds and created general consternation
among them. In 1851 the U.S. government, intent on restricting the
tribes from areas of major emigrant traffic and settlement, opened negotiations at Fort Laramie, in present southeastern Wyoming, to gain the
Indians' compliance. The treaty negotiated there between several of the
plains peoples and representatives of the federal government acknowledged existing tracts for each tribe. For the Cheyennes, that area encom-
passed the region between the upper North Platte River and the Arkansas,
essentially the lands comprising southeastern Wyoming and most of
eastern Colorado. Yet many of the promises made to the Indians at Fort
Laramie went unfulfilled, and not every band (or individual) of every
signatory tribe honored the protocols, realities that brought longstanding confusion and continued distrust on both sides. Meanwhile,

the Cheyennes, Arapahos, and other tribes began asserting their presumed rights to what they believed to be their lands. Eventually, government troops arrived to protect American citizens, and trouble soon flared. In the north difficulties between the army and the Cheyennes arose in the 1850s, particularly during and following the arrival of troops to punish Sioux tribesmen for disrupting citizen travel on the overland trails. At Blue Water Creek in 1855, troops attacked camps of Lakotas, possibly including some Northern Cheyennes, in northwest Nebraska, delivering a disheartening blow and killing as many as eighty-five tribesmen. Exacerbating distrust and mutual enmity, the encounter was one of several signal episodes that came to characterize relations between the U.S. government and the Lakotas and Northern and Southern Cheyennes for the remainder of the century.[8]

It was only a matter of time before warfare with white soldiers directly affected the Southern Cheyennes and their Southern Arapaho allies. By the late 1850s, these peoples ranged across present Kansas and eastern Colorado as they pursued their hunting and warring routine with surrounding tribes, generally ignoring the growing inroads by whites into those lands. Although in 1857 the Southern Cheyennes had an encounter with the soldiers at Solomon's Fork, Kansas, their subsequent attitude toward whites largely remained one of tolerance and avoidance. But besides disease and the ever present military threat by the U.S. government, other matters respecting the presence of whites directly affected the Southern Cheyennes and other tribes in the area. One was the vast river of humanity that was cutting a swath through their lands—an unceasing advance of whites and animals that between 1841 and 1859 totaled more than 300,000 people and probably more than 1,500,000 oxen, horses, cattle, and sheep, all leaving well-worn marks on the environment. Along the Platte and Arkansas, the principal arteries of the westward march, grasses were consumed, while scarce timber was felled and burned from these rivers and adjoining parts of their tributaries. Directly tied to this was the growing competition for game among the plains tribes, now accentuated by competition from whites passing through the country, a factor that constricted food resources for the native peoples. Complicating the situation, a series of searing droughts struck the region between the 1840s and 1860s, drying up water sources and stunting or destroying grasses on which the Cheyennes' horses—and much of their life ways—depended. Moreover, the numbers of buffalo began to decline, possibly because of introduced diseases and overhunting but likely due to the cumulative effects of the droughts. The dearth in supply of—and competition over—the beast on which so many native societies depended for food, shelter, and trade created longstanding hardship and exacerbated other issues that together threatened the rudiments of the culture that had once seemed so alluring.[9] The outgrowth of all this was contention borne of cultural trauma, an instilled resentment motivating behavior ultimately directed against the perceived perpetrators of the dilemma. In 1849 an Indian superintendent who realized the problem wrote that tribal depredations were meant "as a retaliation for the destruction of their buffalo, timber, grass, &c, caused by the vast numbers of whites passing through their country without their consent."[10] Among the Cheyennes, reprisal was most steadfastly pronounced among the Dog Soldiers, who increasingly lost no opportunity to resist the Euro-Americans' westward thrust, but it was manifest among elements of the northern and southern bands as well.

The discovery of gold in 1859 along the South Platte River in present Colorado (then a part of Kansas Territory) only aggravated these conditions. During the resulting rush to the Rockies, and despite the passage of great numbers of whites into and through Kansas Territory, most of the Cheyennes and Arapahos continued their peaceable disposition. Factions headed by noted proponents for peace, like Black Kettle and White Antelope among the Cheyennes and Little Raven among the Arapahos, sought to maintain that harmony. But the unrestricted emigration, together with the movement and settlement of whites throughout Kansas and eastern Colorado along not only the Platte and Arkansas valleys but also those of the Republican and Smoky Hill Rivers, eventually led government authorities to impose new strictures on the Indians who inhabited the region. In 1861 Black Kettle, White Antelope, and Little Raven, among others, signed the Treaty of Fort Wise, an accord that surrendered to the whites almost all of the lands recognized for the Cheyennes and Arapahos ten years earlier in the Treaty of Fort Laramie. The Indians received a triangular-shaped tract adjoining the north side of the Arkansas River in eastern Colorado, where they would henceforth receive annuities from the federal government and learn the rudiments of farming. Yet the document did not represent the views of all Cheyennes and Arapahos domiciled in the Platte country, and those chiefs who touched pen to the treaty attracted lingering indignation from the Dog Soldiers and other Cheyenne bands

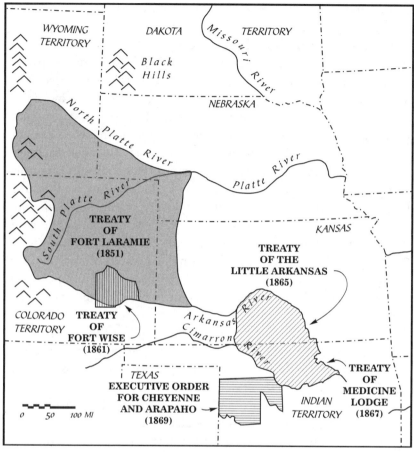

Changing Cheyenne Treaty Lands, 1851–69. Adapted from Berthrong, *The Southern Cheyennes*, 11.

bent upon resisting the land grab. Many of these affected tribesmen, notably the Dog Soldiers, who disavowed the actions of the peace chiefs in agreeing to any such territorially limiting arrangement, remained in the buffalo country, practicing their age-old vocation and refused to be bound by the treaty constraints. Likewise, the Kiowas and Comanches farther south rejected the provisions.[11]

The terms consigning the Indians to a particular tract of land presently coincided with the intention of the governor of the newly created Colorado Territory to gain total compliance from the Cheyennes and Arapahos, the principal tribes inhabiting his region. The Civil War had erupted in 1861, and Governor John Evans and other territorial officials fretted over possible secessionist tendencies among Colorado's population as well as the likelihood of Confederate influences in surrounding regions spilling over to disrupt the territory's relations with its native occupants. Evans and others feared that the tribes might be enticed into a Rebel design to cut communications between east and west by seizing the forts in the Platte and Arkansas valleys. Moreover, in 1862 an outbreak of Sioux in Minnesota had caused consternation among citizens on the plains and, however unfounded, promoted in Colorado an atmosphere of apprehension and suspicion against the Indians. During 1862 and 1863, however, most depredations by Indians involved not the Cheyennes, but the Shoshones and Utes who repeatedly raided the emigrant paths and mail routes in southeastern Wyoming. During the latter year, these activities produced campaigns by volunteer troops from Kansas and California that climaxed with the massacre of a large body of Shoshones at Bear River, in present Idaho, by a command under Colonel Patrick E. Connor. On the plains east of the Rockies, troubles with Indians became mostly confined to bands of Kiowas, Kiowa-Apaches, Arapahos, and Comanches bent upon attacking and stealing from wagon trains passing along the Santa Fe Trail. Elsewhere on the plains, traditional intertribal conflicts continued as in years past, all with little effect on white settlement in the region.[12]

Other circumstances also influenced Governor Evans's determination to rid the Colorado plains of Indians. He was an ambitious visionary committed to clearing the country so that travel and settlement might proceed uninterrupted and safely. Evans also wanted the transcontinental railroad to reach Denver, the territorial capital, and needed the Indians removed so that the project might go forward unimpeded. By concentrating the tribesmen on the Upper Arkansas reservation, as specified in the Fort Wise Treaty, Evans believed that they might be better controlled and thus kept far removed from the arteries frequented by settlers and miners. Hoping to convince the Cheyennes and Arapahos to accede to these plans, the governor invited their leaders to attend a council on the plains east of Denver in September 1863. But neither tribe was interested and no Indians appeared. Most of them regarded the treaty as a fraud and refused to move to the designated tract. They believed that the appointed land held few bison, whereas the plains of Kansas still harbored large herds. The chance killing of a Cheyenne man at Fort Larned, Kansas, also inclined the Indians against further negotiations. Evans saw the rebuff as a signal that the tribes were preparing for war, and he used it in correspondence with Washington authorities to fuel this perception. It is possible that the governor lobbied this viewpoint in order to instigate a situation allowing him to forcibly remove the Indians from all settled parts of his territory.[13]

The evolving scenario between Evans and the Southern Cheyennes and Arapahos would culminate in the Sand Creek Massacre—an event of immediate calamitous proportion for both societies and of significance for the Cheyennes' near future. Governor Evans's accomplice in the unfolding events was a former Methodist minister, Colonel John M. Chivington, an officer who had won several important victories over Confederate troops at Apache Canyon and Glorieta Pass in New Mexico. Chivington commanded the Military District of Colorado within the Department of the Missouri, whose commanders were often engrossed with operations elsewhere, leaving the colonel free to follow his military and political opportunities on the frontier. A reorganization of the military hierarchy in January 1864 placed Chivington's district under Major General Samuel R. Curtis's Department of Kansas, a jurisdiction that remained involved in campaigns in the Indian Territory and eastern Kansas, leaving Chivington on his own. As the war in the East drew more territorial troops away from Colorado, Evans asked for their return and lobbied for regulars to patrol critical supply and communication routes along the Platte and Arkansas. Washington authorities rejected these entreaties owing to then-current manpower deficits.[14]

Despite the transgressions of a few, evidence suggests that the Cheyennes believed themselves to be at peace during this period. Yet Colonel Chivington supported Evans's contrary view and likely sought a pretext for promoting it. In the spring of 1864, after straying livestock turned up in the possession of Dog Soldiers, Chivington interpreted this as a provocation and issued instructions to "kill Cheyennes wherever and whenever found." Troops of the First Colorado Cavalry clashed with the Dog Soldiers at Fremont's Orchard along the South Platte, and during ensuing months, the soldiers attacked other Cheyenne camps, in one case killing the Peace Chief Starving Bear, who had previously met President Abraham Lincoln in the nation's capital. In response, parties of Cheyennes struck back in a series of raids between Forts Riley and Larned in Kansas, but they abstained from igniting a major frontier war. In an effort to forestall further trouble, General Curtis's inspector general advised against further Chivington-like forays and urged conciliation with the Cheyennes and protection of the travel routes. He protested that the Colorado troops did "not know one tribe from another and . . . will kill anything in the shape of an Indian."

By then, such opinions no longer mattered. After more Cheyenne people were murdered, the Indians increased their marauding, and their villages soon contained large amounts of stolen property. Other tribes became involved in the raiding, including Arapahos, Kiowas, and Lako-tas, often without the approval of their leaders, and attacks against white enterprises along the trails bordering the Platte, Smoky Hill, and Arkansas Rivers in Nebraska and Kansas became common. In Colorado the members of one entire white family, the Hungates, were found murdered, and the public exhibition of their corpses brought outrage and fear, causing citizens in outlying areas to seek refuge in Denver. In a frantic message to the War Department, Governor Evans called for ten thousand troops, complaining that unless they were immediately forthcoming, "we will be cut off and destroyed." While the Cheyennes received immediate blame for the Hungate murders, Arapahos later admitted to the deeds.[15]

In July and August 1864, Curtis responded to the growing crisis by sending columns of soldiers to range through the country north, south, and west of Fort Larned, Kansas. The campaign yielded meager results but succeeded in opening the traffic route west along the Arkansas due to increased numbers of troops at the Kansas and Colorado garrisons. Curtis next expanded his control over the area by creating a single command, the District of the Upper Arkansas, overseen by Major General James G. Blunt, to encompass those previously monitoring the Indian situation. Similar administrative changes were made in Nebraska. When Cheyennes in that territory attacked settlers along the Little Blue River, killing fifteen and carrying off others, Curtis mounted a strong campaign of Nebraska and Kansas troops to search through western Kansas, but the soldiers found no Indians. Similarly, in September Blunt headed an expedition out of Fort Larned that presently traveled north after Cheyennes reported in the area. On the twenty-fifth two companies of Colorado troops under Major Scott J. Anthony found a large village of Cheyennes and Arapahos at Walnut Creek and engaged them, with Blunt arriving in support. Blunt's com-mand followed the tribesmen for two days before breaking off pursuit.[16]

Soon after these operations, a sudden Confederate incursion into Missouri drew the attention of Blunt and Curtis away from the Indian situation. The distraction allowed Colonel Chivington to step forward at a time when the tribes began abating their warfare to meet the onset of winter. Buffalo hunting to ensure meat for the months ahead now became of primary importance to the tribesmen, and leaders like Black Kettle, previously inclined toward peace, regained their influence. Black Kettle learned of a proclamation issued by Governor Evans urging the "Friendly Indians of the Plains" to segregate themselves from the warring bands and to locate their villages near army posts to secure protection. Those people who did not so align themselves would be considered hostile. Late in August the chief contacted Major Edward W. Wynkoop, commanding at Fort Lyon along the Arkansas near present Lamar, Colorado, of his desire for peace. In response Wynkoop led his First Colorado Cavalry to meet Black Kettle and the Arapaho chief Left Hand near Fort Wallace, Kansas, at the big timbers of the Smoky Hill River. There the Indians surrendered several captive whites, reportedly received from other bands, and agreed to meet with Evans and Chivington to reach an accord. Then Black Kettle and the other leaders followed Wynkoop back to Fort Lyon.

When Black Kettle and six headsmen arrived in Denver, the city was in turmoil because of the conditions wrought by the Indian conflict. The warfare had halted incoming provisions of food and goods, and citizens were still shaken by the Hungate murders. In August, Evans had published another proclamation contradicting his earlier one, now calling upon citizens to kill all Indians and seize their property, effectually extending an invitation for wholesale bloodshed and thievery. The governor had further received permission from Washington authorities to raise a regiment of one-hundred-day U.S. volunteers to be designated the Third Colorado Cavalry, and Chivington was preparing it for field service. All of these developments rendered Evans's earlier pronouncements insincere, especially with so many of the territory's citizens calling for vengeance. In addition, the governor needed to legitimize with Washington his earlier predictions of war and settle questions concerning the status of tribal lands in Colorado. And if the Indians went unpunished, Evans reasoned that they would be encouraged to renew hostilities the next year.[17]

At the council at Camp Weld near Denver on September 28, 1864, Evans spoke evasively to the chiefs, informing Black Kettle that, although his people might still separate themselves from their warring kin, they must make their peace with the military authorities, in essence giving

Chivington free rein. Black Kettle and his entourage, anxious for peace, accepted all conditions, and Chivington directed them to report to Fort Lyon once they had laid down their arms. But the Camp Weld meeting was replete with "deadly ambiguities." The Indians left the proceedings convinced that since they had already been to Fort Lyon, they had made peace, though neither Evans nor Chivington admitted such. Meantime, a telegram from General Curtis warned, "I want no peace until the Indians suffer more . . . [and only upon] my directions." Governor Evans notified Washington of the Indians' continued animosity and of the need to deal with them forcefully, noting, "the winter . . . is the most favorable time for their chastisement." Yet in consequence of the Camp Weld meeting, Black Kettle prepared his people to accept the Coloradans' terms and surrender themselves as prisoners of war.[18]

First to arrive in late October at Fort Lyon were 113 lodges of Arapahos under Little Raven and Left Hand. Since as prisoners the Arapahos could not hunt, Major Wynkoop delivered rations to the impoverished people while assuring them of their safety. Wynkoop's action, however, directly countered Curtis's policy of disciplining the people, and when word of his charity gained district headquarters at Fort Riley, tempers flared. Wynkoop was summarily recalled to clarify his actions. Major Anthony, of Chivington's First Colorado Cavalry, took Wynkoop's place. On arrival at the post in early November, Anthony denied the Arapahos further provisions and briefly disarmed them. When Black Kettle arrived at the fort, he reported that his lodges were pitched some forty miles away on Sand Creek, a location the major approved because he had no rations to feed the Cheyennes. Anthony told them that he was seeking permission to subsist them at Fort Lyon. Major Wynkoop, who the Indians trusted, had given them assurances of Anthony's integrity, and the Cheyenne leaders had accepted these conditions prior to Wynkoop's departure on November 26. Advised to join Black Kettle's people on Sand Creek, only the Arapaho leader Left Hand complied and started his few lodges in that direction; Little Raven took his followers far away down the Arkansas River.

While all of this proceeded, Colonel Chivington manipulated events in Denver that would result in the confrontation with the Cheyennes and Arapahos at Sand Creek. After a failed statehood vote in which he was defeated as a candidate for Congress, Chivington focused his efforts on preparing the new regiment—locally rebuked as the "Bloodless Third" because its members had yet to kill a single Indian—which was soon to conclude its one-hundred-day enlistment. Having only partly trained officers and men from the local community, the Third Colorado Cavalry had been organized by Colonel George L. Shoup, who had previously served under Chivington. Earlier that fall Chivington had envisioned attacking bands of Cheyennes reported in the Republican River country, but by November (and perhaps secretly all along), he targeted Black Kettle and his people; his every movement appeared calculated to that end, for the tribesmen technically were not at peace and were awaiting Curtis's consent before moving to Fort Lyon. In October, amid this charged atmosphere, Chivington armed his men and, with Shoup commanding the regiment, started companies south to assemble at Bijou Basin, sixty miles southeast of Denver.[19]

On November 14 Chivington himself departed Denver with units of the Third and First Colorado Cavalry Regiments headed toward the Arkansas River. The weather turned foul, and the movement was beset with drifting snows that impeded units from rendezvousing at Camp Fillmore near Pueblo. On the twenty-third Chivington inspected the united command, then all proceeded east along the Arkansas. The troops gained Fort Lyon at noon, November 28, where Chivington's unexpected appearance surprised the garrison. To secure knowledge of his presence and movements, the colonel placed a cordon of pickets around the fort and refused to allow anyone to leave. Major Anthony greeted Chivington and, apprised of his mission to find and destroy Black Kettle's camp as prelude to striking the Smoky Hill villages, gave his whole-hearted support to the extent of providing additional troops and offering guidance to the village. Some officers protested that Black Kettle's people were de facto prisoners of the government, awaiting only General Curtis's permission before they should arrive at the post, and that to strike them would violate promises made earlier by Wynkoop and Anthony. Chivington responded that it was "right and honorable to use any means under God's heaven to kill Indians that would kill women and children, and 'damn any man that was in sympathy with Indians.'"[20]

At around 8:00 P.M. on the twenty-eighth, Chivington led his column out of Fort Lyon along an old Indian trail that headed northeast. Little snow lay on the ground. His command was composed of Shoup's Third Colorado Cavalry and about one-half of the First Colorado Cavalry, divided under Major Anthony and First Lieutenant Luther Wilson, in all about seven hundred men bundled in heavy overcoats.

Mules hauled along four howitzers and the men's ammunition and equipment. Some thirty-seven miles away, along the northeast side of Sand Creek, stood Black Kettle's village of approximately one hundred lodges housing about five hundred people. Other Cheyenne leaders in the camp were Sand Hill, White Antelope, Bear Tongue, One Eye, and War Bonnet, and the few tipis of Arapahos with Left Hand stood a short distance downstream. Although some men were present, many had gone hunting, leaving mostly women, children, and the elderly in the village. Through the night of November 28–29, all were oblivious to the closing proximity of the soldiers.[21]

Chivington's force kept a lively pace through the cold, moonless night, so that the first streaks of dawn on November 29 revealed the white tipis of the Cheyennes a few miles off to the northwest. Advancing closer, the soldiers gained a ridge overlooking Sand Creek from which they could clearly discern the camp. Pony herds ranged on either side of the stream, and Chivington dispatched units to capture and corral the animals before the Indians might use them. As the tribesmen slowly awakened, the troops descended into the dry streambed and moved north along it with the howitzers in tow. Units of the First Colorado rode forward and took position at the east end of the camp. Nearby, Chivington halted the men of the Third Colorado so that they could remove their overcoats and other luggage. He exhorted them about the prospect at hand, then sent them forward toward the camp, whose occupants had gradually become aroused at the noise of the approaching threat. Nearing the lower end of the village, the soldiers deployed their force and fired on the tipis. As the startled Indians ran out of their homes, howitzers hurled exploding shells that drove the people to congregate near the westernmost lodges while their leaders tried to communicate with the attackers. Then shooting from the soldiers erupted everywhere. The leader White Antelope ran forward, arms raised and waving for attention, but a soldier bullet cut him down. Black Kettle, staunch proponent for peace and guardian of his people, raised an American flag and a white flag on a pole near his lodge to announce his status, but both were disregarded in the heat of the onslaught.

Chivington's command continued the small-arms shooting from positions northeast and southeast of the camp. Caught in the crossfire, the warriors reacted by attempting to shield the women, children, and elderly who ran to the back of the lodges. Most of the howitzer rounds fell short of their mark, though some burst over the village. As the soldiers advanced on horseback along either side of the creek, they kept up their shooting, and those on the north bank passed through the fringe of the camp. The people began to flee in all directions for safety, and many ran into and up the creek bottom, which appeared to afford a natural protective corridor leading away from the assault. Riding along either side of the Indians, however, the cavalry troops indiscriminately fired hundreds of rounds into the fleeing villagers and began to inflict large numbers of casualties among them. Meantime, other Indians exiting the camp at the opening of the attack had managed to catch horses and were running generally north and southwest over the open terrain as they tried to elude squads of pursuing cavalrymen. Many of them were chased down and killed.

But it was the mass of people in the streambed that drew the attention of most of the soldiers. As they reached a point estimated to be perhaps one-half mile above the village, these Indians—mostly noncombatants—sought shelter in hastily dug pits and trenches, most of them excavated by hand at the base of the banks. The Sand Creek bottom was several hundred yards wide at this point, and the people sought cover along either side, scooping out hiding places and throwing the sand and dirt outward to form breastworks. Having chased the Cheyennes and Arapahos to this location, the soldiers dismounted on either side of the stream and approached cautiously. Some fired at Indians braced in the pits beneath the opposite banks, while others crawled forward and discharged their weapons randomly over the top of the bank. Trapped, the people fought back desperately with what few weapons they possessed. Shortly, however, the howitzers arrived from downstream, assumed positions on either side of Sand Creek, and began delivering exploding shells into the pits. This bombardment, coupled with the steady fire of the cavalry's small arms, was overwhelming, and by the time the shooting subsided around 2:00 P.M., at least 150 Cheyennes and Arapahos lay dead, most of them killed during the slaughter in the defensive pits above the village or in the streambed as they sought to escape the soldiers. Chivington lost ten men killed and thirty-eight wounded in the attack. Throughout the balance of the day, parties of soldiers ranged over the area for miles around, dispatching any survivors they encountered. Nonetheless, that night many of those wounded during the carnage managed to flee the pits and join other escapees who, over the next several days, journeyed northeast to the Cheyenne camps along the Smoky Hill River. Surprisingly, despite the suddenness and ferocity of the Sand Creek assault, the majority of villagers, including many who were severely wounded, somehow survived.

Those who perished, though, became the objects of widespread mutilation at the hands of the soldiers, particularly of members of the "Bloodless Third." Over the next day, these largely untrained and undisciplined troops, including some officers, roamed the site of the destruction, scalping and otherwise desecrating the dead, compounding the basic butchery of the event. They then looted and burned the village and destroyed its contents. The captured pony herd moved south with Chivington as he continued his campaign, and the dead and wounded soldiers were taken to Fort Lyon. Chivington had planned to inflict similar treatment upon the Smoky Hill camp. Instead, he turned toward the Arapaho village that Major Anthony had earlier sent away from Fort Lyon, but these people had fled by the time the troops reached the Arkansas River. The Third Colorado moved upstream to Fort Lyon before heading back to Denver, where they were greeted on December 22 by a host of cheering citizens celebrating the "victory" of Sand Creek. Scalps from the Indian victims were ceremoniously exhibited at a local theater as the soldiers recounted their participation. As if the true number of deaths were insufficient, Chivington bragged of having killed between five hundred and six hundred Indians in his attack.[22]

Following Sand Creek, as word spread about the ruthlessness of the onslaught, questions arose about Chivington's account of events. The truth shocked and sickened most Americans. In 1865 the massacre became the focus of three federal investigations, one military and the others congressional, looking into particulars of the action. Senator James R. Doolittle (R-Wisconsin), chairman of the Senate Committee on Indian Affairs, directed an inquiry following receipt of information about the event that "made one's blood chill and freeze with horror." In the West General Curtis was directed to find out what had occurred at Sand Creek. The inquiries resolved that Chivington and his troops had conducted a premeditated campaign that resulted in the needless massacre of the Cheyennes and Arapahos and that the atrocities that followed were an abject disgrace. By then, however, the colonel and his men were out of the service and beyond prosecution for their actions. The Joint Committee on the Conduct of the War concluded in its assessment of Chivington that "he deliberately planned and executed a foul and dastardly massacre which would have disgraced the veriest savage among those who were the victims of his cruelty." The committee also resolved that Governor Evans had been "fully aware that the Indians massacred so brutally at Sand Creek, were then, and had been, actuated by the most friendly feelings towards the whites." Ultimately, Evans paid the price for his involvement in events preliminary to the massacre and was dismissed as governor.[23]

The Sand Creek Massacre devastated the Cheyennes. In the lives lost, both they and the Arapahos experienced familial and societal disruptions that have since spanned generations. But the event most directly carried catastrophic physical, social, political, and material consequences among the relatively small Cheyenne population (around three thousand people) and indisputably changed the course of their tribal history forever. Beyond the basic human loss, the massacre of numerous chiefs, occurring at a time when the Cheyennes were already experiencing fragmentation in their system with the evolution of the Dog Soldier band, ultimately had long-range consequences on the structural bonds of Cheyenne society. The Council of Forty-Four, the central entity of Cheyenne government, was ravaged by the loss of White Antelope, One Eye, Yellow Wolf, Big Man, Bear Man, War Bonnet, Spotted Crow, and Bear Robe, besides those of the headmen of three warrior societies. In addition, the losses in material fixtures, including homes, clothing, furnishings, and even artwork during the destruction of Black Kettle's village were immense, with immediate and future repercussions within the tribal community.[24]

For the Southern Cheyennes as a people, the sheer totality of the strike at Sand Creek disrupted the cultural and social fabric of the tribe. Although the people had experienced devastation before, notably in the loss of an entire band during the cholera epidemic of the 1840s, they had never endured such a sudden and complete disaster affecting elements of tribal infrastructure—people, government, economy, and material culture—that would so directly alter its future. It would require generations of recovery before the Cheyennes might regain a semblance of their diverse pre–Sand Creek Massacre leadership. Yet spiritually, the inner strength of the people and their usual reliance on transcendent forces enabled them to move past the calamity and carry on. For the Cheyennes, the true cost of Sand Creek lay in human terms, not ethereal ones.

2

WAR OR PEACE ON THE PLAINS

The Sand Creek Massacre had a major effect on the course of Indian-white relations, notably the implementation of U.S. Indian policy over the following decades. Although largely instigated by federalized territorial forces operating under the license of Colorado authorities, the event and its aftermath promoted an atmosphere of pervasive and nervous distrust between the national government—principally the army—and the plains tribes that confounded their associations and complicated negotiations on virtually every subject. In a single cataclysmic strike, the Colorado troops had eliminated most of the Southern Cheyenne chiefs who had favored peace. News of the treachery spread among the tribes like wildfire. As one official warned regarding an upcoming meeting with Indians when troops might be operating in the vicinity, "An angel from Heaven would not convince them but what another 'Chivington Massacre' was intended." The months after Sand Creek witnessed a spate of warfare across the central plains, with Cheyennes, Lakotas, and Arapahos striking the emigration routes along the North Platte, South Platte, Republican, and Arkansas Rivers. In the north, Sand Creek added fuel to the invasion of Indian lands already underway via the Bozeman Trail, instigating several army campaigns against the tribes as well as an unsuccessful attempt to militarily occupy the region. On the southern plains troops sought to subdue the tribes and impress them with similar campaigns. In 1865, 1867, and 1868, tenuous treaties arranged between the government and the plains Indians attempted to isolate them on prescribed tracts removed from the principal trails westward, but peace remained elusive, and the conflicts of the late 1860s and 1870s throughout the northern- and southern-plains frontier could find their origins, at least partly, in the Sand Creek Massacre and its pervasive, unsettling effects among the Cheyenne people.[1]

George Bent, the mixed-blood Cheyenne who was in Black Kettle's village at Sand Creek, years later gave the most thorough statement of the overall casualties within the various bands involved in the massacre:

> The camp was divided up into several groups of lodges, each band camped with its own chief. The people in each camp all belonged to the same clan [band]. Of these clans, Black Kettle's (the Wutapiu [or Wotapio] Clan) was the heaviest loser. Very few men of this clan escaped. Chief Sand Hill's band (the Heviqsnipahis Clan) had few killed; this band was camped farther down the creek than any of the others and most the people escaped before the soldiers could reach their camp. Yellow Wolf's band (Hevhaitaniu [Hevaitaneo] Clan) lost half its people killed, including the old chief, Yellow Wolf, who was then eighty-five years old, and his brother Big Man. War Bonnet's band (Oivimana Clan) lost half its people. The Ridge Men, Chief White Antelope (Hisiometanio [Hisiometaneo] or Ridge Men Clan) lost very heavily also. Chief One Eye was killed together with many of his band, and the Suhtai [Sutaio] Clan lost a few people, but not very many. The Masikota Clan and the Dog Soldiers, together with some other small Cheyenne bands, were not present. Left Hand was also with us, with ten lodges of Arapahos—say fifty or sixty people; and of these only four or five escaped with their lives.[2]

Following the massacre, the survivors of Sand Creek—perhaps as many as 350 people—made their way northeast, joining other Cheyennes in the Smoky Hill River country. As indicated by Bent, of all the bands represented in the Sand Creek village, that of which Black Kettle was principal chief, the Wotapios, suffered the most loss. It had been at the core of the peace faction of the Cheyennes, the part of the tribe composed largely of followers of the council chiefs who had favored trade and compromise with the whites, and the massacre only compounded an evolving alienation between them and the ascendant Dog Soldiers—the composite militaristic band of Cheyennes and Lakotas that had evolved since the 1830s and came to occupy the headwaters country of the Republican and Smoky Hill Rivers between the Platte and the Arkansas. By the 1860s, the Dog Soldiers—as well as the military societies existing within the various traditional Cheyenne bands—had accrued such great influence that their primary motivation, raiding and plunder, countered the influence of the peace advocates as represented by the traditional council chiefs. The 1861 Treaty of Fort Wise, by which the Cheyenne signatories had accepted a smaller reservation, incensed the Dog Soldiers, and they exercised intimidation over the other bands to renounce it. Even before the Sand Creek tragedy, at the Wynkoop meeting near Fort Wallace in September 1864, at least one of the chiefs, One Eye, had offered to help the whites fight the Dog Soldiers.

Despite the earnestness of Black Kettle and the few remaining peace advocates, Sand Creek effectually validated the military line as embraced by the Dog Soldiers. What happened following the massacre was that those smaller, marginal Cheyenne camps, neither participants in that event nor followers of any particular philosophy, turned their allegiance to the militant societies, thus gravitating away from the council chiefs and closer—physically as well as philosophically—to the Dog Soldiers. Together these people represented the primary core of the Cheyennes' ensuing resistance and conducted much of the retaliatory raiding. Even Black Kettle joined the war fever, despite temporarily losing his position to Leg in the Water and Little Robe, son of the chief of the same name killed at the massacre. In sum, Sand Creek aggravated a social-political schism already at work in Cheyenne society, and subsequent events represented the crescendo of that reality. Those refusing to participate in armed resistance consisted mostly of council chiefs (who had earlier favored peace) and their immediate families, estimated at fewer than 450 persons. By late December 1864, the disparate groups of Cheyennes, including the Dog Soldiers, were assembled along the Republican River, poised with 2,000 warriors to attack the emigrant trails. In early 1865 the Indians opened their campaign, striking Julesburg in northwestern Colorado Territory and beginning a rampage against stations and settlements up the North Platte. After several weeks, Black Kettle, tiring of the warfare, broke away and led his people south of the Arkansas, where they camped with Little Raven's Arapahos and villages of Kiowas and Comanches.[3]

As evidence of the political ascendancy and independence of the Dog Soldiers, as well as of the increasing polarity between them and the council chiefs, trader John Prowers testified at the military inquiry following the massacre that these people had effectually divorced themselves from their kin. "[There exists] difficulty between themselves [Dog Soldiers] and other bands of Cheyennes," said Prowers. "They have drawn off from Black Kettle's band, and refused to have anything to do with him. . . . They do not claim any connection to Black Kettle's band whatever."[4] It is important to recognize the distinction between the Dog Soldiers and post–Sand Creek traditional Cheyenne society because of the later course of U.S.-Cheyenne relations, particularly as they affected events leading to the government's prosecution of these people in 1868, which culminated in the engagement at the Washita River.

One of the principal disputes between the traditional Cheyennes and the Dog Soldiers emanated from the former's signing of the Fort Wise Treaty. Prior to this, the Cheyennes and Arapahos had acceded to the terms of the 1851 Treaty of Fort Laramie (though without Dog Soldier concurrence), which formally designated their territory as that land lying between the North Platte and Arkansas Rivers and from the Rocky Mountains east, embracing southeastern Wyoming, almost all of eastern Colorado, extreme western Kansas, and southwestern Nebraska. It was a vast area, but unfortunately, it straddled the major emigration routes and eventually conflicted with plans of Colorado territorial authorities, who influenced the commissioner of Indian affairs to negotiate a severe constriction of the Cheyennes' land base in 1861. By the Treaty of Fort Wise, the Indians settled for a tract between Sand Creek and the Arkansas River less than one-thirteenth the size of the 1851 reserve. It was this convention, adhered to by the peace proponents, including Black Kettle, White Antelope, Lean Bear, and Little Wolf, that so infuriated the Dog Soldiers and peremptorily turned them away from the Cheyenne traditionalists. The Sand Creek Massacre, which took place within the confines of this district, accelerated the division and pointed up to the Dog Soldiers, at least, the folly of their brethren's ways.[5]

As warfare escalated up the North Platte River in 1865, the government sent forth two expeditions, one headed by Brigadier General

Patrick E. Connor and the other by Brigadier General Alfred Sully, to intimidate, respectively, the Sioux and Cheyennes in what is now Wyoming and the Dakotas. A series of raids by Indians in Kansas beginning in June 1865 likewise prompted the commander of the Military Division of the Missouri to direct full-scale military operations against those tribesmen. But within months, mixed signals from Washington, together with the presence of Senator James R. Doolittle's commission, investigating Indian affairs in the wake of Sand Creek, negated the projected campaign. The Indian agent for the District of the Upper Arkansas, Jesse Leavenworth, also worked among his charges to prevent conflict. In response to the betrayal of the peace advocates at Sand Creek, as well as to attempt to stem the resulting warfare, the U.S. government finally negotiated with the wronged tribesmen the following year, offering indemnities for their suffering and damages. On October 14, 1865, at the mouth of the Little Arkansas River, the Cheyenne and Arapaho peace chiefs, respectively headed by Black Kettle and Little Raven, agreed to terms. When Black Kettle told the commissioners that only eighty lodges of his people were present (excluding, of course, the Dog Soldiers and other traditionalist Cheyennes living north of the Platte River), the federal representatives responded that only those people present would be bound by the protocols and that others might assent within five months. Black Kettle's address to the commissioners at the time conveyed some of the duress under which the chief had labored since Sand Creek. In obvious reference to the circumstances preceding the massacre, he said: "Your young soldiers, I don't think they listen to you. You bring presents, and when I come to get them I am afraid they will strike me before I get away. When I come in to receive presents I take them up crying."[6]

The Little Arkansas Treaty defined a new tract for the Southern Cheyennes and Southern Arapahos. Essentially, the boundary included those parts of the present states of Kansas and Oklahoma framed by the Arkansas and Cimarron Rivers to a point opposite Buffalo Creek on the Cimarron, where an imaginary line then ran north to meet the Arkansas. The Indians relinquished all previous claims to the country lying between the Platte River and the Arkansas, though the commissioners granted them continued residence and hunting rights in "the unsettled portions" of that region pending the extinguishment of other tribes' title to that land and the signatory tribes' removal to the new reserve. As partial redress for the Sand Creek Massacre, each signatory chief was to receive 320 acres within the tract, while each survivor who had lost husbands or parents was to receive 160 acres of land. The government condemned "the gross and wanton outrages" caused by Chivington and his men "while the said Indians were at peace with the United States, and under its flag." Furthermore, for their property losses sustained in the tragedy, the government vowed to compensate the affected tribesmen present at the treaty council "in United States securities, animals, goods, provisions, or . . . other useful articles." Because the Little Arkansas Treaty did not immediately include as participants the Cheyennes still raiding in the area of the Platte River and to the north, it served as but a partial panacea to guide future relations between the federal government and the Cheyennes and their allies on the southern plains. The treaty was ratified in the U.S. Senate on May 22, 1866, and proclaimed February 2, 1867.[7]

Meantime, following the largely unsuccessful army campaigns in the north, many of the Cheyennes and Arapahos, perhaps tired of combating the troops or desirous of hunting in their old lands, began moving south. En route, they attacked whites wherever encountered along the Platte and in one instance killed six people along the Smoky Hill River. These Indians had not been part of the Little Arkansas Treaty; in fact, they seemingly remained unaware of it or of its provisions despite the requirement that its signatories "use their utmost endeavor to induce that portion of the respective tribes not now present to unite with them and acceed [sic] to the provisions of this treaty." Thomas Murphy, director of the Central Indian Superintendency, believed that army attacks along the Platte had generated the reprisals against white emigrants and settlers. The trader William Bent opined that, while many Cheyennes were peaceably disposed, they were hard pressed to counter the influence of the intransigent Dog Soldiers, who were largely responsible for keeping the people from joining their southern kinsmen. Bent suggested that at all costs the Dog Soldiers be kept away from the people with Black Kettle and Little Robe for fear of instigating trouble among them that would threaten the new peace. Yet Interior Department officials appointed Major Edward W. Wynkoop, who the tribesmen had trusted before Sand Creek, to rejoin the disparate elements of the tribe and bring them into accord with the 1865 treaty provisions.[8]

Throughout the winter of 1865–66, the various bands and scattered camps of Cheyennes and Arapahos ranged from the upper Republican

River country of Nebraska south to the Cimarron River. Some, apparently disposed to peace, camped with Black Kettle's people below the Arkansas, and there were reports that even some of the Dog Soldiers had indicated a willingness to talk. In February 1866 Special Agent Wynkoop met with Medicine Arrows (Stone Forehead) and Big Head, who were camped with Black Kettle. Both initially spurned Wynkoop's efforts to gain their support of the Little Arkansas Treaty because neither chief wanted to remain below the Arkansas. Wynkoop managed to convince them, however, and they affixed their marks to a document accepting the treaty. His negotiations also resulted in the Indians' freeing a sixteen-year-old girl, Mary Fletcher, who had been captured along the Platte the previous summer. Wynkoop later met with representatives of the Dog Soldiers, who signed a document attesting to their own intended compliance with the treaty terms. Reporting his success to his superiors, Wynkoop told them that peace had been attained with all of the Southern Cheyennes, an overstatement of fact, but one he doubtless believed. He urged the government to assure the peace by keeping its promises to the people.[9]

As those Indians who subscribed to the Little Arkansas Treaty learned more about its provisions, they began having misgivings. Many were especially distressed about eventually having to forfeit interest in the Smoky Hill country, prime buffalo territory and their favorite hunting ground. Already the region had been compromised by the presence of a trail along that river to facilitate the whites' westward migration. Indeed, some Dog Soldiers threatened war if forced to leave the area, and whites long familiar with the Cheyennes expressed concern that those people would rather die than abandon the Smoky Hill. Ultimately, while ratification was delayed in Congress, Black Kettle, pressured by warriors of the soldier groups, disavowed the cession of the Smoky Hill country specified in the treaty. Wynkoop was dispatched to pacify the tribesmen and to issue a warning: "If the government is obliged to open war upon them, *all* the people will suffer terribly." After lengthy discussions, the agent elicited promises from the Cheyenne chiefs in the Smoky Hill country to comply with the treaty, including a notable statement that if "any of their young men hereafter . . . committed any act offensive to the whites, they would confiscate his property or if necessary for an example, *kill him*." Other chiefs, however, reported that the soldier societies among them, together with the Dog Soldiers, remained determined to close the

Smoky Hill Trail. Within weeks, several violent episodes occurred, resulting in depredations, including the deaths of whites by Cheyenne warriors under Bull Bear. Wynkoop, now appointed agent for the Cheyennes, Arapahos, and Kiowa-Apaches, tried again with his associates to placate Black Kettle, Little Robe, and the other chiefs, this time with gifts. In November, at a council at Fort Zarah, Kansas, he managed to induce the leaders to sign the Little Arkansas Treaty amendments.[10]

But the matter was not over. Although Major Wynkoop reported general contentment among the Cheyennes following the Fort Zarah councils, the military commander of the Department of the Missouri, Major General Winfield Scott Hancock, demanded that the warriors who had committed the killing of whites and the stealing of livestock be turned over or face attack by U.S. troops. Wynkoop was again pressed to investigate the subject and find out which tribe was responsible for the recent forays. Hancock had the support of Lieutenant General William T. Sherman, commanding the Military Division of the Missouri, and in whose administrative province the proposed operations would occur. Initially, Sherman believed that citizen complaints against the tribes were overblown, but he nevertheless projected the removal of the tribes from Kansas and Nebraska to reservations north and south, thereby opening a wide swath for travel and settlement by U.S. citizens. Word in December 1866 of the loss of Captain William J. Fetterman and eighty soldiers near Fort Phil Kearny, Dakota Territory (present Wyoming), at the hands of Teton Sioux and Northern Cheyennes, coupled with Hancock's reports of the Smoky Hill killings also by Cheyennes, served to intensify his view. Of the subject tribes he wrote: "They must be exterminated, for they cannot and will not settle down, and our people will force us to do it." Late in 1866 Hancock, still calling for the surrender of the offending tribesmen while gathering additional evidence against them, began preparations for a spring campaign against the Cheyennes. Further planning to demonstrate the power and authority of the army to tribes throughout the Great Plains, Hancock stated that the Cheyenne people "appear to be as deserving of chastisement as any other."[11]

Aware of the inordinate traffic between the Cheyennes and traders for guns and ammunition, Hancock, on Sherman's direction, in January 1867 ordered all sales of ordnance to the Indians discontinued in the area of the Arkansas River. The dictum touched off a debate between the commissioner of Indian affairs and the army. The commissioner maintained that existing statutes permitted supplying arms to the tribesmen for hunting, but Hancock rejected the argument because of the recent depredations by the Cheyennes. Agent Wynkoop sided with his charges in the exchange, but Hancock pointed to evidence of recent thefts of livestock by the Cheyennes from buffalo hunters and a wagon train as well as weapons and other goods from a trader at Fort Dodge. In the end, with Sherman's sanction and support, Hancock moved forward with his plans. The expedition would move into the Indian country and determine whether the Cheyennes and Kiowas wanted to talk or fight and grant them their preference. He would not initiate a contest. If the chiefs promised to adhere to previous treaty agreements, the army would leave them alone, but Hancock intended to warn them to keep their young men under control in the area of the overland routes. Sherman was intent on setting an example and urged getting among the Indians and killing a sufficient number to inspire the others to stay on the reservation and keep the peace.[12]

While deferring a planned expedition against the Sioux and Cheyennes on the northern plains because of ongoing peace initiatives, Sherman gave Hancock the go-ahead in the south, and that officer opened his offensive in April 1867. Fourteen hundred soldiers convened at Fort Larned, Kansas—troops of the Seventh Cavalry, Thirty-seventh Infantry, and Fourth Artillery. There Hancock met with a small delegation of warriors and chiefs, including Tall Bull, leader of the Dog Soldiers who were encamped at Pawnee Fork of the Arkansas, thirty-five miles west of the post, and delivered a strong lecture about war and peace. The next day Hancock moved his army up to Pawnee Fork to impart the same message to the remaining chiefs. The soldiers' approach startled the Cheyennes and Lakotas in the camp, many of whom feared another Sand Creek–type massacre; many abandoned the village before Hancock's arrival, and those who stayed were gone by the following morning. Hancock interpreted the vacated camp as a sign that the Indians meant war, and he sent troops under Lieutenant Colonel George A. Custer north in pursuit. But the people split into small groups, frustrating the cavalry chase, and by the time Custer reached the Smoky Hill Trail, he found citizens killed, stage stations burned out, livestock stolen, and his quest stymied by insufficient forage. Hancock, meantime, ruminated over whether to burn the abandoned Cheyenne-Sioux village, realizing that its destruction would ensure war with the Indians. Word from Custer of the devastation along the Smoky Hill finally

decided the issue, and over protests from Agents Wynkoop and Leavenworth, the general torched the camp.

With a vengeful reaction from the Cheyennes assured, Hancock
moved on to intimidate other area tribes. He met with chiefs of the Arapahos and Kiowas, cowing them with the same tones, then proceeded
west to Fort Hays, where Custer had repaired to await forage for his
horses. Hancock directed him to remain there until his animals were
strong and then to prosecute a vigorous campaign against the Sioux and
Cheyennes. The general then headed east to his Fort Leavenworth
headquarters, leaving Custer to his own devices. The Indians, meantime, exorcized over Hancock's burning of their village and property,
laid waste to the Platte, Smoky Hill, and Arkansas routes, destroying
stage and mail stations, attacking coaches and wagon trains, and engaging railroad workers. Cheyennes also attacked the garrison at Fort Wallace in extreme western Kansas.

Finally, in early June Custer set out to find and punish the
responsible warriors in an onerous month-long march of a thousand
miles that ranged through the Smoky Hill, Platte, and Republican
River country but that brought few and insignificant actions with the
Sioux. The weary column, some of its men having deserted and its
animals fatigued, struggled back into Fort Wallace with no decisive
encounters. One dramatic clash occurred when Dog Soldiers and
Sioux warriors chanced on a ten-man detachment headed by Second
Lieutenant Lyman S. Kidder, who was carrying orders to Custer, and
surrounded and killed them all. By late summer, however, most of
the peace-prone chiefs had led their followers south of the Arkansas,
leaving the bands dominated by the military societies and the Dog
Soldiers to continue raiding to the north. By then too, Kansas governor Samuel J. Crawford had orchestrated the enlistment of volunteers—the Eighteenth Kansas Cavalry—to help the regulars patrol
transportation arteries in the state. In August 1867 two companies
of the Eighteenth Kansas aided regulars of the all-black Tenth Cavalry in fighting several hundred Sioux and Cheyenne warriors at
Beaver Creek, Kansas. This action, plus Hancock's destruction of the
Cheyenne camp at Pawnee Fork followed by Custer's largely impotent showing (including the loss of Lieutenant Kidder and his men),
constituted the expedition's primary results and initial message of
intimidation to the Cheyennes and their allies. But it left only mud-
dled prospects for any meaningful immediate peace.[13]

Meantime, the chiefs who had generally favored peace and trade with the whites had clearly been intimidated by the prospect of Hancock's expedition. Black Kettle forecasted trouble with the troops and decided to move south with his followers, as did the Comanches, Kiowas, and Kiowa-Apaches, who also anticipated such difficulties. A virulent cholera epidemic that struck the frontier forts in the late summer of 1867 likely also prompted his removal south. Along the north fork of the Canadian River in Indian Territory, Black Kettle settled his people briefly near a Comanche village. There they bartered buffalo robes with white traders before moving on to the south fork of the Canadian, where they learned of Hancock's destruction of the camp at Pawnee Fork and the deaths of Cheyennes in a fight with troops at Cimarron Crossing. Black Kettle's people continued south and, on reaching the Washita River, found Little Raven's Arapahos. A few weeks later the Cheyennes moved up the Washita seeking buffalo and eventually encountered other bands of Cheyennes that had come south out of Kansas. War parties from these assorted bands soon rode back north to take part in and intensify the raids instigated by Hancock's action at Pawnee Fork.[14]

Then on July 20, 1867—in the midst of Hancock's campaign—Congress established a commission to negotiate peace with all of the warring tribes on the northern and southern plains. The commission, authorized in response to the recommendations of Senator Doolittle's report on the condition of the tribes as well as to the demands of both humanitarians and those who wanted the Indians severely punished, included prominent army officers as well as congressmen and political appointees. The purpose of the commission was to separate the "hostile" Indians from friendly ones and to remove all from the routes of western emigration, transit, and commerce. Headed by Commissioner of Indian Affairs Nathaniel G. Taylor, the delegation included Missouri senator John B. Henderson; General Sherman (whose official absence at the southern-plains councils necessitated the temporary appointment of Major General Christopher C. Auger, commander of the Military Department of the Platte); retired major general William S. Harney; Brigadier General Alfred H. Terry, commander of the Military Department of Dakota; Samuel F. Tappan, former officer of the Colorado volunteers, peace advocate, and friend of Agent Wynkoop; and John B. Sanborn, who had helped negotiate the Little Arkansas Treaty. While the commissioners dealt with the northern tribes, preparations ensued for councils to take place with the southern peoples at Fort Larned, Kansas, beginning in October.[15]

When Black Kettle rode into Fort Larned on September 3, 1867, he exercised little influence beyond his own followers. Although the attendant Arapahos openly blamed the Cheyennes for all the depredations that had occurred along the Arkansas, most of the acts had in fact been committed by Dog Soldiers and members of the military societies in the scattered bands of Cheyennes, besides Sioux warriors who customarily ranged the Platte River country. Yet other deeds of plunder were correctly ascribed to young men who left other Cheyenne camps against the wishes of their leaders. Black Kettle, according to George Bent, because of his continued stance for peace, at this time commanded little authority in wider Cheyenne circles and had become an object of ridicule among other Cheyennes. Despite this, he and the peace chiefs of the Kiowas, Comanches, Kiowa-Apaches, and other tribes were ready to hear what the commissioners had to say.[16]

Although the commissioners remained optimistic of results, many army observers felt otherwise. "A general peace will doubtless be concluded,—which will last till Spring," recorded one officer, "though the Commissioners seem to believe that it will be *permanent!*"[17] At the tribes' insistence, the meetings were moved to Medicine Lodge Creek, a traditional Indian ceremonial site in southern Kansas. Among the Cheyennes, only Black Kettle's band offered a certain commitment to attend. After much deliberation and prodding from emissaries sent by Indian Superintendent Murphy, part of the large Cheyenne village that included the Dog Soldiers and Chiefs Tall Bull, Roman Nose, Bull Bear, Big Head, and Medicine Arrows agreed to come to the appointed ground and join in the discussions. Preceding the council, hearings were held regarding Hancock's expedition, the testimony concluding that the operation had been ill conceived. That finding helped clear the air and facilitate a more positive atmosphere. On October 19, when the council opened, 250 lodges of Cheyennes were present, but not all of the soldier-society members appeared. George Bent attended the proceedings with the Cheyennes and later described the physical arrangement of the various Indian groups at the council ground:

> The great camp was in a beautiful hollow through which flowed Medicine Lodge Creek, with its lovely wooded banks. This was a favorite place for the summer medicine-making of

the Indians also for their winter camps. At the head of the camp were the Arapahos, under Little Raven, with about one hundred and seven lodges; next, in a fine grove, were the Comanches, with one hundred lodges, under Ten Bears and Silver Brooch; below them were the Kiowas, under White Bear, Black Eagle, Sitting Bear, and Kicking Eagle, with one hundred and fifty lodges; and next were the Apaches, eighty-five lodges, under Poor Bear. The council grounds were in the center, in a grove of tall elms. Across the creek from the council grounds was Black Kettle's camp of sixty lodges. The remainder of the Cheyennes were camped several miles away on the Cimarron river. . . . Fully five thousand Indians were encamped here, each Indian village being pitched in a circle. Thousands of ponies covered the adjacent hills and valleys near the camp.[18]

With the Cheyennes still smarting over the destruction of their village at Pawnee Fork the previous spring, the presence of five hundred men of the Seventh Cavalry, besides a battery of Gatling guns, which had accompanied the commissioners from Fort Larned, created an air of intimidation at the outset. The Dog Soldiers, however, were not impressed. "When I signed the treaty at Little Arkansas," Tall Bull told the commissioners, "I intended to live by it; but when we were treated as we were by General Hancock, I became ashamed that I had consented to the treaty. I became blind with rage, and what I have done since, I am not ashamed of." Speaking for the commission, Senator Henderson, chairman of the Senate Committee on Indian Affairs, admonished the Cheyennes and Arapahos on the matter of continued warfare. "Why should we war against each other?" he asked. "The world is large enough for us all. . . . War long continued must end in the total destruction of the Indian because his numbers are less."[19]

But many of the Cheyennes did not get Henderson's message. For various reasons, including purported religious ones, the Cheyennes' appearance at the councils was intermittent at best, and it was only late in the proceedings—on October 28, after the gift deliveries to the other tribes began—that the Cheyennes and Arapahos signed the Medicine Lodge Treaty. Black Kettle's stature among the Cheyenne leadership, meantime, already impaired following Sand Creek and the renewal of his position for peace, clearly antagonized the Dog Soldiers. The chief was directed to appear at the Cimarron camps and explain what benefit would accrue by seeking peace. Tall Bull reportedly threatened to kill all of Black Kettle's horses if the chief failed to respond; as a result, Black Kettle journeyed from Medicine Lodge Creek to the Cimarron and talked with his kinsmen.[20]

The Medicine Lodge accords permanently removed and concentrated the signatory tribes on two reservations in Indian Territory (present Oklahoma), one for the Kiowas, Comanches, and Kiowa Apaches, and one for the Southern Cheyennes and Arapahos. For the Cheyennes and Arapahos, the agreement more than halved the land base given them two years earlier in the Little Arkansas Treaty and perhaps too optimistically led off with the salient phrase: "From this day forward all war between the parties to this agreement shall forever cease." In essence granting the Indians all lands lying between the Arkansas and Cimarron Rivers in the present state of Oklahoma, Article 2 of the accord formally stipulated:

> The United States agrees that the following district of country, to wit: commencing at the point where the Arkansas River crosses the 37th parallel of north latitude, thence west on said parallel—the said line being the southern boundary of the State of Kansas—to the Cimarone [sic] River, (sometimes called the Red Fork of the Arkansas River), thence down said Cimarone River, in the middle of the main channel thereof, to the Arkansas River; thence up the Arkansas River, in the middle of the main channel thereof, to the place of beginning, shall be and the same is hereby set apart for the absolute and undisturbed use and occupation of the Indians herein named, and for such other friendly tribes or individual Indians, as from time to time they may be willing, with the consent of the United States, to admit among them.[21]

Besides other things, the Indians conceded emigrant travel over the trails and continued railroad construction, and they accepted the government's proffered schools and inducements for promoting agriculture and severalty among them. The treaty promised the tribesmen clothing and an annual stipend of $20,000 to benefit the people. As for traditional pursuits, the terms allowed the Cheyennes and Arapahos to continue hunting buffalo in the favored Kansas lands south of the Arkansas River, but the Indians were to remain peaceful and commit no further depredations. Specifically, the treaty stated: "If bad men among the Indians shall commit a wrong or depredation upon the person or property of any one, white, black, or Indian, subject to the authority of the United States and at peace therewith, the tribes herein named solemnly agree that they will, on proof made to their agent, and notice by him, deliver up the wrongdoer to the United States, to be tried and punished according to its laws; and in case they wilfully refuse so to do, the person injured shall be re-imbursed for his loss from the annuities or other moneys due or to become due to them under this or other treaties made with the United States."[22]

After signing the pact, the commissioners distributed presents— including ammunition for hunting with promises of more to come— to an estimated two thousand Cheyennes, five hundred of whom were warriors. Those who signed the treaty represented all of the diverse bands of the Southern Cheyennes as well as the prevailing philosophies within them, notably the peace faction, the Dog Soldiers, and the other soldier societies. Cheyenne chiefs acceding at Medicine Lodge Creek were Black Kettle, Bull Bear, Little Bear, Spotted Elk, Buffalo Chief, Slim Face, Grey Head, Little Rock, Curly Hair, Tall Bull, White Horse, Little Robe, Old Whirlwind, and Heap of Birds. Together, these chiefs represented the polarity of Cheyenne convictions regarding peace and war. Arapaho signatories included Little Raven, Yellow Bear, and Storm. In the course of the deliberations at Medicine Lodge Creek, Black Kettle stood out as the principal consistent force for peace among his tribesmen. In so doing, however, some of the newspaper correspondents present believed that Black Kettle personally endangered himself with other elements of the Cheyennes. The Treaty of Medicine Lodge was not ratified in the Senate until July 25, 1868, and was not proclaimed until August 19, 1868.[23] Naturally, the bureaucratic process brought delays in congressional appropriations to enact its provisions. By then too, other factors had come to bear to nullify much of the document's intent regarding war and peace.

Following such an agreement as at Medicine Lodge, there was always a question as to whether the Indians fully understood the results of their action in signing the convention. A Seventh Cavalry officer who was present at the proceedings recorded in his diary his belief that the Cheyennes "had *no idea that* they are giving up, or that they have ever given up, the country which they claim as their own—the country north of the Arkansas. The treaty all amounts to nothing, and we will certainly have another war sooner or later with the Cheyennes, at least, and probably with the other Indians, in consequence of misunderstanding of the terms of present and previous treaties." Perhaps only a small fraction of the Southern Cheyennes were not represented at Medicine Lodge Creek. Beyond the above-quoted provision regarding depredations, however, the treaty did not address matters of intertribal warfare. In November 1867, following a horse-stealing raid against them by Kaw Indians in Indian Territory, Cheyenne and Arapaho warriors mounted several retaliatory strikes that eventually flared into open warfare and once more threatened the Kansas frontier. Added to this was the availability of liquor to the tribesmen, who increasingly bartered buffalo robes with traders for whiskey. Within months of Medicine Lodge, the Cheyennes also complained about the undelivered guns and ammunition promised them for hunting. A trend was also appearing that forecasted further trouble, in that during the time the peace chiefs, including Black Kettle and Little Robe, came into Forts Dodge and Larned to receive provisions, their young men intensified their raiding activities against the Kaws in the area of the Arkansas valley. Agent Wynkoop heard of these continuing intertribal forays and learned that the chiefs endorsed them because the Kaws had instigated the warfare.[24]

During the late fall and winter of 1867–68, intertribal raiding by the Cheyennes against not only the Kaws but also the Osages diminished for the season, but it nonetheless gave every indication of continuance whenever weather permitted. Early in February 1868 Wynkoop reported his Cheyennes to be "congregated in the neighborhood of a point sixty miles south of Fort Dodge." The people, who included Black Kettle's followers, remained perturbed by the delay of the arms and ammunition for hunting promised them, yet Wynkoop described his charges as "very tranquill [sic]" as he anticipated visiting them to turn over the property seized by Hancock the previous spring. A major fear came not from the Cheyennes, but from the Kiowas, who reportedly fell in with some white wolfers, killing one while stealing their equipment. Interpreter John S. Smith urged allowing the Cheyennes to move north of the Arkansas River and away from the negative influence of the Kiowas, but his advice was seemingly ignored.[25]

Delays in Congress in approving the terms of the Medicine Lodge Treaty only increased tensions among the Cheyennes and Arapahos through the winter. Further aggravations came in an ongoing survey of the Osage reservation within the designated boundary, an activity the Indians apparently did not fully understand. Moreover, interpreters strategically placed with the bands (at government expense) to track and report their movements were more interested in promoting private trade. Wynkoop complained, "I never receive any reports from any of them; the only way in which I am able to gain any information in regard to the Indians, is in person or keeping a scout constantly running between them and the agency."[26]

Although the prevailing post–Medicine Lodge calm lasted through most of the winter of 1867–68, there were signs of a burgeoning unrest among the Cheyennes and Arapahos that transcended the political delays keeping goods and arms from the Indian camps. Many of these were grounded in age-old life ways concerning war-practice traditions that white Americans at the time could not fathom, including inter-tribal competition as well as the spiritual, psychological, and social reckoning involved in the attainment of warrior status by the young men of the tribe. For the Cheyennes in particular, chronic intertribal warfare was a cornerstone of their existence on the plains and consti-tuted a deadly enterprise of extenuating facets to guarantee their sur-vival; this reality helps explain the considerably large geographical areas historically claimed by the Cheyennes despite their relatively small numbers. For many young men, moreover, warfare was a rite of passage, and its practice was necessary to attain status within society. Because of the framework of Cheyenne society, the activities of young men bent on gaining prestige through raiding and success as warriors—components that were culturally ingrained and therefore normal exer-cises conducive to establishing a social reputation—were not easily tempered, governed, or eliminated by other tribal members, including chiefs, since they represented ritualized behavior typically affecting personal growth and societal status.[27] This was something white observers could not comprehend.

In the months following the Medicine Lodge Treaty, the attempt to maintain peace unraveled because of a complication of issues, some of them contemporary, some historical, and some cultural. Certainly, the memory of what had happened to Black Kettle's people at Sand Creek was omnipresent, creating a lingering suspicion among them and other Cheyennes and Arapahos that it would happen again. Hancock's per-formance in the events surrounding the destruction of the Cheyenne village at Pawnee Fork confirmed in many of the people's minds the inevitability of yet another military strike—and probably successive attacks—and despite the air clearing at Medicine Lodge, this fear doubtless remained. Also, the Sand Creek disaster seems to have exacerbated existing schisms among the Southern Cheyennes as a whole, especially between leaders like Black Kettle and Little Robe, who still counseled conciliation, and the seemingly vacillating Dog Soldiers and members of the interband military societies, who had but grudgingly and tenuously acceded to the accord. Increased warfare with the Kaws and Osages, longtime enemies, compounded these conditions, promoted cultural responses, and created extraordinary pressures on Cheyenne band hierarchies to control their young men, strictures not only inimical to the tenets of Cheyenne society but also impossible to fulfill. Added to these was political shortsightedness in setting aside the designated reservations and establishing tribal government as called for by the commissioners in their report. And the additional delay in ratification of the treaty, which indefinitely postponed disbursement of anticipated supplies, created dissatisfaction and further distrust. During the early months of 1868, these extant realities and conditions contributed to the evolving scenario that finally led to the punitive army campaign against the Southern Cheyennes.

3

SUMMER DEPREDATIONS

On January 12, 1868, a party of twenty-five Cheyenne and Arapaho warriors, en route to raid the Utes, visited the stage station at Cimarron Crossing and demanded entrance. This denied, they approached a nearby government wagon train loaded with supplies for Forts Lyon and Reynolds, Colorado Territory. The warriors became intimidating in their manner, brandishing revolvers and making threats. Over the next twenty-four hours, they rifled the wagon contents before taking the unarmed trainmen's rations and leaving. Little more than a month later, trouble with the Kiowas arose at Fort Arbuckle, Indian Territory, when they threatened Indian Agent Jesse Leavenworth's party, involved in negotiating the release of white captives taken the previous fall. While no lives were lost, both incidents pointed up the growing turbulence among the Indians in the wake of Medicine Lodge and exhibited frustrations that would accelerate and explode along the Kansas-Colorado frontier over the coming weeks and months.[1]

Although the events of January and February forecasted trouble to military authorities, the agents responsible for the tribes continued to project a sense of amity and understanding that denied reality. In April, Edward Wynkoop professed that his wards were "in a happy and quiet state," though prior to the delivery of emergency rations they were "destitute" and "almost starving." He branded rumors of impending

Indian hostility false, though the static conditions affecting the Cheyennes' and Arapahos' animus toward the neighboring Kaws and Osages
still loomed. When Wynkoop proposed a council of the concerned tribes
to seek peace, the Cheyennes and Arapahos told him they would consider it only after they struck back at their enemies. Despite the supposed concord at Medicine Lodge, uncertainties over the Indian situation began to affect industry and commerce. Officials of the Central
Branch of the Union Pacific Railroad (later renamed the Kansas Pacific
Railroad), then building through Kansas and fearing molestation by the
tribes, petitioned Washington authorities for protection during extension of the line through the Republican valley into Nebraska. Similarly,
troops were dispatched from Fort Wallace, in western Kansas, to protect
the stage route into Colorado Territory.[2]

From afar, the army hierarchy adopted a stance of watchful waiting
to see what happened on the plains during the months following the
peace commission's efforts. The entire region, north and south, fell into
the administrative domain of the Military Division of the Missouri,
headed by General Sherman from headquarters in St. Louis. One of the
subsidiary commands in the division was the Department of the Missouri, which in 1867 consisted of a broad central region comprising the
states of Missouri and Kansas, Indian Territory, New Mexico Territory,
and most of Colorado Territory.[3] In September 1867, following the
highly criticized Hancock expedition, a significant overhaul in the
department saw Major General Philip H. Sheridan succeed Hancock.
The flinty-eyed Sheridan, diminutive and blasphemous, was regarded
as a brilliant strategist. He had fought Indians in the Northwest before
the Civil War, had commanded the Cavalry Corps of the Army of the
Potomac during that conflict, and was one of the front-rank triumvi-
rate of heroes to emerge from the struggle garnering public idolatry,
the others being Commanding General Ulysses S. Grant and Division
Commander Sherman. Like them, and especially Sherman, Sheridan
advocated a doctrine of "total war," supposedly borne of their experiences in the South—the process of subjecting civilian (or "innocent")
populations to the full rigors of intensive physical and psychological
warfare by any means possible on the belief that by doing so, the war
would be shortened and more lives saved in the long run.[4] Sheridan did
not take personal charge of his new command until March 1868, when
he arrived at his headquarters at Fort Leavenworth, Kansas. Within
Sheridan's new command were four military districts: the District of

New Mexico, commanded by Colonel George W. Getty, Thirty-Seventh Infantry; the District of the Indian Territory, commanded since May 1868 by Colonel Benjamin H. Grierson, Tenth Cavalry; the District of Kansas, under Major Thomas C. English, Fifth Infantry, and which included Forts Leavenworth and Riley; and the District of the Upper Arkansas, commanded since May 1868 by Lieutenant Colonel Alfred Sully, Third Infantry.

For various reasons, of all the districts under Sheridan's command, that of the Upper Arkansas had become the most complicated by early 1868. Sheridan concisely described its parameters and circumstances in his annual report for that year:

> The district of the Upper Arkansas embraces nearly all the territory of Colorado, and that portion of Kansas west of a north and south line, through Fort Harker. . . . It had within its limits the territory of the Cheyennes, Arapahoes, Kiowas, and Comanches, which they had agreed to give up in their treaty with the peace commission. The two great commercial highways to Colorado and New Mexico [the Smoky Hill Trail and the Santa Fe Trail], and the lateral roads connecting them, from [Forts] Harker to Larned, Hays to Dodge, and Wallace to Lyon, pass through the district, also the western line of frontier settlements in Kansas, and the eastern line of settlements in Colorado, which, from their scattered and helpless condition, were much exposed, and invited the cupidity of the savages. . . . To guard the lines of the Union Pacific railroad, and the Denver stage road, and other interests in this district, there had been established in 1867 the posts of Forts Harker, Hays, and Wallace, and the outpost of Cedar Point; and to guard the line of the Arkansas to New Mexico, there were the posts of Forts Larned, Dodge, Lyon, and Reynolds, and the outposts of Zarah and Camp Beecher, at the mouth of the Little Arkansas. All these posts were . . . garrisoned by eight companies of the 10th cavalry, 7th cavalry, 5th and 3d infantry, and four companies of the 38th infantry, all very reduced in numbers, which gave me a force of about 1,200 cavalry and about 1,400 infantry.[5]

It was under Sheridan's administration that relations between the government and the Cheyennes sharply deteriorated after Medicine Lodge. Military officers at the Kansas posts made periodic reports to department headquarters of the location, status, and attitude of the various tribal bands in the region below the Arkansas. Most of these reports mentioned visits by different groups to the posts, usually monthly, for the purpose of obtaining light rations of sugar, flour, and tobacco, issues authorized by Sherman through Sheridan in the interests of keeping the peace. These documents are useful indicators of the movements of some of the Indians throughout parts of the region and their motivation beyond receipt of provisions. For example, the reports indicate that all the tribes (Kiowa, Comanche, Arapaho, and Cheyenne) generally remained below the Arkansas within their designated tracts. In the spring of 1868, the Kiowas and Comanches were undertaking an expedition against the Navahos that eventually proved unsuccessful. The Arapahos and Cheyennes were pursuing their own campaign against the Kaws and Osages, and at one time authorities estimated that some eight war parties, totaling eight hundred or nine hundred men from both tribes, were involved in seeking vengeance on those people. Bands of Cheyennes and Arapahos intermittently visited Forts Dodge and Larned for provisions, then returned to their haunts below the Arkansas. A few bodies of Arapahos lingered near the posts, but most of the Cheyennes stayed away. In April 1868 Medicine Wolf and forty-one Dog Soldiers and their families came in to Larned en route to the Smoky Hill to reclaim the remains of that chief's children killed the previous summer. Medicine Wolf pronounced his "intentions peaceable to all whites," and one report erroneously tied this Dog Soldier leader to Black Kettle's people. The chief's village was apparently located near Fort Larned. In May a body of Cheyennes was reported as camped on the middle branch of Pawnee Fork. By July, a particularly large group of 275 lodges, including many Dog Soldiers, stood along Walnut Creek, which military authorities had deemed "at present quiet."[6]

Despite this apparent tranquility, as the spring of 1868 wore on, conditions for open conflict increased. Incidents arose that juxtaposed troops and Indians into an inevitably widening scenario. Some clearly involved warriors who wanted food and clothing and who acted on that need. Because of deep-seated and ongoing intertribal disputes, reported incidents seem always to have involved one or another of the belligerent tribes. Early in May, a party of twenty Indians, tribe unknown, accosted settlers on Big Creek, taking food and garments. Arapahos were suspected because warriors from that tribe also tried to steal cattle from a herd escorted by a cavalry detachment near Wilson's Creek. Other

Indians took food from a nearby rancher. When warriors attacked and killed two men in mid-May near their homes on Walnut Creek, the suspected culprits were thought to be Cheyennes or Osages. Soon afterward, the post trader near Fort Zarah addressed a letter directly to General Sheridan recounting yet another incident of perceived Indian surliness. He described in detail how 125 Cheyennes professing hunger came to his place, which was located off the post. After he fed them, the Indians stayed on to beg for more, only leaving when a government train bound from Fort Lyon to Fort Harker appeared. They approached the train with pistols blazing, then likewise intimidated a Mexican train passing by. Finally, in the night the warriors set fire to the trader's store, destroying it. He reported that the Indians drew their revolvers on, and otherwise insulted, members of the small army detachment at nearby Fort Zarah. Although the official report of the matter suggested that the incident was the work of white men rather than Indians, it referred to the "ill feeling existing among the Cheyennes" over the unfulfilled treaty promises.[7]

Chagrined at these developments in his new jurisdiction, Sheridan responded to the news with a recitation of recent events. He cited four instances of committed or threatened depredations involving the Cheyennes but concluded, "General Sherman's instructions to me do not cover offensive operations on my part, until there is a declaration of war on the part of the President." Instead, Sheridan authorized Colonel Sully, commanding the District of the Upper Arkansas, "to attack and kill any of these marauding parties caught committing depredations." In a missive of May 27, the general told Sully about repeated incidents of "insolence and bad behavior on the part of the Cheyennes. I do not know what this will eventually result in, but it should put us on our guard." Respecting the murder of the two men on Walnut Creek, purportedly by the Osages, Sheridan commented, "I . . . think it was done by the Cheyennes." So consumed by the growing situation did the department commander become that he dictated to Sully remarkably precise instructions for pursuing offending tribesmen: "The Cavalry should be kept well-shod up and in light traveling condition, with sacks large enough to carry on the saddle twenty (20) pounds of grain, which might be made to last five (5) days of swift march, and if Indians were not overtaken in that time let the horses depend on the grass and make the march slower."[8]

More justification for these accusations followed as depredations increased in the summer of 1868. A major event was the long-antici-pated retaliatory raid of the Cheyennes and Arapahos against the Kaw Indians on their reserve near Council Grove, in eastern Kansas, about twenty-five miles southeast of Fort Riley. Council Grove, with about eight hundred inhabitants, stood along the Santa Fe Trail at its juncture with the Neosho River in one of the more settled areas of the state. The Kaw reservation extended east from the town along the river, its agency located some four miles away. On the early afternoon of June 3, two hundred warriors, headed by Little Robe, suddenly appeared at Coun-cil Grove, each brandishing one or more Colt's Navy revolvers or a bow and arrows, some wearing cavalry sabers. The appearance of the Indi-ans decked out for war surely startled the townspeople. Two hours later the Cheyennes and Arapahos attacked the agency buildings but were repulsed by Kaw warriors stationed in the structures, each side sus-taining minimal casualties. Professing peaceful designs, the Cheyenne party called for the return of scalps taken from them by the Kaws the previous fall, but the Kaws refused to speak with them. Before they left, Little Robe told the agent that the Cheyennes would be back with rein-forcements from Black Kettle's band and would seize the scalps by force. Then they turned about, returning through Council Grove to camp west of the town en route back to the plains. On the way, the tribes-men, unable to find game, robbed three settler homes and killed a num-ber of beeves. The events at Council Grove and the Kaw agency instilled fear among area whites, who believed that an Indian massacre of citi-zens was about to occur. The Cheyennes and Arapahos went home via Fort Harker, telling the military representatives there that they had killed cattle at Council Grove because of their starving condition.[9]

This incident served as another example of Indian intimidation of settlers, this time within the relatively settled district of eastern Kansas, and it reinforced a growing trepidation on the part of local whites toward the tribesmen. During July, cases involving the Cheyennes and Arapahos increased. Followers of the Arapaho Yellow Bear threatened ranchmen at Walnut Creek, and a mixed group of Cheyennes and Ara-pahos maliciously stole chickens and fired pistols at another settler. But in their everyday contact with whites, the Indians also had legitimate grievances. They often complained about soldiers randomly shooting at them while they hunted in the vicinity of the water tanks along the

Kansas Pacific Railroad line and "that the passengers fire at them out of the car windows." There were also troubles with the Kiowas and Comanches. In July Sherman wrote Sheridan of the prospect and apparent inevitability of open warfare on the plains despite the efforts of the peace commissioners. "We must try and not inaugurate a war, for the longer it can be deferred the better for us. Of course it will come in the end." It was Sherman's belief that tribesmen guilty of depredations represented their greater tribal groups, and "if they resort to acts of war, you have no alternative but to punish them as a whole tribe."[10] This attitude was critical in the evolving circumstances ultimately leading to direct military intervention on the southern plains in 1868.

That much of the growing problem rested with the fact that the Indians were in a destitute and starving condition, which accounted for many of their actions, was seemingly ignored by many in the Washington bureaucracy. Despite repeated notices from Commissioner of Indian Affairs Nathaniel Taylor and his subordinates, Congress remained sluggardly regarding the Medicine Lodge accords. Time and again Taylor reminded his superiors of the Indians' concerns that the nonratification of the treaty and consequent delay of supplies, coupled with the constant inroads of white settlers into their territories, were threatening peace. If war erupted, wrote Taylor, it "will be brought on by reason of the sufferings and starving condition of the Indians." He urged Congress to take speedy action "to relieve the present wants of the most destitute, and to prevent another Indian war." Yet Taylor called for withholding promised arms and ammunition from the Cheyennes and Arapahos because of "their recent raid into the white settlements," a punishment oddly stemming from their attempt to deal with the desperate circumstances Taylor himself had predicted. When Agent Wynkoop attempted to issue goods to his charges at Fort Larned in July, the Indians refused to take them until they received the promised ordnance.[11]

The delivery of arms and ammunition to the tribes in accordance with the peace-council assurances might have permitted them to hunt in their customary manner and thus might have helped relieve their condition. It is not known whether Taylor saw the irony of his position regarding such distributions, but Secretary of the Interior Orville H. Browning authorized Agent Wynkoop to use his judgment and to issue guns and bullets if he thought it would help preserve peace and if "no evil will result from such delivery." "The great and principal object to be attained," Taylor wrote Indian Superintendent Thomas

Murphy, "is the preservation of peace, not only between the Indians and whites, but, if possible, between the Indians themselves." Consequently, on August 9 Wynkoop issued annuity goods to the Cheyennes and Arapahos at Fort Larned. In accordance with the recommendation of his superiors, and with Colonel Sully's concurrence, the agent delivered the long-awaited firearms and ammunition, amounting to 160 pistols, eight rifles, a dozen kegs of powder, a supply of lead, and 15,000 percussion caps. "They were delighted at receiving the goods, particularly the arms and ammunition, and never before have I known them to be better satisfied," wrote Wynkoop. The tribesmen immediately departed for their hunting grounds, causing the elated agent to remark, "I am perfectly satisfied that there will be no trouble with them this season, and consequently with no Indians of my agency."[12]

On August 10, the day after Wynkoop penned this line, about one hundred Southern Cheyenne warriors arrived at a thickly settled area along the Saline River in north-central Kansas. Most of these Indians belonged to the assemblage of Dog Soldiers at Walnut Creek.[13] Their original purpose had been to attack a Pawnee village in Nebraska, but while seeking food at a settler's home, someone fired upon them. In response, the Indians captured a white woman and took her to their camp, though they later returned her home. Moving on the next day, they reached the north fork of the Solomon, where a party of whites fired on them. Avoiding this group, the warriors attacked a nearby settlement out of revenge, killing several white men and capturing two girls, who were later released. Pursued by a cavalry detachment, the war party divided, with some heading north and with others back to the camp at Walnut Creek. Yet another group turned toward Black Kettle's village near Fort Larned. Formal reports of the raid described how the Indians had raped two women, beat up a rancher, and stolen and destroyed his property, then repeated these acts on others farther down the Saline. Many settlers abandoned their homes and moved closer to the railroad, planning to return when they believed the trouble had ended. Three days later the warriors reappeared, renewed their activities, and moved on to the Solomon, where they continued their destruction until chased off by a cavalry column. An early report mentioned nine men and one boy killed. "One woman was mortally wounded, and two others were horribly abused and violated," wrote Major Thomas English. "Heretofore Indians have been in the habit of visiting this country to hunt and have been kindly treated by the settlers," reported

Colonel Sully, the district commander. "Now the settlers swear they will shoot the first Indians they see." In all, over three days of rampage by the Indians, they had killed fifteen people, including two along the Republican River; raped and wounded several women; and plundered homes and driven off livestock.[14]

Months later, following the Washita engagement, army authorities persuaded the mixed-blood Cheyenne Edmond Guerrier, who participated in the Saline-Solomon raids, to identify the Cheyenne groups from which the warriors had come. Guerrier testified that young men from the bands of Little Rock, Black Kettle, Medicine Arrows, and Bull Bear composed the raiding party. When news of the raids reached the camps of Little Rock's and Black Kettle's Cheyennes at the headwaters of Pawnee Fork, they precipitately moved below the Arkansas River as far as the Cimarron. Ironically, the warriors who conducted the raids did not know that the disbursement of arms and ammunition had ultimately been made to their fellows, they having already departed to attack the Pawnees, and en route were provoked into committing the outrages; Agent Wynkoop later tried to explain how this had happened. But in the end, the frustrated Dog Soldiers' strikes against the settlers of the Saline and Solomon likely signified deep-seated, subliminal, and long-simmering resentments among all Cheyennes against the steadily increasing presence of whites. To them, whites by now had become the chief reason for their ever shrinking land base and for the commensurate competition over game and other natural resources critical to their cultural and physical survival. In the wake of Sand Creek, Pawnee Fork, and the conclusion of less-than-satisfying treaty agreements that further reduced their lands, restrained their movements, and threatened to transform their traditional life ways, the Southern Cheyennes—perhaps more than other area tribes—had reached a defining point in their cultural identity and found themselves at a crossroads they could neither fully understand nor accept. The Saline and Solomon raids symbolized great, ever accreting rage among the Cheyennes over conditions that were gradually overwhelming them as a people and a culture. General Sheridan, in assessing the situation, said, "there was not the slightest provocation offered by the soldiers or citizens for the commencement of this war by the Indians." His statement clearly betrayed an ignorance of the realities of what the tribesmen faced in 1868.[15]

The depredations among the Kansas settlements spawned similar activities elsewhere throughout August along the Kansas-Colorado frontier. In most cases the Cheyennes were identified as the perpetrators. On August 12, even while the Solomon encounters took place, Cheyennes took guns and horses from a government contractor near Fort Dodge and stampeded stock from a Mexican train near Pawnee Fork. Such incidents around that post increased during the month, and the commander complained of not having sufficient cavalry at hand to respond. Farther west, on the nineteenth warriors struck a party of woodchoppers, killing three and driving off their animals. More livestock raids and killings occurred two days later near Pond City. On the twenty-second Indians chased away more livestock at Sheridan City and the next day attacked the stage to Cheyenne Wells. On the twenty-third, between Pond Creek and Lake Station, more warriors struck the Denver stage, and that same day another man, mortally wounded, was brought into Fort Wallace. Four days later 250 Indians challenged an army train, forcing the officer in charge to turn about and return to Big Springs. And the commanding officer at Fort Lyon, Colorado, reported several incidents of Indians running off stock, attacking stagecoaches and ranches, and destroying wagon trains along the Santa Fe Trail. The warriors, identified as Cheyennes, told William Bent that they were on the warpath. Colorado territorial officials, meantime, reported conditions getting out of hand, with one man killed near Lake Station and a stage attacked near Cheyenne Wells. A panicky acting governor reported Arapahos on the warpath and asked that he be permitted to draw troops from Fort Reynolds while he organized volunteer units. Accounting for similar incidents, Sheridan's officers revealed that by the end of August, thirty-five citizens had been killed and nine others wounded. Livestock stolen totaled nearly eight hundred animals, while eight homes and two wagon trains had been destroyed. Included among the fatalities was a prominent scout, William Comstock, part of an intelligence-gathering system organized by the general. He had been shot point-blank near the village of Dog Soldiers at the headwaters of the Solomon; his partner, Sharp Grover, had been wounded in the attack and narrowly escaped being killed.[16]

Of course, most attention remained focused on the Saline and Solomon raids, and Agent Wynkoop sought to learn from his charges the extent of Cheyenne involvement and against whom, directly, blame should be assessed. On August 19 at Fort Larned, he interviewed Little

Rock, the Cheyenne chief whom he had earlier asked to investigate the events and discover the perpetrators. Through an interpreter, Little Rock related the following details:

> This war party of Cheyennes which left the camps of these tribes above the forks of Walnut creek about the 2d and 3d of August went out against the Pawnees, crossed the Smoky Hill about Fort Hays, and thence proceeded to the Saline. . . . There were 10 lodges of Sioux in the Cheyenne camp when this war party left, and about 20 men of them, and 4 Arapahoes, accompanied the party. The Cheyennes numbered about 200; nearly all the young men of the village went; Little Raven's son was one of the four Arapahoes. When the party reached the Saline they turned down the stream, with the exception of about 20, who, being fearful of depredations being committed against the whites by the party going in the direction of the settlement, kept on north towards the Pawnees. The main party continued down the Saline until they came in sight of the settlement; they then camped there. A Cheyenne named Oh-e-ah-mohe-a, brother of White Antelope, who was killed at Sand Creek, and another named Red Nose, proceeded to the first house; they afterwards returned to the camp and with them [brought] a woman captive. The main party was surprised at this action, and forcibly took possession of her, and returned her to her house. The two Indians had outraged the woman before they brought her to the camp. After the outrage had been committed, the parties left the Saline and went north towards the settlements of the south fork of the Solomon, where they were kindly received and fed by the white people. They left the settlements on the south fork, and proceeded towards the settlements on the north forks. When in sight of these settlements they came upon a body of armed settlers, who fired upon them; they avoided the party, went round them, and approached a house some distance off. In the vicinity of the house they came upon a white man alone, upon the prairie; "Big Head's" son rode at him and knocked him down with a club. The Indian who had committed the outrage upon the white woman, known as White Antelope's brother, then fired upon the white man without effect, while the third Indian rode up and killed

him. Soon after they killed a white man, and, close by, a woman—all in the same settlement.

At the time these people were killed, the party was divided in feeling, the majority being opposed to any outrages being committed; but finding it useless to contend against these outrages being committed without bringing on a strife among themselves, they gave way, and all went in together. They then went to another house in the same settlement, and there killed two men, and took two little girls prisoners; this on the same day. After committing the last outrage the party turned south, towards the Saline, where they came on a body of mounted troops; the troops immediately charged the Indians, and the pursuit was continued a long time. The Indians having the two children, their horses becoming fatigued, dropped the children without hurting them. Soon after the children were dropped the pursuit ceased; but the Indians continued on up the Saline. A portion of the Indians afterwards returned to look for the children, but were unable to find them. After they had proceeded some distance up the Saline the party divided, the majority going north, towards the settlements on the Solomon, but 30 of them started towards their village, supposed to be some distance northwest of Fort Larned. Another small party returned to Black Kettle's village.[17]

Little Rock told Wynkoop that many of his people "do not wish to be punished for the bad acts of those who are guilty." The chief agreed to go to his people and try and deliver up the principal perpetrators— Oh-e-ah-mohe-a (White Antelope's brother), Tall Wolf (Medicine Arrow's son), Red Nose, Porcupine Bear (Big Nose's son), and Bear that Goes Ahead (Sand Hill's brother). "Tell them," said Wynkoop, "that I think complying with my demand is the only thing that will save their entire nation from a long and destructive war." Little Rock replied that he would work for his people's welfare, but "if the chiefs and headmen refuse to comply with your demands, I want to know if I can come with my wife and children . . . and place myself and them under your protection," a request Wynkoop obliged.[18]

The cumulative effect of the outbreak and collateral incidents also prompted calls for protection from white residents. Land Office officials in Junction City proposed erecting posts along the Solomon and

Republican Rivers, while Kansas governor Samuel L. Crawford asked for twenty thousand rounds of ammunition so that settlers could protect themselves. He also appealed to the president for permission to raise volunteers in his state. The commanding officer of Fort Zarah, meantime, requested two mountain howitzers with sufficient ammunition "in view of anticipated Indian troubles." While many of the circumstances affecting the encounters along the Saline and Solomon were unfolding, Sheridan left Fort Leavenworth to assess conditions in his department. Arriving at Fort Harker on August 20, the general, dismayed over the issuance of arms to the Indians, met Agent Wynkoop, who expressed perplexity over the outbreak of violence and advanced the belief that Northern Sioux influence possibly accounted for the disturbances. In 1868 the Teton Sioux and Northern Cheyennes had managed to rid the army and settlers from the Powder River country in present Wyoming, and Wynkoop believed that news of this success was being spread among his own charges so that like results might be achieved in the Smoky Hill River country. The agent impressed on Sheridan that not all of the Cheyennes were guilty of the violence, and the officer promised to protect Little Rock's people. Later at Fort Dodge, Sheridan learned that most of the Arapahos had not been involved in the outbreak. He met with Arapaho leaders, including Little Raven, and promised to support them through the winter if they surrendered, a stipulation to which they assented (and later ignored). Nevertheless, anxious to quell the disturbances and reassure settlers, the general took action, writing Crawford: "I will at once order the Cheyennes, Arapahoes and Kiowas out of your state and into their reservations and will compel them to go by force. We will not cease our efforts until the perpetrators of the Solomon massacre are delivered up for punishment."[19]

Meantime, the army had not been immobile during the spate of incidents in the department during the summer of 1868. From his headquarters at Fort Gibson, Indian Territory, Colonel Benjamin H. Grierson in June commanded an expedition to research the defensive needs of the territory. Accompanied by a small party of officers and men of the Tenth Cavalry, Grierson proceeded to Fort Arbuckle, then west to the abandoned Fort Cobb, en route scouting a location for a new post near the Wichita Mountains. The trip was without incident, and the party returned to Fort Gibson within two weeks. Farther north, troops responded to the growing turbulence among the Indians in the District of the Upper Arkansas. From Fort Larned, Lieutenant Colonel Sully reported 300 lodges of Kiowas and Comanches, 200 of Arapahos, and 60 of Kiowa-Apaches camped near the post, with 275 lodges of Cheyennes but forty miles away. Many of the Kiowas and Comanches expressed complaints over their agent, their conditions, and the terms of the treaty that would send them south of the Arkansas and the Kansas border. The Cheyennes (as mentioned) were distressed over their nonreceipt of arms and ammunition following their raid on the Kaws, and directives to district commanders highlighted the need "to act strictly on the defensive and only attack such parties as commit depredations." Indians and even citizens having protested the practice of soldiers shooting at them every time they approached a water tank along the railroad line, Sully ordered his officers to instill in their men the need to exercise caution "and not fire at everything they see." A major concern for Sully were the Kiowa Indians hanging around Fort Zarah, who had a habit of stopping trains over the Santa Fe Trail and forcibly taking their contents. Sully talked with their leaders, and as usual, they blamed the infractions on young boys and old men. "I don't trust these Kiowas at all," reported Sully. "I think they are the meanest Indians on the plains."[20]

After the raiding began along the Saline and Solomon Rivers, Sully put his scattered force on alert and then journeyed to Fort Harker to appraise the situation. On August 13 he sent Captain Frederick W. Benteen and fifty men of the Seventh Cavalry north to try and identify the tribe responsible for the attacks; it was Benteen who later pursued the warriors along the Solomon. Within days Sully had amassed nine companies north of Harker, intent on quelling the trouble and learning the identity of the perpetrators. On the twenty-second he issued the following circular respecting the raids: "Hostilities having broken out with the Cheyennes and other Indian tribes, Commanders of Posts and Detachments in this District are cautioned to be vigilant and on the alert at all times to prevent them from committing depredations in the vicinity of their commands. They will caution all trains and parties passing through to remain at the different posts, until they have a sufficient force to protect themselves; or if they will venture out, they do so at their own risk." To reassure settlers, Sully sent units of the Third Infantry to escort a train of provisions and to erect blockhouses in the areas of the Saline and Solomon, while the commander of the District of Kansas prepared to build one on the Republican River.[21] Companies of the Tenth Cavalry were sent to patrol the ravaged countryside, with orders for detachments to move constantly and to "attack any Indians they may meet, except the Pawnees." Seventh Cavalry companies were ordered to Fort Larned from Forts Reynolds and Lyon, Colorado. Other units of the regiment, under Major Joel Elliott, were dispatched to Pawnee Fork and Fort Larned to scout the country around Walnut Creek and the Arkansas, with similar instructions "to attack all Indians they may see." Seventh Cavalry men posted between Forts Harker and Zarah were cautioned not to interfere with Kiowas or Comanches but to likewise attack those belonging to "hostile bands." At water tanks along the railroad, guards were increased to three men; special orders required them to furnish their dugouts with a barrel of water each along with extra supplies of hardtack and ammunition.[22]

Late in August 1868 Congress finally ratified the Treaty of Medicine Lodge made with the Cheyennes and Arapahos on October 28, 1867. Despite the fact that this had occurred too late to provide adequately for the tribesmen, as had been promised them during the proceedings, government officials instantly seized on elements of the accord to show how its provisions had been abused by the Indians. Article 11, in particular, outlawed such behavior as had occurred at the Saline and Solomon, with specific regard to attacking settlers at home, molesting wagon trains and livestock, taking white women or children, and killing and scalping white men. This interpretation coincided with the swift ascendancy of the War Department in dealing with the tribes. Already Sherman and Sheridan had decreed the Indians' removal below the Kansas line, with orders to pursue and kill them, if necessary, in accomplishing that objective. In view of the army philosophy of holding accountable the entire tribe for the sins of a few members, the position of the Indian Office now became one of trying to protect those people who had not been involved in the depredations. Acting Commissioner Charles E. Mix wrote: "If General Sherman's orders to General Sheridan would not result in the killing of Indians who had had nothing to do with the depredations in question, it would be perfectly right to carry them out to the letter. Those who were engaged in the murders should be punished, and be taught a lesson not to be forgotten; but it would not be right to punish the innocent for acts not committed by them."[23]

On August 10—coincidentally, as the raiding progressed along the Saline—Sherman issued General Orders No. 4 respecting his responsibility for disbursements to the tribes under his oversight on the reservations designated by the peace commission and mandated by the Medicine Lodge Treaty. To manage the various tribes from the Upper Missouri through Indian Territory, Sherman appointed in each region army officers to oversee actual distribution of goods and purchases for the tribesmen. "I will use exclusively Military Agents," he wrote Secretary of the Interior Browning, "simply because I have more faith in their manner of business." Thus, effectually for the time being, the army was to administer Indian affairs with respect to the tribes in Sherman's division. With reference to the country "bounded east by the State of Arkansas, south by Texas, north by Kansas, and west by the one hundredth meridian," reservations specified for the Cheyennes, Arapahos, Kiowas, Comanches, and Kiowa-Apaches, Sherman appointed Colonel William B. Hazen to supervise and control all issues and distribution of goods. In accordance with prevailing opinions of transforming the Indians into husbandmen, purchases were to be limited to beef cattle, meat, grain, and bread, with sparing issues of coffee and sugar in extraordinary cases. The people would also receive clothing for their elderly and young and seeds and tools for cultivating the earth. An 1855 West Point graduate, the mustachioed and goateed Hazen had risen to the rank of major general of volunteers during the Civil War and had won numerous brevets for gallantry and meritorious service. In the postwar army he was colonel of the Thirty-eighth Infantry and considered a competent, if somewhat contentious, officer. His views on the Indian question, however, paralleled Sherman's own, and the general often called on him for such special posts. In compliance with his assignment, Superintendent of Indians Hazen established headquarters for the Southern Indian District at Fort Cobb, an abandoned post in Indian Territory, situated near the mouth of Pond Creek on the north side of the Washita River, near the modern community of Anadarko, Oklahoma. In terms of his appointment vis-à-vis Indian matters, Hazen was directly responsible to Sherman, but for matters regarding army personnel, he deferred to Sheridan, for whom he shared a mutual dislike.[24]

The depredations triggered by the Saline and Solomon raids continued into September. On the second a small party of troops twelve miles from Fort Dodge along the Arkansas River were set upon by warriors, who nearly succeeded in killing them all before they reached the post. Five days later raiders made off with sixty-five animals at a hay camp near Fort Wallace; a cavalry pursuit proved fruitless. Over a fortnight, warriors killed two teamsters and assailed stagecoaches on the road between Wallace and the community of Sheridan. On September 8, Indians drove off stock from a ranch along the Purgatoire River near Fort Lyon, and a cavalry detail went in pursuit while foot soldiers protected area settlements. The horsemen, Company L of the Seventh Cavalry, operating under Captain William H. Penrose, Third Infantry, cornered the warriors about thirty miles from the post and fought a hot engagement in which two soldiers and two Indians were killed. The pursuit continued until the warriors were lost in the distance. Penrose returned to Lyon the next morning after a sojourn of about 120 miles.[25]

Together with the events surrounding the Saline and Solomon depredations, these scattered outbursts presently forced the issue with the Cheyennes and Arapahos. Through the better part of August, Sherman and Sheridan designed and refined a plan to drive the Indians onto the Medicine Lodge-designated lands below the Kansas boundary. The consequences for tribesmen disposed not to go were simple: they would be pursued and killed by the troops. The plan was not immediately enacted, though, delayed because Interior Department officials wanted provision made for those Indians who had nothing to do with the recent disturbances, an accommodation Sherman and his officers firmly resisted. The army believed that because the Indians had neither curbed the guilty parties nor turned them over to authorities as specified in the treaty, they too were as blameworthy and worthy of punishment. Sherman acknowledged, however, that the strictures should apply only to the Cheyennes and Arapahos. His and Sheridan's plan would not affect the Kiowas, Comanches, and Kiowa-Apaches, despite their own proclivities toward raiding in Texas and their frequent instigation of trouble with more-sedentary tribes around Fort Cobb, for they had not been proven responsible for the immediate raids in Kansas. Meantime, Sheridan arrived at Fort Dodge and began organizing an expedition to go after the Cheyennes and Arapahos. The prospect unsettled Wynkoop, who opined to Superintendent Murphy, "the probabilities are that if they strike any Indians at all it will be the wrong parties." But Murphy lined up with the army on the matter of the Cheyennes' and Arapahos' complicity in the disturbances: "Their last annuities had scarcely been distributed to them before they go to war. . . . They have violently broken their treaty pledges, and until they voluntarily abandon the war-path, ask for peace, make full reparation, . . . [and] go and live on their reservation, . . . I would send them no annuities whatever, but would leave these Indians where they now are—in the hands of the military."[26]

Yet the peaceful Cheyennes and Arapahos, including Black Kettle's band, had long since headed into Indian Territory to get far away from the mounting troubles in Kansas, most of which were committed by young men with ties to all the various bands and villages along with core groups of Dog Soldiers. But the parent villages, unfortunately, could never escape the onus of blame, and it became a matter of time before this reality yielded tragic results. Military strategy called for Sheridan to punish the offending peoples severely by means of total war—aggressively instilling terror among noncombatant as well as combatant populations by any means possible, including indiscriminate destruction of their homes and property and rooting out and killing all warriors and others who might give opposition. The deaths of innocents—women, children, and elderly as well as those warriors who had nothing to do with the recent raids—was something that could not be avoided during army attacks on sleeping villages, which was the military's standard tactic on the plains. Moreover, the psychological element of total war meant that as the season turned colder, the Indians might be subjected to tremendous material losses during unbearable climatic conditions; many innocents who survived an attack would likely be thrown out into the cold to starve or die due to vigorous and unrelenting army pursuit. It was this type of punitive winter offensive that Sherman and Sheridan conceived for the Cheyennes and Arapahos in retaliation for their destructive behavior since August.

In preparation, Sheridan augmented his meager force of Seventh Cavalry, Third Infantry, and Thirty-eighth Infantry troops along the railroad and the trails, bringing in seven companies of the Fifth Cavalry to serve in the Smoky Hill and Republican River country in support of the Tenth Cavalry already there. He arranged for his aide, Major George A. Forsyth, to recruit a company of fifty well-seasoned frontiersmen to patrol the railroad in western Kansas around Fort Wallace as something of a special mobile-ranger detachment. In early September, as the different units consolidated, eight companies of the Seventh Cavalry and one of the Third Infantry took station at Fort Dodge along the Arkansas, poised to go after the offending Indians, while four companies of the Tenth moved to Walnut Creek Crossing, along the road between Dodge and Fort Hays to the north. Forsyth and his scouts roamed the country about Beaver Creek north of the Kansas Pacific line.

All of these components watched for Indian trails; most reported signs indicating that the tribesmen had gone south of the Arkansas.[27] With that knowledge, Sheridan prepared to send Sully's command into the treaty lands to effectively chastise and punish the Cheyennes and Arapahos for their role or presumed complicity in the recent violence.

4

MOVEMENTS AND STRATEGIES

The revised toll in General Sheridan's department since August 1868 had stood at 110 citizens killed, thirteen women raped, and more than one thousand head of livestock stolen. In addition, much private property, consisting of buildings, farmhouses, stagecoaches, wagon trains, and rolling stock, had been lost to raiding Indians. During numerous chases and skirmishes with the tribesmen, the troops had been largely unsuccessful in bringing them to bay, and the frustration weighed on Sheridan and his officers with pronounced effect. Still smarting over Lieutenant Colonel Alfred Sully's acquiescence in permitting the distribution of arms and ammunition to the Indians, the department commander nevertheless needed him to take direct action against them. Such was the basis of Sheridan's orders for Sully to go after the Cheyennes and Arapahos and deliver them a sound punishment for their crimes. In addition to being in the spirit of the army's total-war strategy toward the Indians, Sheridan believed that moving Sully below the Arkansas, into Indian Territory, and toward their villages would force the Cheyenne and Arapaho raiders operating in Kansas to fall back and protect their homes and families.[1]

Guided by these assumptions, on the evening of September 7, with Sheridan present to see them off, Sully departed Fort Dodge with a command of more than five hundred men—nine companies (A, B, C,

D, E, F, G, I, and K) of the Seventh Cavalry under Major Joel Elliott plus
one (Company F) of the Third Infantry and a mountain howitzer under
Captain John H. Page, whose principal purpose was to furnish escort
to thirty wagons under the command of First Lieutenant James M. Bell,
the Seventh's regimental quartermaster. The son of the famous painter
Thomas Sully, Alfred Sully at forty-eight had garnered much previous
experience campaigning against Indians. An 1841 West Point graduate, he fought in both the Mexican and Civil Wars, winning brevets in
the latter for his performance at Fair Oaks and Malvern Hill, Virginia.
He was best known for an offensive against the Indians in the wake of
the Minnesota outbreak that culminated in his destruction of a large
Sioux village at Whitestone Hill, Dakota Territory, in 1863.[2] Now, with
Sheridan's concurrence, he forded the Arkansas and steered his column
southwest toward villages reported to be forty miles away along the
Cimarron. The soldiers, with three days' rations in their haversacks,
traveled some thirty miles that night, camping at 3:00 A.M. on a branch
of Crooked Creek. On the eighth, with but a few hours sleep, the
troops continued south, striking an Indian trail at 2:00 P.M. at Goose
Creek and taking up the pursuit until dark.

There is little doubt that the warriors Sully subsequently encountered below the Arkansas were Cheyennes and Arapahos. Whereas
George Bent years later identified them as Kiowas and Comanches,
Sully's own scouts and interpreters—John S. Smith and Benjamin H.
Clark, who knew the Cheyennes and Arapahos well—positively identified the warriors as Cheyennes, in some cases as Dog Soldiers. Although
certain groups of warriors might have included Kiowas and/or Comanches, it seems that the majority were most assuredly Cheyennes and
Arapahos. On September 9, following a delay while the supply train
caught up, Sully marched thirty miles, then sent Major Elliott and four
companies of the Seventh to follow the rain-obliterated trail toward
the Cimarron, while he and the remaining units marched southwest
five miles to Goose Creek to camp and await word from Elliott on the
location of the Indians. "We have not seen any yet, since we started
out," wrote an enlisted diarist, "but they cannot be very far ahead of
us." At 4:00 A.M. the next morning, Sully struck south, meeting Elliott's
command thirteen miles away at the Cimarron. After a march of fourteen miles down that river, a force of warriors suddenly surrounded
the advance scouts, and the colonel dispatched some cavalry forward
to relieve them. During the ensuing skirmish, in which two warriors

and a pony were killed, the tribesmen were driven away. The soldiers camped near the junction of Crooked Creek with the Cimarron. During the night, Indians attacked the troops and the train but were quickly driven away. Next morning, September 11, as the soldiers pulled out of camp, warriors swooped down on two straggling men of Captain George W. Yates's Company F, carrying them away and subsequently killing one and wounding the other, while capturing four horses. Cavalrymen of the rear guard under Captain Louis M. Hamilton pursued the Indians several miles, forcing them to drop the wounded man before abandoning the chase.[3]

This engagement was described by the scout Ben Clark in correspondence of 1904 and probably exemplified the sporadic nature of the action experienced by Sully's men on this expedition. Clark stated that the two troopers, leading two officers' mounts, had been cut off by about one hundred warriors as they prepared to catch up with the command:

As soon as word reached Sully at the head of the column, he sent Capt. Keogh back with a company [apparently Hamilton's] to try to rescue the men. Before the rescuing party could reach the scene the Indians had too great a start to be overtaken and finally disappeared over the hills to the southwestward with the soldiers' horses, equipments, arms and the extra horses belonging to officers as well. It was at first supposed that they had both men still with them alive, but while Keogh was in full chase he came near riding over one of the soldiers who was lying in the tall grass. This soldier was alive but had had his arms taken from him and [was] shot off his horse, being shot clean through his body from the back. He said when he was shot the other man was still in his saddle. This incident still further delayed the pursuing party, which after chasing a mile or two further and searching over the prairie for the body of the other man without success returned to the command with the wounded man who had been placed in an ambulance. . . . In returning to the command some 200 Indians got between us . . . and the rear guard and we had a lively skirmish before getting to the train. We had the ambulance and wounded man with us all the while.[4]

After Sully's column proceeded another five miles, the warriors mounted yet another attack and more or less harried the command all day. Deployed in skirmish formation, the soldiers fought the Indians, now numbering several hundred, for several hours. Sully later reported that his men killed and wounded at least eight warriors "and no doubt a great many more. We had to fight in the hills by detachments. Officers and men report having seen several more [Indians] . . . as having dropped from their horses." Private Winfield Harvey noted that the warriors "did some very bold riding and what a sight it was to see them ride and shoot." The colonel, marveling at the warriors' use of bugle calls to orchestrate their movements, observed: "The Indians were well armed, some with the latest patent inventions of firearms and seemed to be well supplied with ammunition, and were splendidly mounted, much better than our Troops. I noticed one (1) squad of about one hundred (100) who drilled with the bugle. Their calls were different from ours, but yet the Indians understood them. The Guides assert that they were the Cheyenne Dog Soldiers. The Northern Arapahoes were there also. A half breed Arapahoe [scout] recognized one and talked with him." The Indians scattered as the command resumed its march southeast but returned and attacked the rear guard six miles before it reached Beaver River. Sully noted that they "were handsomely repulsed with considerable loss." The soldiers crossed the Beaver, bivouacking on the south side of the river. During the night, warriors tried to stampede the soldiers' animals. Sully's troops, posted beneath the wagons, responded quickly and repulsed them with no losses. Bell remembered that the warriors were "well armed, but still used bows and arrows a good deal."[5]

As the column passed south along the Beaver on September 12, warriors followed, striking again near Kiowa Creek, twelve miles from the troops' crossing point. Here, at about 11:00 A.M., a major skirmish took place, with Sully deploying eight of Elliott's cavalry companies and Page's infantry company. Captain Albert Barnitz reported, "the Indians appeared in force, in our front, and made a vigorous and determined charge on the company which had the advance, but were repulsed by a volley at close range." Exchanging fire with the warriors, the soldiers advanced steadily, finally driving the Indians in all directions with the howitzer. One soldier remarked, "we had fun for about two hours, killing quite a number of them." After going fifteen miles farther, the command camped for the night. On the thirteenth they proceeded southeast along the Beaver to Wolf Creek, twenty-three miles away, with the rear guard under the persistent long-range fire of warriors for much of the day. Believing he was gaining on the villages,

Sully also grew convinced that the Indians were creating blind lodge-pole trails to lead his men into the surrounding sand hills. He explained: "Not having anyone with me acquainted with the country, we crossed the Middle River [Wolf Creek] and got into the trap the Indians laid for us. They occupied all the hills, and were dismounted. The wagon train which we had to keep with us, on account of the broken country, and vigorous attack of the Indians, could not proceed. However, by dismounting my men, I drove the Indians through the heavy sands from hill to hill and withdrew the train from the ambuscade with very little loss and camped for the night on the Canadian near its junction with Middle River." One man described this country as being composed of "the worst sandhills you ever saw." A soldier of Company F, Seventh Cavalry, was killed in this fight before the command afterward turned north, marched three miles to recross Wolf Creek, and bivouacked on Beaver River.[6]

On September 14, the day after this encounter, a weary Sully reassessed his situation. The families, he decided, had escaped beyond his reach. Furthermore, he was satisfied that he could no longer pursue the tribesmen through such broken country with a wagon train and under circumstances where "the Indians had every advantage of attacking, or retreating, at their option, [and continuing] would only result in wearing out my stock."[7] Simply put, the sand hills had defeated him. Sully concluded to start home to obtain supplies, ammunition, and additional troops to protect his train, then to outfit another column to act in concert with his own. The decision did not sit well with all of his officers, Captain Barnitz included: "I . . . was quite mortified to find that it was determined to retreat 'for rations' as it was said—though we had enough to last us till the end of this month—of everything except forage, and I was very sanguine, from all indications, that within two or three days more we should have overhauled their villages, and ended the campaign—whereas to retire then was only to protract the matter and render it more tedious as well as difficult." Sully's command passed over the Beaver and journeyed twenty miles, the Indians still harassing his flanks before withdrawing. The troops encamped along Buffalo Creek. In a view somewhat contrary to that of Captain Barnitz, Private Harvey recorded his observations of the day: "The Indians followed us until about noon, thinking they had given us a big thrashing, but it was not the case. We were out of rations and could not help ourselves."[8]

The colonel turned his men north on September 15, a cloudy blustery day, fording the Cimarron and reaching Bluff Creek in Kansas after covering thirty-two miles through sage-covered sand hills and "an exceedingly broken red earth country" abounding with so many buffalo that the soldiers killed scores of them. From that point, Sully forwarded his sick and wounded, a broken ambulance, and his empty supply wagons to Fort Dodge, the latter for reprovisioning so he might resume his campaign. "There is no doubt," he declared, "that all of the Cheyennes and nearly all of the Arapahoes are engaged in this war." The colonel opined that the Kiowas and Comanches might soon join these Indians, and he urged "that we operate as soon as possible with force enough, not only to oppose the hostile Indians but to crush them." Two columns of troops would succeed where one could not, he believed, and "will keep those Indians moving and so uncomfortable that they will be glad to make peace on any terms." Sully estimated that his campaign had resulted in killing at least twenty or thirty warriors and wounding about the same number. "It is too much the custom to report a very large number of the enemy killed, but the above is far within the limits of what is supposed to be the actual loss." Disheartened over the meager results of his eight-day sojourn, Sully finally headed back to Fort Dodge, leaving the Seventh Cavalry companies under Elliott to patrol for Indians below the Arkansas.[9]

Sully's plan for a resupplied and rejuvenated campaign to prosecute the Indians did not materialize as rapidly as he had thought. It took time for the widely scattered infantry units to reach Fort Dodge, and by the time they arrived, any momentum the colonel had hoped to salvage had long since vanished. From a military perspective, the campaign had been a failure. The Cheyennes, determined to prevent the soldiers from striking their homes and families, had forced Sully to withdraw when seemingly at their doorstep, their constant harrying having worn down the soldiers before any material gain could be achieved. On balance, Sheridan's hope of punishing the tribes and preventing recurrent raids in Kansas did not materialize. General Sherman did not mince words: "I think Sully made a botch of it on the Canadian," he told a colleague. The colonel drew criticism for having conducted his campaign from an army ambulance, in which he traveled much of the time. Major Elliott wrote a friend: "I had the honor to command the cavalry on that expedition and if it was *fighting*, then Indian wars must be a huge joke." He cautioned the recipient of his remarks not to make them public because Sully "is an amiable fellow and I would not like to hurt his feelings." Another critic was Edward S. Godfrey, then a first lieutenant. In 1927 he reminisced how the colonel, in passing over the Arkansas the evening of departing Fort Dodge, had likened it to having "crossed the Rubicon" and, on deciding to retire after a week of mostly barren results, had given as his reason the "interminable" nature of the sand hills. Despite all the problems, maintained Godfrey, Sully "seemed perfectly satisfied with the results of the expedition."[10]

For the army, about the only positive feature resulting from Sully's operation was his issuance, on September 26, of General Field Orders No. 3, which, based largely on his recent experience, broadcast procedures for dealing with the Indians while on campaign. It was a remarkable document, one of the few ever to offer prescriptions for combating warriors, resulting from a trying, hard-fought, and frustrating—though perhaps all too brief—campaign. The orders addressed the warriors' strategy to "never attack except they have the advantage, and never to make a stand for resistance, except we are lucky enough to strike their villages; their plan will be to harass us in small parties, endeavoring to draw the troops from the direction in which they may be going, or to entice us to an unsuccessful pursuit, whereby they can break down our animals." Regarding the recent encounter in the sand hills, the orders warned officers to be on guard for trails that looked fresh, "for it is an old trick of the Indians to fasten Lodge poles to their War horses' saddles and then make a trail to lead you where they most wish you." The remainder of the document offered carefully contemplated rules, from recent hindsight, to assure success for future area field commands.[11] It was under these principles the colonel wished to operate during his subsequent expedition.

While Sully's campaign had been afield, other events had taken place in Sheridan's department. On September 15 a company of the Tenth Cavalry protecting the stage road between Fort Wallace and Denver came under attack along Sand Creek. The troops, commanded by Captain George W. Graham, drove the warriors off with reported casualties of eleven killed and an unknown number wounded.[12] Two days later the command of scouts under Major George A. Forsyth was attacked by at least seven hundred Cheyennes along the Arikaree Fork of the Republican River in eastern Colorado. Forsyth's small contingent dug in on a sandbar at midstream and managed to hold off the warriors, who mounted numerous charges against the men. Lieutenant Frederick H. Beecher, Third Infantry, and four of the scouts were killed in the engagement, while fifteen more were wounded. Forsyth himself endured two severe wounds. The men, constantly under siege, lived on horseflesh over the next week until troops of the Tenth Cavalry found and relieved them on September 25.[13]

Delays in forwarding reinforcements resulted in the commensurate loss of provisions for Sully's command—the rations were consumed by his troops on patrol and those at Fort Dodge. With that, Sheridan and Sherman turned to a more contentious strategy, believing that if the offending tribes were to be adequately punished, a more potent strike force had to be readied for the job. Justification for such aggression lay in the Indians' abrogation of stipulations of the Medicine Lodge Treaty. "They have not restrained those who have [committed depredations], nor have they on demand given up the criminals as they agreed to do." Sherman had already complied with Sheridan's request for more men, sending six companies of the Twenty-Seventh Infantry and two of the Second Cavalry under Lieutenant Colonel Luther P. Bradley to patrol the forks of the Republican—they had arrived there in time to take part in the rescue of Forsyth's command. Late in September seven companies of the Fifth Cavalry under Major William B. Royall arrived at Fort Harker and were immediately dispatched to range the Beaver Creek country of northwestern Kansas above the railroad. (This stream was a tributary of the Republican and is not to be confused with the Beaver River of Indian Territory, where Sully had recently maneuvered.) The purpose of these units was to operate through the winter and "clean out all hostile Indians near to and between" the Platte and Smoky Hill overland roads. Deeming his total force still too small to contend with warrior bands that now possibly included those from the Kiowa and Comanche tribes, Sheridan, with Sherman's approval, called on the governor of Kansas to raise twelve hundred cavalry for operations in his department. Sherman's design, as he enjoined his department commander, was "to remove all Indian Agencies from the lines of the Railroad, and to establish them down on the Canadian, so that we may induce some Indians to go thither, compel others, and treat all others as hostile. . . . Until that is accomplished, peace with the Indians is impossible."[14]

Concerned over the inability of the troops to distinguish between what he considered the "well-disposed" as opposed to "warlike" tribes-

men, and doubtless hoping to assuage apprehensions of Interior Department officials that the army would attempt no such distinction, Sherman directed agents for the former people to bring them to Fort Cobb,
where Hazen would superintend them. "It will simplify our game of
war, already complicated enough, by removing them well away from the
field of operations." Hazen geared his efforts to stabilizing the Kiowas
and Comanches who had not yet become involved in the escalating
troubles. On September 19 and 20, Hazen and Sheridan met with the
Kiowas and Comanches at Fort Larned, during which those tribesmen
agreed to join Hazen at Fort Cobb and avoid hostilities. Meantime,
Sherman urged their agent to join Hazen in distributing food and clothing to ensure against the people joining the Cheyennes and Arapahos.
"The latter [peoples] should receive nothing," he concluded. "Now that
they are at open war, I propose to give them enough of it to satisfy them
to their hearts' content, and General Sheridan will not relax his efforts
till the winter will put them at our mercy." Believing that he would not
reach Fort Cobb before the peaceful tribes arrived there, Hazen arranged
for a surrogate to meet them. Captain Henry E. Alvord, Tenth Cavalry,
appeared at the post in mid-October and began disbursing rations and
talking with leaders pending Hazen's arrival.[15]

Between the time of Sully's return and the resumption of major
campaigning under the edicts laid down by Sherman and Sheridan,
most of the Seventh Cavalry remained afield, ranging around the area
of Bluff Creek for the balance of September, seeking adequate grass and
water for their stock while remaining poised for serious operations.
"There is no news of where we are going to go," wrote an enlisted man
at Fort Dodge on September 18. "Some say to winter quarters and some
say on a campaign; not knowing which yet."[16] Three days later, however, rumors floating among the soldiers held that Lieutenant Colonel
George A. Custer was coming to assume command of the regiment.
Based on the disappointment prevalent in the ranks in the wake of
Sully's barren movement, that news likely sparked excitement. On
October 1, moreover, Indian warriors struck boldly at troops bivouacked
near Fort Dodge. Private Harvey described the assault:

> This morning at daybreak, the Indians came charging down on
> our camp. . . . I was sitting by the cook fire eating my break-
> fast, when I first saw them. They charged on some working
> men [soldiers] just about one-half mile from here, but the men

ran and made their escape. One was badly wounded, afterward dying. Our company soon got into line and started after them on a dead run, sometimes coming very close to them, but our Company Commander, being an old card, would not let us charge them. There was a wagon train coming up the river at some seven miles from the post and the Indians seeing that they had a chance, charged it, capturing four wagons and killing two teamsters, [and] also wounding the wagon master, afterwards dying. After we drove them off south of the Arkansas, we fell back to camp, took dinner, drew one day's rations, [and] started again down to Big Coon Creek to meet another train on its road to this place. . . . No more of today.[17]

That same day more warriors, some reported to be Kiowas, struck Fort Zarah and several civilian wagon trains in its vicinity. Farther north on the Solomon, warriors struck again. On October 9, near the town of Minneapolis, they killed four people, wounded one, and carried away twenty-three-year-old Anna Belle Morgan, a homesteader's wife. The Indians were tentatively identified by Morgan's husband as belonging to Black Kettle's band of Cheyennes. Regardless, Morgan eventually landed in a village of Dog Soldiers, who might, in reality, have been the perpetrators of the new Solomon raids.[18]

Thus Sully's fruitless campaign, instead of cowing the tribes, produced something of a backlash and brought a flurry of renewed raiding to the area. Partly inspired, at least, by the mild autumn weather in the region in 1868, at least seven incidents involving Indian attacks on citizens or trains occurred between October 2 and October 14. One of these became especially noteworthy in light of later events. On the morning of Tuesday, October 6, a train of eight ox-drawn wagons departed Boggs Ranch en route to Fort Dodge. The party was in the charge of a Mr. Owens and consisted of ten men, one woman, and a boy. The woman was Clara Blinn, wife of Richard Blinn, who was also along, and the boy was their two-year-old child, Willie. The next day, some ten miles east of the mouth of Sand Creek on the Arkansas, a force of seventy-five Indians attacked the train, wounding one man, stampeding the teams, making off with four of the wagons, and taking Mrs. Blinn and her son. All day and night the party fought the warriors, whose number gradually increased to around two hundred. On the afternoon of the eighth, most of the Indians drew off, forded the Arkansas

River, and camped on the south bank, only to return and renew the attack that night. On Friday the ninth, they attacked yet again, this time keeping the party under fire for four more days before crossing the river and heading southeast. On October 12 one of the besieged got away and reached Fort Lyon, where Captain Penrose dispatched troops to their relief. Cavalrymen scoured the countryside for evidence of Mrs. Blinn and her son. Approximately four miles from the scene of the late havoc, they found a note from the woman "saying her & the child was well and that the Indians were going to keep them & asked her husband to do all he could for her." Owen identified the leader of the Indians as Satanta, the prominent Kiowa, thus establishing the presumed guilt of that tribe for the deed.[19]

These incidents compelled General Sheridan to move rapidly in his recourse. As strategy for fulfilling Sherman's objective of delivering a debilitating blow, with memories of Sully's impotent movement in mind, Sheridan invoked the concept of multiple military columns marching from several directions simultaneously to converge on a common area where the Indians were known to be located. Both Sherman and Sheridan saw winter—when the people were at their most vulnerable—as the perfect time for launching a punitive strike. Sheridan received authority for such a movement on October 9. By then, he believed, the warriors had mostly removed from the area north of the railroad, where troops were constantly patrolling, to the tract below the Arkansas River, where their families congregated, reportedly in the area of the headwaters of the Red River, in the Texas Panhandle, and south of the Antelope Hills in Indian Territory. To converge forces on this area, Sheridan directed Colonel George W. Getty, commanding the Military District of New Mexico, to organize a column composed of six companies of the Third Cavalry, two of the Thirty-Seventh Infantry, and four mountain howitzers to move east from Fort Bascom, New Mexico. This force, rationed until January 1869, would range along the South Canadian (then Main Canadian) River. Another force from Fort Lyon, Colorado Territory, under Major Eugene A. Carr, composed of four companies of the Tenth Cavalry and one of the Seventh, would move east along the Arkansas, then maneuver south toward the Antelope Hills and the Red River. These two columns Sheridan regarded as "beaters in," driving any outlying tribesmen to the central village area. A third column constituted Sheridan's principal component. Consisting of troops of the Seventh Cavalry and the Nineteenth Kansas Volunteer

Cavalry (to be raised by the state's governor), it would proceed to a point near the junction of Beaver River and the North Canadian in Indian Territory, establish a supply depot, and strike south, hitting the winter camps somewhere along the headwaters of the Washita River or farther south in the area of the Sweetwater and Red Rivers. There would be "no terms with the hostile Indians except unconditional surrender." The objective of the operation, according to Sheridan, was "to strike the Indians a hard blow and force them on to the reservations set apart for them [by the Medicine Lodge Treaty], and if this could not be accomplished to show to the Indian that the winter season would not give him rest, and that he and his villages and stock could be destroyed; that he would have no security, winter or summer, except in obeying the laws of peace and humanity."[20]

On October 9, 1868, the day Sheridan received authority for the campaign from Sherman, he wired Kansas governor Samuel J. Crawford, calling on him to provide a regiment of mounted volunteers for six months' service against the Indians. The directive stipulated that the regiment should consist of forty-one officers (colonel, lieutenant colonel, three majors, twelve captains, and a like number each of first and second lieutenants), the requisite noncommissioned officers (as specified in existing army regulations), and twelve companies of one hundred men each. The soldiers were to be recruited and mustered in at Topeka and later to be mustered into the service of the United States, with appropriate arms, equipments, clothing, and horses provided at that time. Sheridan anticipated that the regiment would be in the field by November 1.[21]

Another decision by Sheridan was to be of historic moment. Following Sully's abortive campaign, the general determined to energize his command with the addition of Lieutenant Colonel George A. Custer, who was then waiting out a suspension from duty following his court-martial the previous year for actions connected with his service on Hancock's expedition; the gossip circulating within the ranks of the Seventh Cavalry had merit. Sheridan formally requested the remission of the remainder of Custer's sentence and on September 24 wired him to report for duty immediately. "Eleven companies of your regiment will move about the first of October against the hostile Indians from Medicine Lodge and towards the Wichita Mountains." Custer joined his command on October 11 at Bluff Creek. By coincidence, the troops' bivouac came under attack that very evening, and the soldiers formed

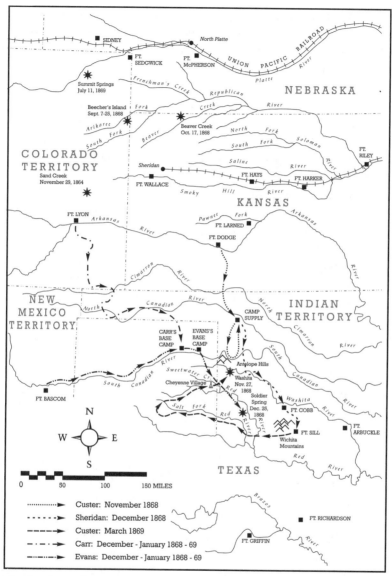

The Southern Plains War, 1868–69. Adapted from Utley, *Frontier Regulars*, 146.

as skirmishers and eventually drove the warriors away without casualty on either side. Custer immediately sent out columns looking for the tribesmen. Over the next two weeks, he led the ten companies of the Seventh in scouting operations between Bluff Creek and Medicine Lodge Creek and the environs of the Big Bend of the Arkansas, the regiment covering a distance of approximately 250 miles during the remainder of the month. These scouts proving fruitless, the command returned to Bluff Creek before moving to a point on the Arkansas a few miles southeast from Fort Dodge to await and prepare for Sheridan's major winter offensive.[22]

The entree of Custer into Sheridan's campaign plans brought an almost instant infusion of animation to the companies of the Seventh Cavalry, largely demoralized following Sully's tepid performance. Custer, one of the brash young officers who had endeared himself to the public during the Civil War, had pursued the Cheyennes in Kansas, Nebraska, and Colorado during Hancock's expedition, which comprised his only experience with Indians. An 1861 West Point graduate, Custer rose meteorically during the Civil War through prowess in battle and inspirational leadership. He attained the rank of brigadier general of volunteers following a valiant performance at Aldie, Virginia, thereby becoming, at age twenty-three, one of the youngest generals in the Union army. He led the Michigan Cavalry Brigade at Gettysburg, Yellow Tavern, Trevilian Station, and Winchester with such imposing effect that in 1864 he received command of the Third Cavalry Division. He fought under Sheridan in the Shenandoah Valley in 1864–65, leading the division at Tom's Brook, Cedar Creek, and Waynesboro as well as in the war's closing operations at Five Forks, Sayler's Creek, and Appomattox Station. By war's end, Custer's continuous service had netted for him promotion to major general of volunteers and numerous brevet appointments in both the regular and volunteer service.

Reduced in grade to captain in the regular army during the postwar reorganization of the army, Custer won appointment as lieutenant colonel of the newly formed Seventh Cavalry in 1866 and played no small part in readying the regiment for service on the plains. Hancock's campaign had been Custer's baptism of fire in the West. Its aftermath represented the nadir of his military career and brought on his courtmartial and dismissal from duty for a year. The incident reflected much of Custer's rash and impetuous nature that brought him either admiration or disdain from his associates. The press, which had captivated the country with his daring wartime persona, coupled with his own writings, contributed to bring him considerable fame, and by the time of his death eight years hence along Montana Territory's Little Bighorn River, Custer was the country's most celebrated Indian fighter. Standing nearly six feet tall, lithe and sinewy, the blue-eyed, blond-haired

officer cut a striking figure. His remarkable energy, coupled with enthu-
siastic demeanor, skilled perceptive faculties, and dashing physical
appearance gave him a reputation of accomplishment within military
circles, and it was these qualities that Sheridan tapped to recharge his
uninspired troops.[23]

Word among the officers of the Seventh held that Sheridan's campaign would begin before the end of October. The movement would
be in the direction of the Wichita Mountains in the southwestern part
of Indian Territory. Its purpose was to disrupt the Cheyenne and Arapaho camps and keep them moving, to thus wear down the warriors'
ponies until spring, when the army would bring all of its resources to
bear against the tribes. But the schedule for starting troops south was
postponed when anticipated supplies failed to reach Fort Dodge. Captain Barnitz complained to his wife: "Rations and all manner of supplies sufficient to last a force of this size for six months, at least,
should have been stored at a post like Fort Dodge, at all times. . . .
Now we see the result! An Expedition of some magnitude is indefinitely delayed."[24]

Elsewhere, however, other parts of Sheridan's command succeeded in meeting the Cheyennes, though the results of the engagements were inconclusive. On October 14 a command under Major
William B. Royall, Fifth Cavalry, operating in the Republican River
country had been attacked by Dog Soldiers on Prairie Dog Creek, losing two men killed and twenty-six horses stolen by the warriors. The
day before, Major Carr, escorted by some one hundred troopers of
Companies H and I, Tenth Cavalry, under Captain Louis H. Carpenter,
departed Fort Wallace to seek out and join the companies of the Fifth
under Royall. On striking Beaver Creek, the soldiers and their supply
wagons journeyed fifty miles northeast down its course, searching for
Royall without success. On October 18 the command was suddenly
attacked by a body of several hundred Cheyennes—apparently many
of the same ones who had besieged Forsyth's scouts at Beecher's Island
three weeks earlier. The fighting raged for nearly six hours in intermittent, long-range fashion before the troopers drove the warriors
away, whereupon Carr withdrew with minimal casualties back to Fort
Wallace. On the twenty-second, the colonel, accompanied by fifty
scouts, joined and took command of the seven companies of the Fifth
at Buffalo Tank along the Kansas Pacific Railroad and set out to find
the Dog Soldiers. Three days later the battle was joined near Beaver

Creek, and over the next five days, a running fight occurred until the twenty-seventh, when the warriors withdrew and departed the area. Carr headed his exhausted men back to Wallace to ready them for Sheridan's campaign to finally subjugate the Southern Cheyennes and Arapahos and their affiliates.[25]

5

CAMP SUPPLY

By mid-October, as autumn continued to turn the plains into a drab and lifeless palette, the targeted tribes of Sheridan's movement huddled their villages along the streams far below the Arkansas, hopeful that the period for army campaigning was at last over. Despite the seasonal changes, however, war parties composed largely of Cheyenne and Arapaho warriors from those camps took advantage of the relatively mild days, moving with ease to strike unsuspecting civilian trains and wayfarers on the Kansas trails.[1] The troops at Fort Dodge, meantime, still awaiting provisions, spent the days preparing for their imminent departure south to chastise those Indians for their perceived cumulative wrongs, all of which had thus far occurred with impunity.[2]

On October 28 the companies of the Seventh Cavalry, which had lately combed the country along the Arkansas, took station below Fort Dodge at Camp Sandy Forsyth, so named in honor of Major George A. Forsyth of Beecher's Island fame. Custer wrote Sheridan at the general's Fort Hays headquarters of his regiment's need for horses and arms, particularly Colt revolvers, but concluded, "I can move on the proposed campaign in good condition in half an hour's notice." He added, "While I would be glad to see every man armed with a revolver, I would not delay a day to receive them. I find that in a charge against Indians the revolver often would be of great service when neither the sabre or carbine can be used." Custer also registered with Sheridan his concern over Lieutenant Colonel Alfred Sully's likely participation. "Sully did not say whether he was going with the expedition or not. If he goes I hope he will not break the 7th up in to two or more columns." He wrote, "As to the campaign, I feel great confidence in being able to do something decisive." Plans called for the command to depart for Indian Territory on November 9.[3]

In 1868 the Seventh Cavalry was but two years old, having been organized at Fort Riley, Kansas, on authority of Congress granted in July 1866 and designated by the War Department in November. Its colonel was Andrew J. Smith, on extended leave of absence through most of 1868, leaving Custer, its lieutenant colonel, to command after returning from suspension. There were three majors, Alfred Gibbs, in ill health and commanding Fort Harker; Joseph G. Tilford, also on leave of absence; and Joel Elliott, on duty with the regiment. Below them in rank were a host of captains and lieutenants, not only many with service credentials dating back to the Mexican and Civil Wars but also some newly commissioned officers, West Point graduates and men commissioned from civil life. The enlisted corps consisted of both seasoned veterans and relatively recent enlistees. They came from all walks of life—former soldiers (including officers), sailors, shoemakers, tailors, teachers, carpenters, laborers, lawyers, farmers, rough-hewn bowery types, foreign-born and natives, educated and unlearned, temperate and bibulous. Throughout the army, their noncommissioned overseers were typically (though not universally) older, seasoned veterans with years of experience. They actually ran the company units; some were domineering brutes who tormented their charges to the extent that many were driven to desert. By the early fall of 1868, the various units of the Seventh had experienced baptisms of fire in twenty-two actions with Indians since its organization. As it now readied for Sheridan's campaign near Fort Dodge, the regiment's available components consisted of eleven companies—A, B, C, D, E, F, G, H, I, K, and M (Company L remained stationed at Fort Lyon, Colorado Territory), totaling twenty-nine officers and approximately 844 enlisted men. In addition, five companies of infantry (one of the Fifth, one of the Thirty-Eighth, and three of the Third), under Captain John H. Page, Third Infantry—plus the various civilian teamsters and white and Indian guides and scouts—brought the total expedition to over seventeen hundred personnel. (Moreover, the planned addition of the Nineteenth

Kansas Volunteer Cavalry would raise that figure to around twenty-seven hundred.)[4]

While at Camp Forsyth, the Seventh, plagued by many and frequent desertions in its early history, received a large number of recruits, which helped bring each company's strength to its authorized level.[5] The new arrivals required a commensurate number of new horses, arms, and equipment, and more ammunition was necessary for the upcoming operation, which was estimated to last for two months. Then the regiment began "refitting, reorganizing, and renovating." The units of the Seventh practiced cavalry drill and marksmanship (including taking shots on parties of Indians that occasionally harried the command). So important was the emphasis on accurate shooting that a special unit of sharpshooters was created, based on the results of twice-daily target practice and composed of forty of the regiment's best marksmen. Exempted from guard and picket duty and allowed to march together, these troopers were headed by First Lieutenant William W. Cooke. (The unique character of the unit made wags in the regiment designate it the "Corps d'Elite.")[6] The post commander of Fort Dodge turned over to the Seventh Cavalry two thousand Spencer carbine cartridges for use during the expedition. Officers received directives requiring them to familiarize themselves with the Manual of Signals and to train a number of enlisted men in those procedures. Medical Department personnel received instructions to join senior medical personnel at Fort Dodge; one of them, Assistant Surgeon George M. Sternberg, was appointed chief medical officer for the campaign. Custer recommended that his men receive "an issue of vegetables" before getting underway. First Lieutenant Henry J. Nowlan was appointed acting commissary of subsistence for the expedition, while First Lieutenant James M. Bell, quartermaster officer of the regiment, oversaw preparations regarding clothing, equipment, and other supplies. Hundreds of wagons arrived for hauling materials for building the forward supply base as well as many more to carry rations and provisions for the command. Oxen and mules were brought in to draw the wagons and ambulances, which were assigned under the following guidelines: "One six mule and one four mule wagon (with their teamsters) for every Troop present with the regiment, one six mule wagon for the Band, one six mule and one four mule wagon for the Field and Staff, one six mule and one four mule wagon and seven ambulances for the Medical Department of the Regiment, two citizen Blacksmiths and tools necessary for them, and one wagon master will also be retained by Bvt. Maj. Bell."[7]

For a cavalry regiment to perform properly, its horses had to be healthy, and their maintenance in the Seventh during the regiment's preparations became an ongoing concern. Some of the mounts were jaded from past service, and Sheridan sent fifty new horses for dismounted men and to replace those animals deemed unserviceable. Company farriers stayed busy shoeing all of the regiment's horses. The general also arranged for Custer to receive 550 Colt Army revolvers requested for his men, but the colonel asked for more for the remainder of the regiment: "All the troop commanders are very anxious to have their men armed with them."[8] Custer also reassigned the horses to his companies based on their colors—"coloring the horses" it was called—and each company commander, based on rank and seniority, selected his choice of color. According to Lieutenant Edward S. Godfrey, there were "four troops of bay horses, three sorrel, one each black, brown and gray, the band and trumpeters gray, and the eleventh troop the odds and ends of all colors." The change did not sit well with all of the officers, and Captain Albert Barnitz called Custer's order "foolish, unwarranted, [and] unjustifiable."[9]

Through Sheridan's offices, and evidently on the recommendation of Governor Crawford, authorities recruited a dozen Osage Indians to serve as scouts for the expeditionary force. The Osages not only knew the country in which the troops would be operating but also were in a constant state of war with the Cheyennes and Arapahos. At Camp Forsyth, orders directed the quartermaster to issue each man a blouse and a cavalry hat and tassel, this in order "to distinguish these Indians from those of the Hostile tribes." The Osages, who "look as savage as the enemy we seek," were also slated to receive eight hundred rounds of cartridges for the campaign.[10]

The soldiers received winter clothing, which would serve them well when temperatures plummeted. Their basic clothing kit consisted of an issue pullover shirt, flannel drawers, woolen sack coat or cavalry shell jacket, pattern-1861 mounted greatcoat, and leather boots with buffalo overshoes or commercially made vulcanized "arctics." In addition, fur or woolen caps and privately manufactured mittens or gauntlets of buffalo or other fur were available. Each man wore an 1855-pattern leather saber belt with a pattern-1851 brass-and-German-silver eagle belt plate. Mounted upon the belt were a leather pistol holster, percussion-cap pouch, pistol-cartridge box, and carbine-cartridge box. Weapons were the .50-caliber Model 1865 Spencer seven-shot repeating carbine (carried by the soldier on a leather carbine sling with steel snaphook that fitted across his shoulder), the .44-caliber Model 1860 Colt Army revolver six-shooter (some troopers apparently still carried the .44-caliber Model 1858 Remington revolver [New Model Army]), and the Model 1858 light cavalry saber. Officers normally wore higher-quality clothing of different design and manufacture. On campaign, however, they wore and used many of these same clothing items and equipments, some of which were privately purchased or otherwise appropriated from issue stocks.[11]

Officers and men spent considerable money at the post-trader's store, where, one observer noted, prices rose rapidly, with blue flannel shirts and pairs of cotton socks commanding nine dollars and one dollar, respectively. Other clothing improvements were effected after the troops reached Camp Supply, as described by Private John Ryan:

> Some lined their overcoats with woolen blankets, while others made leggings from pieces of condemned government canvas. Although in those days the cavalry overcoat was very warm about a man's body, while sitting in the saddle his legs were very cold. By lining the skirt of the coat they were made very comfortable as far down as the knees, and then the leggings, in addition to the long cavalry boots, kept the men pretty warm. The government also issued us buffalo overshoes, made from buffalo skin, with the fur side in, and buckled up in front. They were very warm, but clumsy. The gloves that were issued to the enlisted men were made of the same material as the socks, with a thumb and forefinger to each glove, and although they were clumsy they were warm. We were provided with little shelter tents, . . . and just try to imagine a man getting out of his tent and putting his clothes on in the snow outside.[12]

Custer probably dressed similarly to his officers and likely wore a fur coat and fur hat on the campaign. Overall, throughout the first eleven days of November, the command worked its way into fighting trim. "The halt, lame and the blind, both men and beasts, were culled out," remembered Second Lieutenant Francis M. Gibson, "and everything not of vital value to a fighting column was eliminated."[13]

General Field Orders No. 6 directed that the Seventh Cavalry, along with Page's infantry battalion, be ready to move on November 9. The expedition did not, however, get under way until three days later, with Colonel Sully commanding, when the cavalry marched from Camp Sandy Forsyth with the wagons and their escort of five companies of the Third Infantry; the Kansas volunteers had not arrived. A correspondent described the appearance of the outfit: "The regiment moved off in column of divisions or platoons, in which the horses were arranged by colors, as chestnuts, blacks, bays, greys, sorrels, browns, etc., presenting a magnificent appearance in the bright sunlight of a clear, cool morning, with just enough breeze to display the flags and guidons to the best advantage, and to waft down the column the strains of music from the Seventh Cavalry band, which was mounted on fine greys in the advance. . . . The band took occasion to remind us of 'the girl we left behind us.'"[14]

Fording the Arkansas, the cavalry troops filled their canteens, then bivouacked five miles south on Mulberry Creek, where the wagons and infantry joined them. Next morning, after a tedious stream crossing, the column took up the march south. "We are coming in to the Indian country, but have not seen any yet," penned Private Harvey. "If General Custer comes across them he will hurt some of them."[15] Much as in the manner prescribed in Sully's directive of September 26, two companies of cavalry rode in advance, with three more as flankers on each side and two others serving as rear guard. The wagons advanced inside this moving perimeter, enclosed by a cattle herd, then encircled by the infantrymen, who, as the day wore on, gradually piled themselves into the wagons. As Godfrey remembered, "the leading troop on the flanks would march to the head of the train, halt and graze until the rear of the train had passed it, thus alternating so as to save dismounting and yet cover the flanks of the train. The advance guard of one day would be rear guard the next day."[16] Each night the company wagons were placed at the front of each company's bivouac, some thirty or forty feet apart, and a picket rope tied from the rear wheels of one to those of the next. Along this line the horses were tied. The troops placed canvas covers on the animals to protect them from the cold, but they managed to reach back and tear them off each other.[17]

Sully issued explicit directions governing the daily responsibilities of the cavalry and infantry:

The Commanding Officer of the 7th Cavalry will detail, "every morning," one (1) Troop of his Regiment as advance guard and one (1) as rear guard. These troops on arriving in camp will act as pickets around the campground. While on picket duty they will have their horses by day and [be] dismounted at night. This advance and rear guard will be relieved every morning.

On breaking camp at the signal "Boots & Saddles," the advance guard for the day will move forward with the guides to the distance of a mile (more or less) according to the nature of the country to allow the supply train to string out of camp; then halt until ordered forward by the commander of the expedition. The rear guard will remain in camp until the command has moved out and comply with the instructions contained in *General Field Orders No. 3* from these Headquarters in regard to marches.

The Commanding Officer of the Infantry Battalion will detail (daily) one (1) company to accompany the ox train which will move out as promptly as possible every morning but not beyond the advance of the advance guard. The rest of the Battalion of Infantry will be distributed along the line of wagons so as to be able to repel an attack at any point.

The commanding officer of the Infantry Battalion will furnish a guard of (1/4 in number) of his command every evening on arriving in camp (six (6) Sentinels and two non-com-officers) as guard for these Headquarters and the rest of the guard to guard his camp and the supply train during the night. He will also detail one (1) Commissioned Officer as Office of the Day, who will report to these Headquarters for instructions.

The Commanders of the troops detailed as an advance and rear guard, will also report for instructions, and the ranking officer will be ordered on duty during the day as Acting Field Officer of the Day.[18]

Over the following days, the command marched to Bluff Creek, then to Cavalry Creek and Bear Creek, and on south to the Cimarron, which was reached November 15. The troops experienced considerable difficulty "getting our heavily loaded wagons through the sands and soft bottom." The day was cold and snowy, with high winds buffeting the

column. That night the officers feasted on buffalo, brought down by
Custer and the guides. (Cooke's sharpshooters also bagged a number
of buffalo and pronghorns during the trip.)[19] Meantime, District Quartermaster Major Henry Inman's ox train, which had been unable to keep
up, pressed on south to the Beaver, accompanied by a squadron of cavalry and three companies of infantry. On the sixteenth the expedition
covered twenty-five miles—the most of any day thus far—and reached
Beaver River, moving east the next day, crossing Sully's old trail, and
camping along that stream. On the eighteenth, as they wended along
the valley of the Beaver, the column passed over the fresh trail of a war
party headed north, surmised to be going to attack the Kaw or Osage
villages. Here Sully refused Custer permission to go on the back trail
with cavalry and attack the village from whence the warriors came,
believing that the camp would be on alert and the troops would be
ambushed. It was, concluded Custer, "a fine opportunity neglected."[20]
Later that afternoon the column camped on the peninsula formed by
Wolf Creek and Beaver River, about 2.5 miles above their confluence.
(The total distance marched since leaving the Arkansas was approximately 110 miles.) Here on the floodplain, the troops stopped and began
work raising the cantonment, termed in the orders "Camp Supply."[21]

Plans for the post had been executed at Fort Dodge by Sully's acting engineer officer, First Lieutenant Henry Jackson, Seventh Cavalry,
before the expedition got underway. According to orders, this construction was to be "a temporary work built of logs" to be occupied by
the infantry battalion while the cavalry ranged south to find and strike
the Indians. On Thursday, November 19, the soldiers began laying out
and erecting the new station, a project that occupied the next several
days. Major Inman, noted Captain Barnitz, "begins to unload his vast
supply of axes, spades, shovels, grindstones, doors and casings, win-
dow casings, sashes, boards &c &c—a large pile of paulines [sic] being
among the latter."[22] The post, built near where Sully skirmished with
the Cheyennes in September, was intended to provide an advanced
supply facility not only for the present campaign but also for future
ones into Indian Territory. The work progressed quickly; orders directed
that "troops accompanying the mowing parties and those in the timber will *not* return at noon for dinner, but will carry that meal in their
haversacks" so they would not have to pause too long from their work.
Armed with axes and saws, the men harvested wood from the surrounding countryside. Using bull teams, they "snaked" hundreds of

logs to the site, then raised a ten-foot-high stockade, complete with loopholes for musketry and secured at its base by a perimeter of excavated trenches. The palisade wall had two blockhouses at the northwest and southeast diagonal corners besides storehouses. Soldier quarters formed lunettes of half dugouts at the open northeast and southwest corners, each extending in an angled "V," with front-to-rear sloping roofs permitting protective fire against an attack. Sully issued orders prohibiting the destruction of boxes, barrels, and gunnysacks and directing that they be turned over for use in constructing the field works. The men also dug wells to provide water for both men and beasts, and mowing machines cut dead grass in the environs for use as forage. But "Camp Supply" eventually turned out to be something of a misnomer. Said one officer: "While there was a partial supply of everything, there was not an adequate supply of anything, at least for such a prolonged and far reaching campaign." Barnitz registered that the Seventh would probably remain at Camp Supply for two weeks, "for the infantry have no idea of being left 'unprotected' before the new Post is completed." The Seventh Cavalry likely went into camp on ground a short distance west of the stockade.[23]

At Camp Supply, the growing rift between Sully and Custer resurfaced. Custer fumed over Sully's earlier rebuff. Both were lieutenant colonels, but Sully commanded the District of the Upper Arkansas (which lay beyond Indian Territory), Custer only his regiment. Anticipating the arrival of the Kansas troops, both men realized that Colonel Crawford (the recent governor) outranked them and technically might assert his command prerogative. The Articles of War stipulated that whenever volunteer and regular troops maneuvered together, brevet, or honorary, rank would apply. To assure himself command following the arrival of the Nineteenth Kansas, Sully, therefore, began exerting authority by virtue of his regular-army brevet rank of brigadier general. Realizing that Sully was operating beyond his district boundary, Custer followed suit, claiming command authority by virtue of his own regular-army brevet rank of major general. But since the Kansas troops had not yet arrived—and concern over their whereabouts was growing—the matter for the time being became moot, and Sully continued in charge. On the nineteenth he revised his earlier edict, directing that the Seventh Cavalry and the ten companies of the Nineteenth Kansas, once arrived, would move out, provisioned for thirty days, to find and strike the Indians. "We intend to make a raid after the red skinned devils and

kill them as we can get them," wrote Private Harvey. The next day
Sully ordered that discharge papers be prepared for all men (except for
those reenlisting) scheduled for release from the army before the end
of the month. Those scheduled for discharge would be offered positions
in the Quartermaster Department to continue helping construct the
post.[24]

Two days after work began on Camp Supply, General Sheridan
arrived, accompanied by two companies of the Nineteenth Kansas that
had earlier been sent from Topeka to go with the Seventh Cavalry against
the Indians. Deeming the winter campaign "an experimental one"
requiring his presence to ascertain the extent of the troops' privations,
Sheridan had departed Fort Hays on November 15 with a contingent
of scouts and one company of the Tenth Cavalry, but freezing rain and
snow had delayed his march. He reached Fort Dodge on the afternoon
of the sixteenth and continued on the next morning. At Bluff Creek he
rendezvoused with the two volunteer companies en route from Forts
Hays and Dodge, then continued south through another snowstorm.
As they proceeded, the general and his party spotted small bodies of
Indians, the pickets firing on them at one bivouac. At one point they
encountered a strong trail leading northeast, possibly the same one that
Sully and Custer had feuded over days before. Sheridan reached Camp
Supply on the evening of the twenty-first. Almost immediately he settled the Sully-Custer "conflict of rank" by sending the less-than-aggres-
sive district commander north to Fort Harker, leaving Custer in command of the expedition. Privately, Sheridan deemed Sully "incompetent"
and wrote Sherman, "If Genl Sully had permitted him [Custer] to follow backwards the trail of a war party coming from the Canadian, . . .
his command might have or could have captured a very large village
then encamped on the Canadian."[25]

The question of the whereabouts of Colonel Crawford and the
remainder of the Nineteenth Kansas Volunteer Cavalry, expected to
reach Camp Supply no later than the twenty-fourth, piqued the curios-
ity of all. Sheridan wrote Sherman: "The Kansas troops have not yet
arrived. I fear the snow has set them astray." He was right. The same
storm that had delayed the general's arrival had also played havoc with
the troops advancing from Topeka. Governor Crawford had issued a
proclamation on October 10 calling for the organization of the regiment. By October 26, the twelve companies were practically full, and
a training camp was established at Topeka. Five hundred Spencer

carbines were delivered to them by the federal government, and copies of *Cooke's Cavalry Tactics* had been requisitioned. His term in office set to expire shortly, Crawford resigned the governorship and assumed duty as the regiment's colonel. The enlisted men represented a discordant mix of green recruits and veterans with past army service, while many of the officers had garnered Civil War experience; the regiment totaled some twelve hundred officers and men. In early November Companies D and G entrained west, ostensibly to accompany the Seventh Cavalry and the supply train south from Fort Dodge. Should these two companies—designated a squadron—not reach the Seventh or the supply camp in time, they were to push on and overtake the command as it headed for the targeted Indian villages. Meanwhile, on November 5 the remaining ten companies of the Kansas troops, meagerly rationed, set forth with their supply train directly for the projected Camp Supply.[26]

The journey to meet Sheridan's command coincided with the onset of bad weather. As they passed southwest near Emporia, a heavy rainstorm drenched the men before changing over to snow. On November 12 at Camp Beecher near present Wichita, the troops bivouacked and shoed horses; promised rations did not materialize there, yet Crawford believed those on hand would last until the command reached Beaver River. Guided by two white scouts, Jack Stilwell and William "Apache Bill" Seamans, the regiment proceeded to the Ninnescah River, where, cold and wet, the soldiers encamped in a grove of cottonwoods. That night a blizzard swept in, collapsing the tents, imperiling the men as well as their animals, and precipitating a number of desertions from the ranks. Nonetheless, after marching another three days, during which the troops subsisted on buffalo, they reached Medicine Lodge Creek. There three hundred of the hungry horses suddenly stampeded, and only about one hundred were ever recovered. Again on the night of the twenty-first, bad weather struck, and the volunteers pressed on next day—walking much of the time because of the condition of the horses—amid a blowing, driving snowstorm until finally camping in the area of the Cimarron.

By now, though, Apache Bill—the lead scout—had become thoroughly lost. Crawford, after consulting his officers, decided to continue while one of his most experienced officers, Captain Allison J. Pliley, moved ahead with fifty men to try and reach Sheridan's force and get relief. The balance of the command, now desperate for food for themselves and their beasts, ranged about in hunting parties and scraped away snow so that the horses could munch the shriveled buffalo grass. Many animals collapsed and died while on the picket lines. On Tuesday, November 24, Crawford's troops moved on slowly, reduced to eating dried hackberries and some buffalo meat acquired during the day's march. To make matters worse, the next day the men learned that Apache Bill had guided them too far south. At this, Crawford decided to mount part of his command on the best remaining horses and proceed forward and find Sheridan, leaving the rest, 360 men, to stay behind with the wagon train awaiting relief. On the twenty-sixth Crawford's shrunken column negotiated gullies and ravines, finally crossed the Cimarron, and turned west. Next day they reached the North Canadian River and turned upstream, and on the twenty-eighth the Kansans encountered a group of scouts from Camp Supply, only five miles away. When they straggled into the post, they found tents, bedding, and plentiful rations awaiting them. Pliley had arrived three days earlier, then departed for the Cimarron with wagons and an escort. They eventually reached the balance of the troops, still subsisting on hackberries, and together made it in to Camp Supply on December 1. Besieged by winter conditions and near starvation, the Nineteenth Kansas had persevered without major casualties despite several cases of frostbite and pneumonia. The only permanent losses to the regiment had occurred through desertion.[27]

As of the evening of November 21, the Seventh Cavalry awaited only the arrival of the Kansas troops before moving south to find the Indian encampments. Next evening they received word that Sheridan had directed Custer to proceed the following morning at six o'clock (reveille at 3:00 A.M.) with enough supplies in the wagons to last a month in the field. Sheridan may have given this order even earlier, based on his previous observation of the Indian trail leading northeast: "Believing that an opportunity offered to strike an effective blow, I directed Custer to call in his working parties and prepare to move immediately, without waiting for Crawford's regiment."[28]

The eleven companies of the Seventh Cavalry that prepared to ride out of Camp Supply on November 23 represented a mixed lot of experience and ability. While the officer corps probably typified that of other period cavalry regiments in the army, the unit's affiliation with Custer and his own subsequent history have drawn inordinate attention to the composition of the Seventh's commissioned cadre. Some of the officers identified more closely with the regiment's lieutenant colonel than did others, and it is fair to say that a schism based on personality, temperament, and allegiance to Custer existed that became exacerbated in the wake of the Washita campaign. Because of their varied roles in the activities of the expedition, many of the officers deserve more than passing notice. Among them was Custer's second in command, Major Joel Elliott (1839–68), an Indiana native who had risen through the enlisted ranks of that state's troops during the Civil War to achieve a regular commission. Elliott fought at Shiloh, Perryville, Stone's River, and Corinth and had taken part in Benjamin Grierson's famous cavalry raid in Mississippi. Twice wounded and the recipient of two brevets, he mustered out in 1866. Elliott took an exam, qualified as major, and following some political machinations, in 1867 accepted an "original appointment" in the newly organized Seventh Cavalry. Custer considered him "a young officer of great courage and enterprise," and as the senior major present during Custer's suspension, Elliott had commanded the regiment during its operations in Kansas.[29]

Among the company commanders was Captain Frederick W. Benteen (1834–98). From Virginia, he had served as an officer of Missouri cavalry during the Civil War and was engaged in numerous actions, including Wilson's Creek, Pea Ridge, Tuscumbia, Vicksburg, and Tupelo, attaining several brevets for his meritorious performance and appointed a colonel of colored troops after the war ended. Assigned to the Seventh in 1866, Benteen had led Company H against Indians in Kansas since then and had recently participated in the operations following the Saline-Solomon depredations, for which he was later brevetted. He was known as a brave, dependable, and competent officer but was also considered an avid drinker, argumentative, and prone to carry a grudge. Benteen was clearly a man of petty jealousies, and he seemed to relish embarrassing confrontations with the younger Custer, whom he despised. A fellow officer said that his "weakness was vindictiveness, which was pronounced. He was indifferent to the minor matters of discipline, and always had the poorest company in the regiment." Yet his tenuous relationship with Custer seems not to have affected his military performance in 1868, and Benteen was regarded as a dutiful leader.[30] One of Benteen's junior officers was First Lieutenant William W. Cooke (1846–76), born in Canada, who was a veteran of the New York volunteer cavalry during the war and had served at the Wilderness, Spotsylvania,

Cold Harbor, and Petersburg. Mustered out in 1865, Cooke received an appointment as second lieutenant with the Seventh in July 1866 and was promoted a year later. He was detached from Company H to command the corps of sharpshooters during the present expedition.[31]

Captain Louis M. Hamilton (1844–68) commanded Company A. Scion of a prominent New York family and grandson of both Alexander Hamilton, the first secretary of the Treasury, and Louis McLane, secretary of state under President Andrew Jackson, he had served with his state's volunteer infantry at Harper's Ferry. Family connections netted him an appointment in the Third U.S. Infantry, and he won brevets for duty at Chancellorsville and Gettysburg; he also fought at Petersburg and Appomattox. Appointed a captain in the Seventh Cavalry in July 1866, Hamilton was well liked and respected by his peers as well as the enlisted men. Custer termed him "an officer of great presence of mind as well as undaunted courage." Reportedly the youngest captain in the army, he was known as a conscientious officer who could be counted on in all instances to do his duty. His contemporary in the Seventh was Albert Barnitz (1835–1912), captain of Company G. As with Hamilton, Barnitz began his army career in the echelons of the state forces during the Civil War, fighting in the Kansas-Missouri border country as well as in the Virginia theater, the latter under Sheridan and Custer. He garnered brevets for gallantry and meritorious service, was wounded, and attained the grade of major by the conflict's end. He joined the Seventh as captain in 1866 and had spent the two years following in pursuing Indians on the prairies and plains of Kansas.[32]

Other officers of note include Captain Robert M. West (1834–69), Company A, who had served as an enlisted man in the Mounted Rifles before the Civil War. During the war, he served with Pennsylvania troops and rose to the rank of colonel, attaining several brevets (including one as brigadier general of volunteers for his service at Five Forks, Virginia). Like his fellows, West received an appointment as captain in the Seventh Cavalry in July 1866, but he would resign from the army in March 1869 as a result of illness aggravated by a severe drinking problem. His principal subaltern was First Lieutenant Edward S. Godfrey (1843–1932), who joined the regiment in Kansas upon his graduation from West Point in 1867. Godfrey had served as a private of Ohio troops in 1861; he would log a distinguished career in the Seventh lasting a quarter century, participating with the regiment in nearly every one of its major engagements with Indians between 1868 and 1890. An officer with

Company M was First Lieutenant Owen Hale (1843–77), who had spent the Civil War as an enlisted man and officer in the New York volunteer cavalry, had been mustered out of service in 1865, and joined the Seventh at its organization.[33]

Captain Thomas B. Weir (1838–76) commanded Company D of the Seventh. An Ohio native, he served with Michigan cavalry troops during the war. Weir took part in the siege of Corinth and in the operations around Mobile, and in 1862 he spent six months as a Confederate prisoner of war. Later brevetted for his Civil War service, he was mustered out of the volunteers a lieutenant colonel in 1865 and later served in Texas under Custer, with whom he was friends. When the Seventh was organized, Weir accepted a commission as first lieutenant with the regiment and served as its commissary officer until promoted captain in 1867. Francis M. Gibson (1847–1919) of Pennsylvania was second lieutenant of Company A, having joined the regiment scarcely a year earlier in October 1867. He would one day author an account of the Washita expedition. His company officer was First Lieutenant Thomas W. Custer (1845–76), younger brother of the field commander and whose military career depended largely on that relationship. Custer had spent three years of the war as an enlisted man with Ohio troops, fighting at, among other places, Stone's River, Chickamauga, and Atlanta before gaining a commission in the Sixth Michigan Cavalry. He subsequently received numerous brevets and two Medals of Honor (for capturing Confederate battle flags three days apart, the latter effort resulting in a severe wound to the face) before joining his brother in the new regiment in July 1866. An irreverent prankster, he also could be a heavy drinker. In battle, however, he had garnered a respectable record for bravery and reliability. (Tom Custer would later die with his brother at the Little Bighorn.)[34]

First Lieutenant James M. Bell (1837–1919) was the regimental quartermaster in charge of the supply wagons and their contents during the trip south. Bell, from Pennsylvania, served with Ohio and Pennsylvania troops in the war and won brevets for his performance in the Wilderness Campaign and at Reams's Station, Virginia. Mustered out in 1865, he joined the Seventh as a second lieutenant in 1866. Another veteran officer was Edward Myers (1830–71), a captain in the regiment since its organization. A German immigrant, Myers had served as an enlisted man in the dragoons before the Civil War, and during that conflict had continued with the redesignated First U.S.

Cavalry as a lieutenant through Appomattox, winning brevets to captain, major, and lieutenant colonel for his gallant and meritorious conduct. He also joined the Seventh Cavalry in 1866 and commanded Company E. His service, however, was somewhat marred by his temperament, his actions often bordering on incompetence, and general bad health. George W. Yates (1843–76) was captain of Company F. A New Yorker, Yates had served with Michigan and Missouri troops in the Civil War and had been awarded brevets for "conspicuous gallantry" at Fredericksburg (where he was wounded); Beverly Ford, Virginia; and for Gettysburg. After the war he had served with the Second Cavalry as a second lieutenant and transferred to the Seventh as captain in 1867.[35]

The oldest officer in the regiment was William Thompson (1813–97), who commanded Company B and was fifty-five in 1868. Varied in background, the Pennsylvanian had been a lawyer and had served with the Iowa territorial legislature as chief clerk, eventually becoming a representative from that state in Congress. He later practiced law and edited an Iowa newspaper. During the Civil War, he captained a unit of state cavalry; served in Missouri and Texas, meriting two brevets; and became colonel of his regiment. Thompson joined the Seventh as a captain upon its organization. First Lieutenant Samuel M. Robbins (1832–78), a New Yorker, became a captain in the First Colorado Cavalry in 1861, took part in the Battle of Apache Canyon in 1862 (which halted the Confederate invasion of New Mexico), and later served as chief of cavalry in the District of Colorado until 1865. He joined the Seventh Cavalry in July 1866 and in 1868 served with Company D, though on the campaign he was detailed as Custer's aide-de-camp.[36]

Other officers of note in the coming campaign were First Lieutenant Charles Brewster and Captain Myles W. Moylan. Brewster (1836–1904), commanding Company I vice its captain, Myles W. Keogh, who was detached as a member of Colonel Sully's staff, was from New York, saw service with that state's cavalry during the war, and aided in suppressing the New York City draft riots of 1863. He later served with Custer in the Shenandoah Valley and was captured by Colonel John S. Mosby's Partisan Rangers. He was brevetted at war's end for "efficient and meritorious services." Brewster joined the Seventh Cavalry as a second lieutenant in July 1866 and won promotion to first lieutenant in February 1867. He was not considered a good or competent officer and would leave the army under a cloud in 1870. Conversely, the Massachusetts-born captain Myles W. Moylan (1838–1909) was considered one of the most capable officers in the regiment. He had risen through the enlisted ranks during the 1850s and 1860s to reach commissioned status by the end of the Civil War. Moylan served with Custer during the war, fighting at Gettysburg and Brandy Station among other places. Dismissed from the Fifth Cavalry on a trivial charge in 1863, he enlisted in the Massachusetts cavalry under an assumed name and was soon after commissioned again, taking part in the operations around Petersburg and Appomattox. After the war Moylan enlisted in the army and in 1866 was assigned to the Seventh Cavalry, where he quickly advanced to first lieutenant and served as regimental adjutant.[37]

Second Lieutenant Algernon E. Smith (1842–76), a New Yorker, was commissioned with that state's volunteer infantry and fought at Richmond, Petersburg, and Cold Harbor, Virginia, and Fort Fisher, North Carolina, where he was badly wounded and for which action he received one of several brevets. Smith, who became a devoted Custer disciple, joined the Seventh Cavalry in 1867 and took part in various expeditions around Fort Dodge, Kansas. First Lieutenant Henry J. Nowlan (1837–98), also from New York, served in the state's cavalry forces during the Red River Campaign of 1863. Held prisoner for nearly two years, Nowlan escaped and took part in Sherman's drive through the Carolinas. He was later severely wounded while serving in Texas after the war, but joined the Seventh Cavalry as a second lieutenant in July, 1866, and was promoted the following December. Assistant Surgeon Henry Lippincott (1839–1908) was from Nova Scotia, and served during the Civil War as surgeon with California troops. In 1866 he was appointed assistant surgeon and first lieutenant and was assigned to the Seventh Cavalry from March to November 1867, and later, in October 1868, for the duration of the campaign.[38]

Besides the officers, a number of hired civilian personnel would play significant roles in the expedition. Perhaps, ultimately, the most useful civilian employee was Benjamin H. Clark (1842–1914), known as Ben Clark, who was carried on Quartermaster Bell's "hired" rolls as a "Guide and Scout," one of five such paid at the rate of one hundred dollars per month (two other civilian guides received seventy-five dollars per month). Lean and mustachioed, Clark was from St. Louis and had earlier served in a volunteer unit during the Mormon War in the 1850s and in the Sixth Kansas Volunteer Cavalry during the Civil War. Much of this latter service occurred in the Kansas-Missouri border country, and he spent the years since the Civil War guiding freight trains through the Indian country, by which means he became proficient as a scout. Known as a brave, responsible, and levelheaded frontiersman, Clark had joined Sully for his late summer campaign in 1868, an assignment that continued under Sheridan and Custer. A contemporary described Clark in these terms: "He is a man of excellent judgment and superior intelligence, and his thorough knowledge of the country makes his services doubly valuable. He is . . . [of] medium height, [and] has long, light hair, falling below his shoulders. He has none of the bravado common to many frontier characters, but in address is plain, unassuming, and treats everybody with the utmost courtesy."[39]

Another prominent scout was Moses "California Joe" Milner (1829–76), a Kentuckian who had gone west and become a trapper and mountain man. A scout of vast experience, he had served under Colonels Stephen Watts Kearny and Alexander Doniphan during the Mexican War, joined the gold rush to California in the early 1850s, and established an Oregon cattle ranch in 1853. He prospected in Idaho and Montana, then moved south to New Mexico and began scouting for the army in 1866.[40] Fitted out with corncob pipe and broad-brimmed hat, Milner was truly a character to behold, and a decided proclivity for liquor sometimes complicated his otherwise discerning abilities as a scout. One soldier reminisced about him: "[California Joe] understood the Indians and their language thoroughly, but, like many others, he liked his fire water. . . . He was generally togged out in a buckskin suit. His hair and beard he wore long. He was armed with a government rifle and rode a small government mule. There was nothing very attractive about Joe's appearance, but being a jolly fellow he was well liked. One time he absented himself from the camp, became intoxicated and returned after a short time, alarming the camp by yelling and making gestures as he rode in. General Custer placed him under arrest, but after a short time he was released." Milner's proclivity to drink cost him his position as chief of scouts, which subsequently fell to Ben Clark.[41]

Another "Guide and Scout" was the swarthy mixed-blood Raphael Romero (1843?–1908), of Mexican or Indian origin and possibly of Mexican-Arapaho mixed descent. A young man who had lived for years among the Indians (and reportedly had been stolen by them as a boy), he was valued for his knowledge of the frontier as well as for his linguistic skill with Cheyenne and neighboring tribal tongues. During the Civil War, Romero had served with the Second Colorado Cavalry in 1862–63. The officers in the command dubbed him "Romeo," "a sobriquet to which he responded as readily as if he had been christened under it." Yet other civilian guides and scouts carried on the rolls were E. V. Carr, Jack Corbin, W. E. Stone, Louis McLoughlin, and Jack Fitzpatrick. Gweso Chouteau was hired as interpreter (one hundred dollars per month) for the twelve Osage scouts. Osage chiefs Little Beaver and Hard Rope (seventy-five dollars per month each) led the delegation, the balance of whom (fifty dollars per month each) were known as Little Buffalo Head, Draw Them Up, Sharp Hair, Patient Man, I Don't Want It, Big Elk, Little Black Bear, Lightning Bug, Little Buffalo, and Straight Line.[42]

It had originally been proposed to approach the Utes to scout against the Cheyennes, Arapahos, and Kiowas, offering them rations and "all the plunder they might capture," but on Governor Crawford's recommendation, Sheridan had finally settled upon recruiting Osages from the nearby reservation in southeastern Kansas. Of those who signed on, Hard Rope was a chief, and during the Civil War, he had reportedly battled Confederate troops near the community of Independence, Kansas. Little Beaver, also a chief, was also known as John Beaver or Little Beaver II. The Osages who volunteered would receive pay, clothing, weapons, and horses during their service. When they joined the troops, Custer had described them as "a splendid-looking set of warriors. . . . They are painted and dressed for the war-path, and well armed with Springfield breech-loading guns. All are superb horsemen. We mounted them on good horses, and to show us how they can ride and shoot, they took a stick of ordinary cord-wood, threw it on the ground, and then, mounted on their green, untried horses, they rode at full speed and fired at the stick of wood as they flew by, and every shot struck the target."[43] The Osages, along with the civilian scouts and guides, would factor importantly in the army's campaign.

As the weather worsened on the evening of November 22, the troops and their officers, along with the diverse array of supplemental personnel, huddled in rude quarters and tents at Camp Supply. Doubtless each man contemplated the morrow and speculated over what it might bring, yet they prepared to make the most of the conditions in advancing as quickly as possible to breach the secluded winter quarters of the Cheyennes and Arapahos.

6

CLOSING PROXIMITY

General Sheridan's directive for Custer to take the field was motivated by the earlier discovery of an Indian trail headed northeast, and he feared that the tribes to the south would flee once they realized that troops were operating in their vicinity. He later learned that the war party consisted of Cheyennes and Arapahos. "They had been north, killed the mail carriers between Dodge and Larned, an old hunter at Dodge, and two of my expressmen, whom I had sent back with letters from Bluff Creek to Dodge." Enthused over his assignment, Custer recorded his explicit instructions, which were to move out with thirty days' rations, "go south from here to the Canadian River, then down the river to Fort Cobb, then south-west towards the Washita [Wichita] mountains, then north-west back to this point, my whole march not exceeding two hundred and fifty miles."[1] Although the presence of a fiercely blowing snowstorm changed the plan to move up Beaver River and find the Indian trail, it did not deter the projected movement to find the Cheyennes and Arapahos. In fact, it was eventually seen as beneficial. "We could move and the Indian villages could not," recalled Custer. "If the snow only remained on the ground one week," he told Sheridan, "I promised to bring the General satisfactory evidences that my command had met the Indians."[2]

The train of wagons was made ready; the troops, equipment, and horses all inspected; and but a few tents loaded; officers and men made arrangements to take along only the "clothes on their backs." Some officers tried to get around Custer's stricture on extra clothing. Private John Ryan recalled that when one wagon became mired crossing a creek, Custer ordered it unloaded, whereupon he found a trunk belonging to Lieutenant Owen Hale. "The trunk was burst open and the contents, consisting of long topped boots, corduroy pants, velvet pants, etc., dumped out, and the men were given orders to help themselves, which they promptly did. The owner of the clothing could do nothing, as he had disobeyed orders. I thought it kind of hard to see enlisted men of the company riding along and wearing some of the clothing belonging to this officer, which he could not claim." Reveille came at 3:00 A.M. on the twenty-third, and over the next three hours, the troops groomed and saddled their horses, belted and adjusted their weapons and equipments, downed meager breakfasts, and awaited the signal to mount.[3]

At 6:00 A.M., beneath leaden skies, "Boots and Saddles" sounded, and the soldiers lifted themselves into their saddles and moved out in column of fours, the band at the front of the column blaring out the old Civil War favorite "The Girl I Left behind Me."[4] The snow kept coming down as the troops, their greatcoat capes buttoned about their heads, passed down the line of infantry tents, the foot soldiers cheering their departure, then out onto the plain, fairly buried in a foot-deep accumulation. "We were off to a winter campaign in a country never traversed by any man in our outfit," recalled an enlisted man. The white-out that enveloped everyone and everything hindered the scouts and guides in spotting distant landmarks and thus leading the way. Under these circumstances, Custer personally took over, guided by a hand-held compass, and the command groped its way southwest, reaching the hills and ridges on the west side of Wolf Creek about 2:00 P.M. and halting after a march of fourteen miles. Eventually, the storm fell away, yet the struggle through the heavy snow proved fatiguing for both man and beast, and the wagons, numbering some thirty-seven, were delayed. As the temperature warmed, "the snow balled on the feet of our shod animals causing much floundering and adding to the fatigue of travel," wrote First Lieutenant Edward S. Godfrey. Moreover, the rawhide seats of many of the saddles became soaked, warping their trees when dried and causing painful riding. Wielding axes, the men felled sufficient timber and built fires, and once the wagons appeared, the officers raised their tents and meals were served. That night the men feasted on rabbit stew made from the plentiful local quarry. Private Winfield Harvey recorded, "at night we had to lay in snow eighteen inches deep with our clothes all wet and freezing, although we have plenty of wood and good fires to keep us warm." The Indian scouts made their camp apart from the troops, and "the monotonous sound of beating the tom-tom was heard at all hours."[5]

At reveille Tuesday morning (November 24), the soldiers found that the storm had stopped during the night, leaving a total accumulation of about eighteen inches; it melted quickly beneath a glaring sun that brought on some cases of snow blindness. Movement southwest proceeded after breakfast, though on Custer's orders, several of the wagon masters and teamsters were arrested and forced to wade through the snow with the column for several hours as punishment for delaying the departure of the command. The day's march led up the south side of the valley of Wolf Creek, tracing the sand hills; the troops crossed the Wolf and camped along its banks that afternoon after passing sixteen miles. Trooper Ryan years later reminisced over details of the march (doubtless referencing both the movement to the Washita and back):

The rivers were frozen over, but the ice was not thick enough to hold up our horses, and the first companies to enter the stream broke the ice for the other companies. The water was quite deep, in fact, so deep that quite a number of the men wet their feet and legs in riding through it. After crossing these rivers and getting our wagons through I remember we had quite a time drying ourselves before fires made of dry bushes, weeds and wild prairie grass—anything that would make a blaze. In making camp at night we could take shovels and clear the snow from a place about five or six feet square and then build a fire on the ground. When the ground became thoroughly dried and warm we would shovel the snow away from another place and move the fire there. Then we would spread down the remnants of the horse covers that could not be kept on the horses, and our saddle blankets. The rest of our blankets were used for covering. We placed our saddles on the ground and used them as pillows, the men sleeping three or four together in what they called spoon fashion. Of course the side next to the ground would be warm on account of the fire, but the upper side would be very cold. When one man was uncomfortable and wished to turn over, they would all have to turn over together to warm the other side. We also had to sleep with our boots and clothes on, for if we took off our boots they would be so frozen in the morning that we could not get them on. . . . Each man had to do his own cooking by making a fire out of dry brush, dead wood and grass, and holding his cup of coffee over the blaze. Our horses suffered terribly in being tied to the picket ropes. When a number of horses were tied together, they backed around to the storm and stood as close as they could with heads down.[6]

On the twenty-fifth, a clear day, the march resumed due south as the Osages steered the command up and over a divide and toward the South Canadian River near the Antelope Hills, ever nearer to the upper Washita drainage, the area suspected to harbor the Indian villages. The weather turned warm, and large numbers of game animals, driven to shelter by the storm, appeared in the timber along the stream. The scouts were able to approach huddled clusters of buffalo and shoot them easily; groups of soldiers then butchered the beasts and placed the cuts for storage on the slow-moving wagons lurching behind the column. Occasionally, officers, including Custer, left the column to pursue and kill buffaloes. As the march approached the Canadian, the troops saw the Antelope Hills rise in view. Some of the horses and mules began to play out from exhaustion, necessitating the doubling of teams at stream crossings. After traveling eighteen miles, late that day, as darkness loomed, the soldiers took up a bivouac along a timbered tributary now called Commission Creek, about a mile from the north bank of the Canadian. Both teamsters and soldiers cut bark from the cotton-woods to feed their animals, which could not reach the grass beneath the snow. In anticipation of finding a trail—perhaps *the* trail, or the returning path of those who made it, lately discovered above Camp Supply—Custer consulted with his Indian and white scouts. He then determined to send on the morrow three companies—G, H, and M— under Major Elliott to scout for signs of the tribesmen up the north side of the Canadian.[7]

The next morning before dawn, Elliott and his men, including several white and Osage guides, all duly armed and rationed, started out. "The morning was excessively cold, and a dense fog prevailed," observed

Captain Barnitz. "It was necessary to dismount very often, and walk in order to prevent our feet from freezing. As the snow was a foot deep, with a hard crust, which broke beneath our feet, walking was exceedingly difficult and tiresome." The scout was to travel as far as fifteen miles and, if a trail was found, would start in pursuit, sending news back to the main command of the supposed composition of the party and the direction they were headed, at which Custer would move cross-country to intercept them, if possible. The colonel, meantime, intended to ford the Canadian and move south past the Antelope Hills, a sharply rising escarpment pinnacled by several small buttes reaching as high as three hundred feet, and camp along an upper tributary of the Washita. Of major concern was a place to bring the wagons across the rising and fast Canadian, laced with ice chunks and slush, but this was eventually accomplished. Meantime, Custer and some of his officers ascended the hills to look over the country and found themselves momentarily engulfed in a frozen mist of sundogs and prismatic shades—natural phenomena that could not be seen at lower elevations. After three hours getting the wagons across, Custer readied his column to resume the march south on the plains east of the hills. Before he could, though, a courier from Elliott, Jack Corbin, rode up with news that two large Indian trails, one less than twenty-four-hours old and reflecting use by as many as 150 warriors, had been discovered twelve miles distant heading south-southeast across the Canadian from Elliott's position. Moreover, an abandoned Indian camp lay nearby. Custer sent word back via Corbin, astride a fresh horse, telling Elliott to stay on the trail and notify the colonel of any directional deviation, and at 8:00 P.M., if the columns had not yet joined, to halt and await the arrival of the balance of the command. (Corbin reached Elliott at about 2:00 or 3:00 P.M., and another courier arrived shortly after dark.)[8]

After finding the trails, Elliott's command proceeded across the Canadian and ascended the high divide separating its drainage from that of the Washita River. His soldiers followed the fresh trail most of the day, finally stopping along a Washita tributary after Corbin reached them. Custer, meantime, assembled his officers and laid out his plan. He would leave one officer and an eighty-man detachment with the larger part of the wagon train, with instructions to follow as conditions might permit, and made ready to angle southeast cross-country with the balance of his men to find Elliott. A smaller detached train of two wagons, containing forage and "light supplies and extra ammunition," and four ambulances, personally commanded by First Lieutenant James Bell, would roll out closely on the trail of Custer's men. Each trooper, armed with his Spencer carbine and Colt revolver, would carry one hundred rounds of ammunition and hardtack, coffee, and forage for his animal. In outfitting, remembered Custer: "Every man and officer in the command was vigorously at work preparing to set out for a rough ride, the extent or result of which no one could foresee. Wagons were emptied, mess chests called upon to contribute from their stores, ammunition chests opened and their contents distributed to the troopers. The most inferior of the horses were selected to fill up the detail of eighty cavalry which was to remain and escort the train; an extra amount of clothing was donned by some who realized that when the bitter, freezing hours of night came we would not have the comforts of tents and campfire to sustain us." As the command prepared to pull away, Captain Hamilton, who as officer of the day would normally remain with the train, approached Custer and beseeched him to be allowed to accompany the soldiers. Custer relented, provided the captain could find a substitute; eventually, Lieutenant Edward G. Mathey, afflicted with snow blindness, remained in charge of the wagons in Hamilton's place. Soon the command pulled out, Captain Yates's Company F in the van, and rode hard south without resting. Late in the day Custer's scouts located the Indians' and Elliott's trails. The weary command overtook the major's bivouac at approximately 9:00 P.M., having marched thirty miles that day. It was Thanksgiving night, and the soldiers, after unsaddling and feeding their mounts and taking care to conceal their fires, dined on coffee and hardtack.[9]

Custer's command, in the quest to strike the Indian villages, passed into the drainage system of the southeastwardly flowing South Canadian River. This region includes the tributary streams of that watercourse as well as those of the Washita, which run south of and roughly parallel to the Canadian, which is itself an eventual tributary of the Red River.[10] The country is characterized by rolling hills and undulating plains interspersed with wooded creeks and streams that typify the transitional topography between woodland prairie and open plains. In the valleys of the rivers and streams grow assorted plants that afford shelter for game; for the tribes that harbored there, it fostered the safe passage of the winter months. The valleys, generally lower than the surrounding plains, offered the Indians shelter from cold winds while providing water, firewood, and areas of grass, trees, and brush where pony herds might graze on whatever sparse vegetation remained. The people could also hunt game in the form of deer, rabbits, wild turkeys, and prairie chickens to augment their diet of dried buffalo meat. Occupation of the stream valleys was seasonal and had doubtless been recurrent in the region for generations.[11]

Along one of these streams, the Washita, stood Black Kettle's village. Since moving below the Arkansas following the Saline-Solomon raids in August, these people had gravitated associatively with other Cheyenne bands. During mid-October, they had settled on the South Canadian, not far from the Antelope Hills, along with some Lakotas and the Arapahos of Little Raven, and they bartered with Mexicans who had come to trade. Some of the livestock captured during the late raids into Kansas was given to the Mexicans, along with buffalo robes, for guns and ammunition. During the first part of November, the camps relocated southeast to the Washita, known to them as Lodge-Pole River. Drawn by the presence of water, firewood, and timber, the Indians also found the place appealing for the abundant winter grasses on which the ponies could feed. Most of the Cheyennes raised their tipis beside a long north-sweeping loop of the river, southeast of Little Raven's Arapaho camp, which lay toward the north end of the loop, and west of Kicking Bird's small village of Kiowas (the lodges of Satanta, Lone Wolf, and Black Eagle having earlier repaired to the area of Fort Cobb), with camps of Comanches and Kiowa-Apaches not far away. This large Cheyenne assemblage included the followers of Medicine Arrows, keeper of the Sacred Arrows, along with those of Little Robe, Sand Hill, Stone Calf, Old Little Wolf (Big Jake), and Black White Man. Just below this large village lay another, smaller camp of Cheyennes under Old Whirlwind; together these two villages totaled 129 lodges. Several miles to the west, across the bend at a point where the Washita assumed a more east-west alignment, Black Kettle's people raised their lodges. Black Kettle, as an advocate for peace with the whites, had tried unsuccessfully to control some of the young men in his camp who had sporadically participated in the war parties mustered against enemy tribes and the white settlements in Kansas. The onset of cold weather and the retarding effects of snow accumulations had, for the time being, largely halted these activities. Altogether, the population of the various Indian camps on the Washita in November 1868 totaled approximately six thousand people.[12]

By late that month, Black Kettle's village stood on the south side of the Washita between two gently rising ridges approximately two miles apart on either side of the stream. The location afforded a shelter from the sometimes fierce, galelike freezing winds that swept over the land. The lodges occupied the generally flat, or terraced, area of the red-clay floodplain about one mile east of the confluence of a northward flowing tributary of the river (presently called Plum Creek) and approximately one mile west of the confluence of a northeastwardly flowing one (now called Sergeant Major Creek). Between these the Washita, which likely averaged from nine to twelve feet in width along its course at this point, knifed briefly southeast, then shot north, before finally circling back south in its west–east passage, and in this latter, roughly crescent-shaped bend, which formed something of a sheltered pocket about three-quarters of a mile wide encompassing about thirty acres, most of the lodges were raised. The banks of the stream were somewhat steep above the river channel, which was shallow at this season. Black Kettle's own lodge stood beneath a cottonwood tree near the smaller bend, along with those of several other Cheyenne families.[13]

Beyond the south riverbank stood a near perpendicular embankment some fifty feet high, its top composing the rising prairie that undulated away to the south. The embankment paralleled the Washita for several miles downstream, gradually lessening in height until it joined the level tract bordering the river. The land on the north side of the Washita swept away spaciously, then formed spurs that gradually and finally merged into high red-sandstone hills in the distance. The number of tipis with the village totaled fifty-one and included two of visiting Lakotas and two of Arapahos. As many as 250 people occupied the camp. Among the families present with Black Kettle were those of Big Man, Wolf Looking Back, Clown, Cranky Man, Scabby Man, Half Leg, Bear Tongue, Roll Down, and Little Rock. The latter represented the sole council chief remaining with Black Kettle since Sand Creek. Beyond the tipis, and scattered to forage in the different gullies and washes west of the village, were the ponies. Near Black Kettle's lodge, a pony trail crossed from the north side through a shallow part of the Washita, skirting the village, then running west to the sand hills where the large herds of Cheyenne ponies grazed. The remote location of Black Kettle's village from that of the principal concentration of Cheyennes might simply be coincidence. In 1930, however, a Mrs. Blackhead, approximately eighty years old and a survivor of the Washita attack, claimed that after Sand Creek, Black Kettle "never camped with the main body of Cheyennes. He always pitched his village a distance from the main camp."[14]

In the years since the Washita engagement, there have remained questions about whether the Cheyennes and Arapahos had legal justification, with reference to the provisions of the Treaty of Medicine Lodge, to have located themselves at the Washita River. Article 2 of that document, ratified during the summer of 1868, specified that the Indians would occupy a district essentially comprising the lands enclosed by the south boundary of Kansas, the Arkansas River, and the Cimarron River. While the difficulties with the army increased following the Saline and Solomon encounters, the tribesmen had gravitated farther south to the South Canadian and then to the Washita, both of which remained south of and removed from the new reservation. Yet Article 11 of the treaty conceded and "reserved the right to hunt on any lands south of the Arkansas so long as the buffalo may range thereon in such numbers as to justify the chase." There was no question as to the availability of buffalo in the region; even Custer's men had taken advantage of their presence during their advance. And since there was no provision ordaining the length or frequency of such hunts, a sustained tribal presence through the winter might clearly qualify as such under liberal interpretation of the treaty. Thus, the Indians normally should have enjoyed relative security in their position.

The problem at hand, however, was that the third, fourth, and fifth paragraphs of Article 11 specified that the Indians "will not attack any persons at home or traveling, nor molest or disturb any wagon-trains, coaches, mules, or cattle"; "that they will never capture or carry off from the settlements white women or children"; and that "they will never kill or scalp white men, nor attempt to do them harm." All of these stipulations had been violated by various Cheyenne and Arapaho elements who had conducted many of the raids throughout much of 1868 and especially since August. Under the War Department's interpretation (most notably the concurring views of Generals Sherman and Sheridan), however, the entire population—not just the offending individuals— was to be held accountable for the depredations. Moreover, under provisions of Article 2, U.S. Army troops, considered as "officers, agents, and employees of the Government," were specifically authorized to enter and pass through the reservation "in discharge of duties enjoined by law"; technically, however, since the present military operations were taking place beyond the prescribed reservation boundaries, this particular stricture did not apply. Thus did the legalities and circumstances of their situation place Black Kettle's people—as well as the other villages of Cheyennes and Arapahos along the Washita—in immediate jeopardy of army attack. In the final analysis, the government's view, as manifested through the War Department and belatedly by the Bureau of Indian Affairs through its superintendent, was that the tribesmen had breached the Medicine Lodge treaty and therefore should face the consequences of their actions.[15]

The man whose people unknowingly lay in harm's way had been a staunch advocate for peace with the whites for many years. Black Kettle, who was then sixty-seven years old, was born near the Black Hills in 1801, a Suhtai, and the eldest son of Swift Hawk Lying Down. His brothers were Gentle Horse and Wolf, and his sister was Wind Woman. As a youth and young man, he exhibited traits that characterized a good warrior and leader and took part in several war parties and horse-stealing expeditions against neighboring tribes, particularly the Kiowas, Comanches, and Kiowa-Apaches, when the Cheyennes were enemies of these people. In 1838 Black Kettle and others had located enemy camps before joining the Arapahos in battling them along Wolf Creek below the Cimarron River. Ten years later, while Black Kettle led a war party against Ute tribesmen, his wife, Little Sage Woman, was taken by the enemy near the headwaters of the Cimarron River, and despite subsequent efforts to get her back, she was never found. He then married a woman of the Wotapio band and lived with her people. When the chief of that band died in 1850, Black Kettle, who had long demonstrated leadership abilities, succeeded him. Available photographic imagery of Black Kettle discloses a Cheyenne leader of medium to tall build, his hair parted in the manner of his people, with a thoughtful yet resolute countenance.

In 1861 Black Kettle and other chiefs signed the controversial Fort Wise Treaty, which restricted the Southern Cheyennes' land base and ultimately provoked the conflict that culminated in Sand Creek and the deaths of more than 150 Indians, including several council chiefs. Many other Cheyennes had refused to abide by the Fort Wise provisions, and after Sand Creek they viewed as futile Black Kettle's continued attempts to foster peace, which coincided with the rise of the Dog Soldiers and a political schism in Southern Cheyenne society. Black

Kettle's signing of the Little Arkansas Treaty in 1865 further aggravated the discord and cost him and other chiefs influence among their people in the treaty councils that followed at Medicine Lodge, where the Cheyennes, at best, presented but a disjointed front. The chief's inability to keep his young men from participating in the depredations during the summer of 1868, while reflective of the dynamics of Cheyenne society, perhaps represented the key contributing factor to the U.S. Army, however oblivious to his identifiable presence, moving to strike at his people.[16]

It was with the hope that such trouble might be averted that Black Kettle had recently gone to speak with federal representatives at Fort Cobb, some eighty miles southeast of the Washita villages. There, in early November, Colonel William B. Hazen, General Sherman's designee to oversee Indian affairs, had arrived to relieve Captain Henry Alvord's temporary stewardship. Alvord had already met with the Kiowas, Comanches, Caddoes, Wichitas, and neighboring tribes and distributed what little food provisions were available. On October 31 he learned from the chiefs of the projected arrival at Fort Cobb of a delegation of Cheyennes and Arapahos for the purpose of expressing friendship. Alvord had heard that the Cheyennes, as recently as November 1, had camped on the South Canadian near the Antelope Hills, had attempted to entice the Kiowas and Comanches into hostilities, and had been receiving merchandise, including ammunition, from Mexican traders. By the time Hazen appeared, a large number of Caddoes and Wichitas, together with some smaller groups, had arrived at Fort Cobb, where Alvord had distributed to them provisions. Hazen, on Sherman's direction, was to provide them food and protection and thus keep them from becoming involved in the imminent warfare. Sherman told Hazen of Sheridan's move against the Cheyennes and Arapahos, stating that Sheridan, in possibly operating in the vicinity of Fort Cobb, would attempt to "spare the well-disposed" tribes.[17]

Black Kettle headed the delegation of Cheyennes that rode into Fort Cobb on November 20. With him were Little Robe, Little Rock, Big Man, and Wolf Looking Back of the Cheyennes, and Big Mouth and Spotted Wolf, who headed the Arapaho delegation. The chief, for whom the issue of peace was now vital, told Hazen that he wanted peace for his band but claimed that he had no control over any other body of Cheyennes. Speaking for all of his people camped at the Washita, Black Kettle told Hazen:

The Cheyennes, when south of the Arkansas, did not wish to return to the north side because they feared trouble there. . . . The Cheyennes do not fight at all this side of the Arkansas; they do not trouble Texas, but north of the Arkansas they are almost always at war. When lately north of the Arkansas, some young Cheyennes were fired upon and then the fight began. I have always done my best to keep my young men quiet, but some will not listen, and since the fighting began, I have not been able to keep them all at home. But we all want peace, and I would be glad to move my people down this way; I could then keep them all quietly near camp. My camp is now on the Washita, 40 miles east of Antelope Hills, and I have there about 180 lodges [meaning the total number of Cheyenne lodges along the Washita]. I speak only for my own people. I cannot speak [for] nor control the Cheyennes north of the Arkansas.[18]

Big Mouth spoke for the Arapahos, likewise appealing for peace. Knowing the status of these Indians in Sherman's mind, however, Hazen told them forthrightly that he could not make peace with them and that, furthermore, they must not come to Fort Cobb and jeopardize the peace for those Kiowas and Comanches presently there. Speaking of the current military maneuvers, Hazen said: "North of the Arkansas is General Sheridan, the great war chief, and I do not control him; and he has all the soldiers who are fighting the Arapahoes and Cheyennes. Therefore, you must go back to your country, and if the soldiers come to fight, you must remember they are not from me, but from that great war chief, and with him you must make peace." Hazen told the chiefs that he would forward their words to the Great Father, and if he approved their treatment as friendly Indians, Hazen would send for them to come to Fort Cobb. He told them that they must not come in again unless he sent for them and that they must keep well out beyond the friendly Kiowas and Comanches. Yet it was Hazen's belief that, in order to prevent more such outbreaks by young warriors and to gain a sustained peace, the entire people must suffer the army's punishment.[19]

Superintendent Thomas Murphy believed that most of the affected tribes, including the Cheyennes and Arapahos, would assemble at Fort Cobb to get clear of the army while obtaining their annuities. Aware of Sheridan's strategy of converging columns, he complained, "in all these military movements I fancy I see another Sand Creek," a view with which Commissioner Nathaniel Taylor disagreed. Taylor was still obsessed of the notion that the army was punishing the innocent to get the guilty and that patience would have been more productive: "I am satisfied the delivery [of the guilty for the Saline-Solomon raids] was not effected on their [the Cheyenne leaders'] part only from want of time." Yet Hazen also feared potential conflict if the Cheyennes came to Fort Cobb, and while he explained what he had done, he asked for clarification on the peace issue: "To have made peace with them would have brought to my camp most of those now on the war path south of the Arkansas; and as General Sheridan is to punish those at war and might follow them in afterwards, a second Chivington affair might occur, which I could not prevent. I do not understand that I am to treat for peace, but would like definite instructions in this and like cases. To make peace with these people would probably close the war, but perhaps not permanently. I would prefer that General Sheridan should make peace with these parties." Hazen also complained, "the young men who accompanied these chiefs expressed pleasure that no peace was made, as they would get more mules, and that next spring the Sioux and other northern bands were coming down and would clean out this entire country."[20]

Following their meeting with Hazen, the chiefs started back to their villages on November 21 and 22. Captain Alvord wrote: "Parties of Cheyennes and Arrapahoes leave here . . . after in vain attempting to arrange with General Hazen for a removal of their people to this vicinity to remain peaceable. They seem quite astounded at the novel fact that the war is not to cease at their pleasure." Alvord reported that the chiefs were well armed with rifles, carbines, and revolvers and had plenty of ammunition. Following their departure, Hazen and Alvord plotted to send several Padouca Comanche spies to the villages "to ascertain the substance of the council which will take place . . . on their arrival, and information as to the change of their camps, which will doubtless follow."[21] Within days the captain would report: "the camps of all the Cheyennes and Arrapahoes south of the Arkansas River have been consolidated, from 16 to 20 miles west-southwest [*sic*—east-southeast] from the Antelope Hills [at] the Washita River forks. At that fork, the large main camp of these hostile Indians, with their families and all their stock . . . , was situated on the night of the 22 inst—four days ago." Alvord reported that his intelligence had confirmed that a Mrs. Blinn and her son, captured in early October near Fort Lyon, were being held in the Cheyenne-Arapaho camp. By November 26, when Black Kettle and the others had returned to their villages along the Washita, Hazen, upon learning that these leaders had "talked badly of fight[ing]" after having left Fort Cobb, requested as a precautionary move two companies of the Tenth Cavalry from Fort Arbuckle.[22]

The return trip of Black Kettle's party to the Washita villages must have been anguished, for in effect, the Cheyennes and Arapahos had been told by Hazen that to avoid warfare and imminent direct attack by Sheridan's soldiers, they must somehow fend for themselves in negotiating a settlement. As a cold winter's storm set in, the leaders set out from Fort Cobb, carrying foodstuffs provided by a trader, and pressed north into the mounting blizzard. They reached the villages late on the evening of the twenty-sixth, six days after their departure, and two Cheyennes, Big Man and Magpie, ate a supper of buffalo meat, crackers, and coffee in the chief's lodge, fretting over what steps to take. Later Black Kettle convened a meeting with his headmen and told them of the distressing news about troops being afield. Lasting late into the morning hours of November 27, the council decided that a delegation should seek out the soldiers and attempt to explain the Indians' position once the foot-deep snow cleared. To that end, runners would go out to find the military commands. They also decided to move Black Kettle's camp to a more secure location closer to the downstream villages.[23]

While Black Kettle and the other chiefs ruminated over what to do, Custer's cavalry continued its approach. The trail that Major Elliott had found and Custer had finally gained was that of a war party of young men coming home from the Smoky Hill country. This group, originally numbering as many as 150 warriors, had traveled north during the past summer to assist the Dog Soldiers in their combat with the whites along the Saline and Solomon. Some belonged to Black Kettle's camp, while others had come from the villages of Medicine Arrows, Little Robe, and Old Whirlwind farther downriver. Desirous of reaching their home camps by the shortest route, the war party had divided into two groups at the South Canadian. One group forded the river and kept bearing south via the Antelope Hills, seeking the larger village on the Washita. The other traveled down the South Canadian, intending to cross over to the Washita and reach Black Kettle's camp. The first group entered the larger Cheyenne villages on the evening of November 25. The other party crossed the Canadian and proceeded south to the Washita, where they found evidence that the camp had moved. They continued southeast, finally gaining Black Kettle's village later that same evening.[24] That night a war party of Kiowas that had been out west raiding the Utes returned and, while passing through Black Kettle's village, reported having seen near the Antelope Hills a large trail in the snow heading toward the Washita camps. The Cheyennes reportedly discounted the information, disbelieving that soldiers would be operating that far south in such wintry conditions. The Kiowas went on to their own village, though one named Trailing the Enemy elected to stay the night with friends in Black Kettle's encampment.[25]

Following their hour-long repast along the tributary of the Washita, the Seventh Cavalry troopers mounted their animals in the darkness and pressed forward on the trail of the war party, the slow-moving column led by Hard Rope and Little Beaver, who moved forward dismounted. Custer and the remaining Indian and white scouts rode several hundred yards behind the two Osages but ahead of the troops, arranged in column of fours and following as much as a half mile in the rear for fear that the loud crunching noise of their horses walking on the crusted snow might somehow alert nearby tribesmen. Years later Lieutenant Charles Brewster remembered that night: "What a weird serpentine specter was this body, outlined upon the white snow. As it wound around the tortuous valley it had the semblance of a huge reptile, stealthily creeping to destroy its victim or foe." Trumpet calls were prohibited. Precautions were taken to tie equipment down so that it might not rattle. Smoking was not permitted, and the men conversed only in whispers as they passed the miles in the cold, beneath scattered clouds that partly hid the moon. "It . . . became necessary 'to make haste slowly,'" recalled Lieutenant Francis Gibson. "Frequent short halts were made, necessitated by the very deliberate, stealthy and cautious progress of the scouts in advance, who had evidently no intention of walking into a trap or ambush." Moreover, the winding nature of the stream required numerous crossings that further delayed the movement. Presently, as they passed along the Washita valley, the Osages out in front smelled smoke, then a mile on spied the smoldering embers of a wood fire recently abandoned by herders out watching ponies, indicative of the proximity of a village.[26] The discovery, wrote Custer, "produced almost breathless excitement." On painstaking examination, the disturbed snow in the area revealed the tracks of many ponies and the traces of lodge poles being dragged. At this Custer sent word to stop the column, then took the two scouts and advanced cautiously from ridge to ridge, finally surmounting a low height that overlooked the valley of the Washita from the northwest. From that point, probably at about midnight, Little Beaver stole to the crest and sighted a large herd of ponies about a half mile away toward the river. Custer joined him, and together they lay in the snow peering at the sight below. The colonel at first thought the animals were buffalos, then barking dogs and a tinkling bell in the herd confirmed the presence of ponies and of a likely village nearby.[27] But the lodges, hidden in the darkness by the timber along the stream, could not be easily discerned. As Custer prepared to return to his command, another affirming sound broke through the crisp predawn air: a baby's cry.

Custer returned down the slope to the larger body of scouts, where he sent orders to "halt the cavalry, enjoining complete silence and directing every officer to ride to the point we then occupied." Custer directed Ben Clark to advance and determine whether the camp lay to the north, south, or astride the Washita. Clark moved out with Jack Corbin and Rafael Romero, descending into the valley toward the river, about a mile away, careful not to disturb the ponies or camp dogs. They reached the riverbank and from there could see many of the fifty-one lodges silhouetted in the starlight and stretching along a flat bordering the south side of the Washita for a distance of perhaps a quarter mile. From this point Romero crept ahead into the camp, seeking more information, then all withdrew back to the hill to the north where Custer and his officers waited. Clark reported the estimated warrior strength of the village to be around 150, less than one-fifth that of the command. Armed with this information, Custer ordered his troops to countermarch and remove themselves from the area so as to prevent their discovery by the Indians while plans were formulated for an attack. Fearing that Bell's wagons, following on the trail about one mile behind the cavalry, might likewise alarm the camp, he sent a courier back to tell the lieutenant to stop where he was, that an attack would be made at dawn, and that he must wait until he heard the firing before advancing.[28]

When his officers arrived, Custer had them remove their sabers so that their noisy clanking would not carry forward to the village, then moved up the ridge to its crest so they might comprehend what lay before them in the darkness.[29] Captain Barnitz observed of the moment: "We could see, though not distinctly, the course of the Washita, on our right, with what appeared to be tributaries entering from the left and possibly from the right, and the summits of steep bluffs were seen looming up on all sides of the valley, but the herds of ponies, and teepes [*sic*] were not visible although the tinkling of a little bell could be distinctly heard at times, and some of the officers who looked through a night glass were of the opinion that they could discern herds of ponies."[30] From the sounds of the barking and infants' cries, as well as the tinkling of the pony bells, the relative positions of the core village and the herd was projected. Leaving two officers and an Osage on the hill to watch the village, the others crept down the slope and retrieved their sabers. Then Custer deliberated with them his plan of attack.[31]

"The general plan," wrote Custer, "was to employ the hours between then and daylight to completely surround the village, and at daybreak, or as soon as it was barely light enough for the purpose, to attack the Indians from all sides." The tactic was a mainstay during the Indian wars—both before and after Washita—troops in loose-order formation surrounding a village whose occupants were asleep and then attacking from all sides simultaneously, preferably at dawn, killing and wounding the residents, capturing their ponies, and destroying their property.[32] To accomplish this here, Custer divided his command of approximately eight hundred men into four detachments. Major Joel Elliott commanded a battalion composed of Companies G (Captain Albert Barnitz; Second Lieutenant Thomas J. March), H (Captain Frederick H. Benteen), and M (Captain Owen Hale, Second Lieutenant H. Walworth Smith) that would move left, or east, of the main force, keeping behind the string of ridges and knolls to the north, to quietly encircle the village's rear, or east side, and assume a position in the timber near the stream to attack it from the east or northeast as the lay of the ground might allow. Captain William Thompson, commanding a squadron composed of Companies B (First Lieutenant David W. Wallingford) and F (Captain George F. Yates, Second Lieutenant Francis M. Gibson), would countermarch to the right of the main column, swinging down the slope to the west and south of the village; cross the Washita, keeping well beneath the hills on the right bank to a position opposite the camp; and coordinate his attack with that of Elliott. At the signal, Thompson's force would close on the camp on horseback. Captain Edward Myers was to take Companies E (First Lieutenant John M. Johnson, Second Lieutenant Algernon E. Smith) and I (First Lieutenant Charles Brewster), move down to a position in the woods approximately three-quarters of a mile to Custer's right and well south of it, cross the stream, advance to within sight of the camp, and then prepare to strike it from the timber on the west, a position also preventing the escape of occupants fleeing in that direction. Finally, from the discovery ridge, Custer, aide-de-camp First Lieutenant Samuel M. Robbins (detached from Company D), and regimental adjutant First Lieutenant Myles Moylan would accompany and oversee two cavalry squadrons commanded by Captain Louis M. Hamilton (Companies A [First Lieutenant Thomas W. Custer] and C [First Lieutenant Mathew Berry]) and Captain Robert M. West (Companies D [Captain Thomas B. Weir] and K [First Lieutenant Edward S. Godfrey, Second Lieutenant Edward Law]), themselves accompanied by First Lieutenant William W. Cooke's sharpshooters and the Osage and other scouts. Medical officers accompanying this column were Assistant Surgeon Henry Lippincott and Acting Assistant Surgeon William H. Renicke.[33] The attack would be executed simultaneously from all directions, but it was important that each column knew the proximity of the others and stagger its appearance accordingly in order to avoid inflicting "friendly" casualties once the assault began. A contingency plan held that should the Indians discover any of the enclosing columns, "the attack was to be made at once." As Barnitz reported, "The signal of attack was to be sounded at daybreak by the band, which was to play on the summit of the ridge from which Genl. Custer's column was to advance, and instantly, at the appointed signal, or at the firing of a gun, the advance was to be made from all directions—all were to go in *with a rush* and this was particularly enjoined upon all the officers by Genl Custer, as he fully realized the importance of concentration." The colonel sent Lieutenant Godfrey back to Bell's train with an order for Captain Benteen's squadron, Companies H and M, which had been rear guard with the wagons, to come forward. The camp guard, consisting of four or five sick men along with a few deserters, stayed behind to protect the train.[34]

Some time after 2:00 A.M., Elliott started his soldiers east, G Company in advance, tracing along a string of hills and ridges well back from the river to avoid detection. Battalion officers directed the men not to smoke, to talk only in whispers, and to carry their cups in their haversacks to keep them from clanking against saddles or other equipment. Thompson, and later Myers, likewise started their men moving south and southwest to assume their positions. As Elliott's men passed east along the ground, they crossed over several well-worn trails leading in the direction of the Indian camp. Ascending the bluffs at one place, Elliott decided that he was moving too close to the camp and that the horses stepping along the crusted snow would alarm the Indians. He descended and countermarched his column, then moved farther north behind the bluffs as they pressed downstream to their assigned spot. At some point during the movement, Elliott discovered that the regimental band, which was supposed to remain with Custer, was following him, and he ordered it back. He also discovered that Benteen's squadron had not yet advanced with the column.

At an outlying point, the major and Barnitz ascended what Barnitz later described as a "very steep conical hill" on their right and opposite the camp, which he subsequently termed "Sugar Loaf." Keeping low to the snow-encrusted ground, the two officers squinted their eyes, trying to see the village in the darkened valley beyond. Again, however, the "short, snappish barking" of the Cheyennes' dogs betrayed its presence. Descending from the hill, they found a number of baying foxhounds that had somehow broken away from the wagon train parked all the way back on the South Canadian River and followed on the troops' trail. Fearing discovery, Elliott ordered the animals killed by strangulation and with knives. Then the battalion entered a deep rocky draw leading toward the river, through which the troopers passed in single file, finally climbing up the steep sides by holding onto their horses' manes.[35] Soon afterward, they encountered a herd of ponies individually tethered in a grove of trees and shortly gained the Washita some three-quarters of a mile below the village. Elliott and Barnitz then reconnoitered across the stream, finding even more ponies.

When Benteen arrived, the combined forces started west through the woods toward the camp. In the final dispositions Benteen's companies (H and M) took position on the north side of the stream, while Barnitz placed Company G on the south side, the men in dismounted skirmish formation so that their right flank adjoined the Washita. Ten mounted soldiers under Sergeant Francis McDermott took position on the left of Barnitz's line to work in concert with Company F of Thompson's battalion and with Myers's troops in closing off escape routes to the south and southeast. Private John Ryan, of Company M, recollected the ensuing wait: "[We] were obliged to sit in our saddles, as we were under orders not to dismount. We were pretty cold, especially our feet, and we tried two ways of keeping them warm; first, to take the feet from the stirrups and let them hang down, thus allowing the blood to circulate; then to kick the feet against the stirrups and keep the blood stirring."[36]

Meantime, the column under Captain Thompson crossed the Washita, but it possibly had trouble negotiating the broken ground in the dark in assuming its position to the south-southwest of the village. Lieutenant Gibson, who accompanied this battalion, remembered: "Daylight never seemed so long coming, and the cold never so penetrating. It was an infraction of orders to talk or move about, so there was nothing left to do but to remain perfectly quiet and immovable, thus maintaining a death-like silence, while spending the night in moody meditation, broken occasionally by spasmodic shivers and involuntary shakes."[37]

Following the assignments and the departures of Elliott's, Thompson's, and Myers's columns, the squadrons of Hamilton and West (with Custer) passed the remaining four hours until dawn in excruciating discomfort. Fires were not permitted, and the early morning cold debilitated the troops, who were ordered not to stamp their feet or pace for fear of the noise of crunching snow reaching the silent camp. The men stood with their horses or lay down in the snow, holding the reins and waiting, some chewing hardtack, listening to the barking dogs in the valley. "[We were] cold, wet, and mad!" remembered one man. Officers clustered together in quiet discussion, while others slept on the hard-packed snow crust, their capes wrapped about their heads. The Osages gathered separately, wrapped in blankets and filled with paranoia that the troops might find too many Indians in the village and offer up their Indian scouts as hostages for their own deliverance. In the precautionary mood of the moment, Custer's greyhound, which tended to bark after the dogs in the valley, was at first muzzled, then garroted with a lariat, to silence him.[38] Two hours before daybreak, the moon disappeared, plunging the scene into pitch darkness until the hint of dawn appeared on the eastern horizon. Behind the ridge, as Custer awakened his officers, a phenomenon appeared to the southeast, resembling a signal flare and startling them that the village had somehow been alerted. It was a morning star, and its rising above the ridge and seeming to hover directly above the Cheyenne camp momentarily brought consternation and anxiety among the officers until it was correctly identified.[39] Meantime, far below, the Indian village hardly stirred in the freezing morning twilight, oblivious to the danger lurking just beyond the darkness.

7

WASHITA

As daylight grew, the troops with Custer's battalion received orders to remove their greatcoats, haversacks, canteens, and blanket rolls so they might move more freely. Then they mounted and advanced to positions behind the ridge.[1] West's squadron formed in line on the right; Custer, his staff, and the regimental band—numbering but sixteen men—took the center; and Hamilton's squadron arrayed on the left. Cooke's sharpshooters, dismounted, arranged themselves in skirmish formation in advance of Hamilton's companies. Officers passed the word not to fire until the signal was given. (The units of Elliott, Thompson, and Myers had earlier been instructed to advance on the camp as closely as practicable before daylight; Myers was also to approach with one-half of his command dismounted.) Then the companies crested the ridge and at a walking gait began their descent toward the village, approximately a mile away, Custer and the regimental band advancing in the center of the line. Presently they reached a lower ridge, where they halted briefly, poised to renew the advance in the growing daylight.[2] Dogs in the village were now yelping furiously at the soldiers, but still no one stirred in the lodges, and a fleeting fear passed through some of the officers that the camp was deserted like that at Pawnee Fork. The movement of the horses over the crusted snow proved noisy, and on reaching the Indian herd, the ponies quickly turned away from the columns. More animals were located on the hillsides south of the village, while others were picketed among the lodges. Captain West rode over to Lieutenant Godfrey, with Company K at the extreme right of the line, and told him to charge through the camp and round up the herds. The troops closed on the white tipis scattered beyond the thickly growing timber along the Washita. Smoke could be seen emanating from the tops of some of them. Trumpeters sounded "Charge!" Then, as Custer turned to signal the band leader, a shot ripped through the morning air, fired from a point across the camp, and immediately the band struck up the opening strain of the Seventh's marching song, "Garry Owen." At that instant, from all sides, the troops rushed toward the village.[3]

In a moment all was tumult. Cooke's sharpshooters pulled farther to their left, opening a corridor for the cheering troops with Custer who, momentarily slowed by the steep banks, came splashing across the Washita on a northwest-southeast diagonal directly into the Cheyenne camp, shooting into and through the tipis.[4] Awaking in the shock of the attack, the warriors and their families, many unarmed, scrambled out of their lodges, attempting to run before the thundering onrush of the army horses. Almost abruptly, the band's instruments froze up in the icy air, the measured notes replaced by a cacophony of shooting, screaming, barking, and yelling, accompanied by the pounding din of hundreds of horses' hooves storming over the frigid terrain.[5] Custer led the attack of the larger battalion, his black stallion bounding across the river and into the camp, where he fired at one tribesman and ran his horse over another as he, accompanied by Ben Clark, streaked through the camp and up the southern slope to a point on elevated ground about a quarter mile beyond the stream. There the colonel took position on a rising hillock to oversee and direct movements on the field. In the opening melee West's and Hamilton's soldiers galloped into the camp, discharging their pistols at the people fleeing in all directions. One of the first army casualties was Captain Hamilton, who, riding on Custer's left, was heard to call to his men to "keep cool, fire low, and not too rapidly" shortly before a Cheyenne bullet found its mark, knocking him dead from his saddle.[6]

The component battalions simultaneously entered the fray. From the west and south, Myers and Thompson drove toward the village, but Thompson's cavalrymen, late to arrive, failed to extend their enclosing line on the east, opening a wide gap between them and

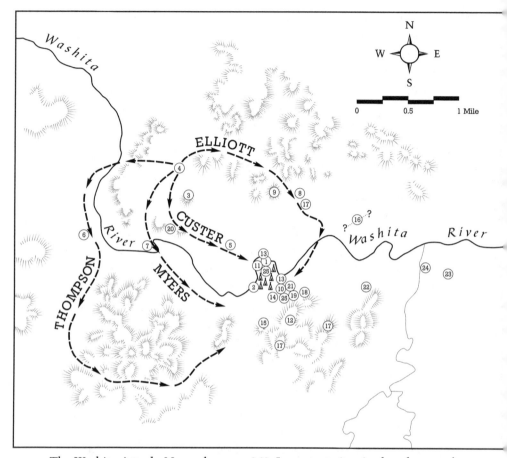

The Washita Attack, November 27, 1868. Important sites in the advance of Custer's battalions at daybreak and the subsequent engagement are keyed as follows: 1. Black Kettle's Village; 2. Site of Black Kettle's Lodge; 3. Observation Ridge; 4. Army Preattack Staging Area; 5. Custer's Attack Route; 6. Thompson's Attack Route; 7. Myers's Attack Route; 8. Elliott's Attack Route; 9. Sugar Loaf Butte; 10. Custer's Knoll; 11. Hamilton Death Site; 12. Barnitz Rock Circle; 13. Cheyenne Stand Areas; 14. Magpie's Escape Route; 15. Twin Knolls; 16. Godfrey's Advance Downstream; 17. Areas Where Warriors from Downriver Villages Assembled; 18. Possible Skirmish Line Site Southwest of Village; 19. Elliott's Departure Point; 20. Route of Bell's Advance; 21. Pony-Kill Site; 22. Sergeant Major Kennedy's Death; 23. Deaths of Blind Bear and Hawk; 24. Destruction of Major Elliott's Command; 25. Locations of Scott Monument. For a discussion of each site, see appendix A.

Barnitz's troopers through which many of the people escaped.[7] Myers's column acted primarily as a containment force. Barnitz's soldiers, positioned on a low plateau behind a swale full of tree stumps, did not directly drive into the camp, but after the initial attack by the mounted commands, the dismounted reserves "followed [them in] with more deliberation to support the attack and to complete the victory." Barnitz believed that his movements in the brush east of the camp and south of the river were responsible for opening the attack when they spooked a number of Cheyenne herders, possibly boys, who ran toward the village. The captain's dismounted troopers followed them but did not fire. "We had just reached the edge of a shallow ravine beyond which we could see the clustered tepees, situated among wide-branching cottonwood trees, when a shot was fired in the village, and instantly we heard the band on the ridge beyond it strike up the familiar air 'Garry Owen.'" Following the signal, Benteen's squadron galloped forward in line from the northeast. Thus, largely hemmed in from all directions, many of the people, warriors among them, ran to the riverbank and jumped in the freezing waist-deep water, turning to fire defensively over the bank at the soldiers. Other men, women, and children fled down to the river and into the stream, finding refuge behind a large chunk of earth that had collapsed into the water from erosion and now formed a natural barricade paralleling the north bank. Still others sought protection in ravines and behind trees, fallen logs, and driftwood, anywhere they might attempt some form of counterattack with their meager resources. The Indians, said Custer, fought "with a desperation and courage which no race of men could surpass." From near their lodge on the west end of the encampment, Black Kettle and his wife together mounted a single pony and started for the Washita. Reaching and entering the stream, they were knocked off the animal and into the water, killed by soldier bullets.[8]

Within minutes of the assault, the troops controlled the village. The tribesmen, scattered among the surrounding topography, fought back as best they could against the soldiers, who rooted them out of lodges and hiding places. Some of the women came at the troopers brandishing pistols and were shot. One group of women and children tore across the rising prairie southwest of Custer's command knoll, pursued by men from Captain Myers's command who were shooting at them, "killing them without mercy," said Clark. "I was riding to the south, when I came in view of fully half of Myers's men, chasing the

panic-stricken women and children." The scout immediately brought
Custer's attention to the activity, asking the colonel if the people were
to be killed, whereupon Custer directed Clark to immediately intervene,
halt the pursuit, and take the captives to a guarded lodge in the mostly
deserted camp.[9] Some noncombatants, however, remained in their lodges
throughout the attack, passing the anxious moments likely singing
prayer songs. According to Ben Clark, much of the killing of women
and children lay with the Osages. They "shot down the women and
mutilated their bodies, cutting off their arms, legs and breasts with
knives."[10] Presently, the camp area was largely cleared, many of the
occupants having fled downstream, pursued by cavalry.

But as one trooper recalled years later, "the real fighting . . . began
when we attempted to dislodge them from ravines or ambush." Other
people took refuge in the woods bordering the stream, and officers directed their men to dismount and advantage themselves of the terrain in
rooting them out. The sharpshooters apparently took part in this activity, working their way far downstream, clearing out pockets of resistance. Gradually, the troops' firing proved too much, and those who
escaped this shooting joined others behind the stream bank. At the place
where the people were hidden behind the length of collapsed embankment, the sharpshooters killed a number of noncombatants, including
women. Farther downstream, however, a party of warriors occupied a
ravine, driven there by Barnitz's dismounted line, with only their heads
visible when they rose up to fire. This group succeeded in registering
a number of casualties among the troops, and it was only after Cooke's
sharpshooters sent rounds at them from concealed positions that they
were all killed.[11] As a matter of policy, throughout the field, any wounded
warriors discovered by the soldiers were promptly shot to death. Once
the village was secured, Custer sent the interpreter Romero to the
lodges, with assurances that the women and children would not be
harmed. These noncombatants were collected in the designated tipis.
"This was quite a delicate mission," wrote Custer, "as it was difficult
to convince the squaws and children that they had anything but death
to expect at our hands."[12] Custer later talked to the prisoners to assure
them of good treatment; through Black Kettle's sister-in-law, Mahwissa
(Red Hair), he learned the identification of the camp and presumably of
the death of the chief, as well as that of Little Rock, in the attack. Meantime, the surgeons established a hospital in the center of the camp, and

the wounded as well as the fatalities, Hamilton among them, were brought in for their attention.

While the attack unfolded, some of the troopers went after the ponies. California Joe employed two captive Cheyenne women in rounding up nearly three hundred. The animals were tightly guarded to prevent their recapture or stampede by the warriors. Lieutenant Godfrey, meantime, followed his instructions from West to seize the ponies. On fording the Washita west of the village, he reformed his platoon of about twenty men and rode directly through the camp after the mounts, though many of the animals had run toward the lodges during the alarm. Godfrey assembled a herd on the slopes south of the camp, then, sighting some dismounted tribesmen running away on the north side of the valley, he left the herd in the custody of Lieutenant Law and crossed to that side of the Washita and started downstream along the ridges looking for the escaping Indians. Godfrey's platoon followed a trail for perhaps three miles. When accompanying sergeants admonished him about proceeding too far, Godfrey scaled a promontory to scan the valley. He was shocked to see the hundreds of lodges of the lower camps and large numbers of warriors moving rapidly in his direction. The lieutenant trotted away but soon came under fire of the warriors. He halted his men, returned fire, laid out a skirmish line, and began a steady withdrawal from ridge to ridge back toward the Cheyenne village. As he recalled: "Under the cavalry tactics of 1841, the retreat of skirmishers was by the odd and even numbers, alternating in lines to the rear. I instructed the line in retreat to halt on the next ridge and cover the retreat of the advance line. This was successful for the first and second ridges, but at the third I found men had apparently forgotten their numbers and there was some confusion, so I divided the skirmishers into two groups, each under a sergeant, and thereafter had no trouble."[13]

As the troops withdrew, they could hear sharp firing to the south and across the Washita; trees and vegetation obscured from them the source of all that shooting. The Indians finally fell away from Godfrey's front, and the lieutenant completed his withdrawal and reported his sightings to Custer, who seemed surprised in the knowledge of the lower camps and questioned the officer intently about what he had seen. Godfrey later told the colonel about the sounds of heavy firing that had drawn his attention to the south bank and that the profusion of trees near the river had screened any view of activity there. The lieutenant suggested that the shooting might be related to a group headed by Major Elliott that had earlier gone in that direction and might be fighting downstream, but Custer informed him that Myers had been fighting in that vicinity and that the shooting probably came from his action.

But the reality was that Elliott was probably under attack. He and Barnitz had seen a large body of Indians racing from the village and passing their left flank over some sand hills toward ponies ranging to the southeast. Barnitz ordered his men to fire on the people, then sent Sergeant McDermott and his mounted soldiers to head them in the direction of Thompson's column, anticipated to arrive from the bluffs to the southwest. Attempting to locate Thompson, Barnitz spurred his horse to pass through the running Indians and learned that they were elderly women; some had babies on their backs, while others dragged children along by their arms. He saw one woman with a child straddling her neck as she ran while leading two others with her hands. While his troops rounded up these noncombatants (forty-eight women, according to Barnitz), the captain continued southeast, following some running warriors. As he approached, two unleashed arrows at him, and he shot both. A third man discharged a rifle at him, wounding the captain as he simultaneously fired, hitting the Indian. The injured Barnitz then turned back as his soldiers pursued the other warriors. He slowly rode toward the village, finally paused on a hilltop, dismounted, and crawled into a depression, with the clear expectation that he was dying. Later some of Barnitz's men found him, placed him on a buffalo robe, and transported him to the hospital area, where Drs. Lippincott and Renicke, both under the effects of snow blindness, pronounced his wound fatal.[14]

At the same time, in an attempt to corral some Indians seen fleeing through the unclosed gap between his command and that of Captain Thompson, Major Elliott and Sergeant Major Walter Kennedy assembled a group of sixteen volunteers, who took off downstream after the tribesmen. Ben Clark recalled seeing Elliott standing atop a hill east of where he and Custer had been at the outset of the fighting.[15] The twenty-eight-year-old major stood with Kennedy, looking through his field glasses at a number of men and boys hiding in the timber below, then called for troops to accompany them and took off.[16] It was between 9:00 and 10:00 A.M. Reportedly, Elliott had shouted to Lieutenant Hale,

"Here goes for a brevet or a coffin," as he galloped away in the lead.[17] Meanwhile, the men continued east along the south side of the Washita valley for some distance and apparently captured a number of refugees. But at a point along the river approximately two and one-half miles east of the village and near the confluence of the tributary now called Sergeant Major Creek, Indians from the downriver camps converged from several directions out of the timber on Elliott's small force. It is not known if in his peril Elliott grasped the significance of the Indians coming against him from the east. His men tried to hide in tall grass, but the warriors closed in, shooting bullets and arrows from a distance, then rushed the position. Soon, Elliott and his entire detachment lay dead.[18]

This fight, though presently unknown to Custer, presaged a perilously unfolding situation. Godfrey had reported the existence downstream of a great number of lodges, and increasingly cognizant of something wrong at Black Kettle's camp, hundreds of Cheyenne, Arapaho, and Kiowa warriors gradually began ascending the heights bordering the north side of the Washita, cautiously approaching to discover what was happening. Custer's women prisoners confirmed that other wintering camps lay less than four miles downstream, and the colonel quickly realized that, despite his troops' success in seizing the Cheyenne camp, his position was by no means secure. As the afternoon wore on, he anxiously watched through an eyeglass the mounting numbers of armed, war-bonneted figures perched on ponies atop the hills bordering the valley floor in several directions, believing that an attack was all but inevitable. Custer realized that with his prisoners and wounded, and with the large numbers of ponies and captured property—to say nothing of his own diminishing ammunition supply—he would be unable to press forward toward the downstream villages. The latter predicament was rectified with the arrival shortly before noon of Lieutenant Bell with the wagon train. After Benteen's departure from the train to join Elliot, the wagons and their tiny escort had advanced on the trail for about a half mile. At the sounds of shooting, Bell again moved forward but was delayed crossing the Washita approximately one mile above the village. Then, following on Custer's trail, he ascended the steep grade and saw the ongoing fighting below. Finally, the train penetrated a loose cordon of warriors arriving from the downstream camps. These men disrupted the effort to claim the soldiers' greatcoats and other equipment left behind in the initial advance, and the Cheyennes seized the material while the train, drawn by galloping mules, raced down the crusted slope, forded the stream some distance west of the fighting, and entered the village. The wheels of one of the wagons was in flames because of friction on the tarred axle, and upon reaching the lodges troops overturned the vehicle to save the ammunition, using snow to extinguish the fire.[19]

After Bell's arrival, ammunition was distributed to the troops. Determined to finish his business in the village, Custer now threw out skirmishers beyond the camp to watch and engage the distant warriors. Company C, under Lieutenant Matthew Berry, composed at least part of the skirmish line. According to Clark, the Indians continued shooting into the camp from the area where they had confiscated the soldiers' overcoats, and Custer sent Berry to dislodge them. Those troops then remained in that position overlooking the village from the northwest. The remainder of his command Custer set to destroying the fifty-one lodges and all of the material that might be of value to the Indians. By this time, the village was littered with clothing, blankets, and robes tossed by the fleeing people. The soldiers now toppled the lodges (though one particularly handsome one was packed into a wagon for Custer), and their contents of dried meat and other food, flour, clothing, coffee mills, kettles, frying pans, hatchets, axes, weapons, powder, and ammunition were piled together and consumed in several raging bonfires.[20] Looting by the soldiers was not permitted because it would encumber their march. During this action, the men purportedly found evidence of the village's complicity in the Kansas raids, including unopened mail, photographs, and various household goods taken during the attacks on the settlements. Clark stated that he saw "four white and three Indian scalps" in the camp. Lieutenant Godfrey's Company K accomplished much of the destruction: "I began . . . at the upper end of the village, tearing down tepees and piling several together on the tepee poles, set fire to them. . . . As the fires made headway, all articles of personal property—buffalo robes, blankets, food, rifles, pistols, bows and arrows, lead and [percussion] caps, bullet molds, etc.—were thrown in the fires and destroyed."[21]

From the raging flames, the sounds of exploding powder and ammunition punctuated the day, and as the blackened smoke from the fires filled the valley, the warriors from the lower camps glowered intently from the hills surrounding the north side of the valley. Some challenged the soldiers to come get their overcoats, then began a series of mounted feints toward the soldiers' line, as if trying to penetrate the prostrated skirmishers, but in each instance they kept their distance. Custer now went on the offensive, sending squadrons under Benteen, Myers, and Captain Thomas Weir (who had succeeded Hamilton) to advance on the tribesmen. The adversaries traded charges, the squadrons supporting each other in their movements until the warriors finally fell back.[22]

Realizing that Elliott and his men had not returned, and having reports of brief shooting heard from downriver, Custer dispatched Captain Myers downstream to try and locate the major's party. The colonel queried other officers about the major's whereabouts without gaining any precise knowledge, while Myers reportedly searched for two miles, then returned. "I had previously given him up as killed," Custer recalled, "but was surprised that so many of the men should be missing, and none of their comrades be able to account for them. All the ground inside of the advanced lines held by the Indians who attacked us after our capture of the village was closely and carefully examined, . . . but with no success."[23] Mindful of his train halted at the South Canadian, Custer also feared that if he remained at the Washita camp overnight, the warriors would discover and attack the advancing wagons and their eighty-man escort. In addition, there was the matter of the large number of Cheyenne ponies and mules. As Custer explained:

By actual count we had in our possession 875 captured ponies [and mules], so wild and unused to white men that it was difficult to herd them. What we were to do with them was puzzling, as they could not have been led had we been possessed of the means of doing this; neither could we drive them as the Indians were accustomed to do. And even if we could take them with us, either the one way or the other, it was anything but wise or desirable on our part to do so, as such a large herd of ponies, constituting so much wealth in the eyes of the Indians, would have been too tempting a prize to the warriors who had been fighting us all the afternoon, and to effect their recapture they would have followed and waylaid us day and night, with every prospect of success, until we should have arrived at a place of safety.[24]

Now armed with an abundance of ammunition following Bell's arrival, Custer gave orders to slaughter the herd. The animals had been difficult to capture and manage and instinctively recoiled at the soldiers' presence, frantically trying to escape. Details of the men corralled the beasts, drove them to a position beneath a high bluff southeast of the village, and then waited while the women prisoners and Osage scouts— as well as some officers (including Custer)—selected a number to accommodate their needs.[25] After attempts to kill the spirited beasts by slitting their throats failed, four companies of dismounted cavalrymen shot them to death. Ben Clark remembered that the animals "were bunched against the steep bank south of the village." The destruction of the ponies continued for at least one and one-half hours and "was done by platoon shooting." Far across the Washita valley, warriors observed the killing of the animals, enraged by what they saw.[26]

During the attack, a number of incidents occurred to, or were witnessed by, members of the army command. In one near the outset of the charge, Captain Benteen, while leading his squadron forward, encountered a mounted Cheyenne youth, about fourteen years old, who rode directly at the officer and twice discharged a revolver at him. Benteen initially regarded the boy as a noncombatant and hesitated in his response. But the youth continued to fire at him, and one shot wounded his horse; with all sense of appeal gone, and with the boy reaching for another pistol, Benteen leveled his own revolver at him and fired, killing him. (This Cheyenne has been tentatively identified as Blue Horse, a twenty-one-year-old nephew of Black Kettle.)[27] Elsewhere, Lieutenant H. Walworth Smith raced through the camp, followed closely by an enlisted man. While passing a group of women wrapped in blankets, Smith instructed his companion not to fire on them, when suddenly one of the "women" let loose an arrow that struck the soldier in the temple and then slid around slicing through his scalp. The trooper managed to stay mounted and, passing by, sent a bullet into the Indian, whom it was discovered was an elderly man equipped with bow and arrow. According to Custer, the trooper took the Indian's scalp.[28] During the engagement, Ben Clark witnessed a Mexican captive of the Cheyennes named Palar (or White Bear) carry a little girl to the soldiers. Delivering her over to a sergeant who told him to run, the man turned and started away, whereupon the sergeant shot him in the back, killing him. And an incident reported in the *New York Herald* accounted for an Osage scout who was in mourning for the recent loss of his wife. Once the shooting began, one of the other scouts, aware of this fact, took action to help his comrade get beyond his grief. The warrior, "having shot a Cheyenne, rushed upon his fallen foe and in an instant with his knife severed the head from the body. With a wild whoop he took the ghastly object to the mourning warrior and threw it down before him. The warrior seized the trunkless head and in an instant had the scalp." Thereafter, the sorrowed warrior was in the midst of the fray with his fellows.[29]

By late in the day, the extrication of Custer's command from what appeared to be a steadily worsening threat from the Indians of the downriver camps now became paramount. "We had achieved a great and important success over the hostile tribes," wrote the colonel. "The problem now was how to retain our advantage and steer safely through the difficulties which seemed to surround our position." As dusk settled, the men prepared the dead and wounded for the journey ahead; all, including wounded Cheyenne women and children, were placed in the wagons. Cavalry trumpets recalled the scattered force into the area of the village, the soldiers mounted, the band struck up "Ain't I Glad to Get Out of the Wilderness," and with guidons flying and skirmishers leading the way, the regiment crossed to the north side of the Washita and started downstream toward the other villages. "I . . . had recourse to that maxim in war which teaches a commander to do that which his enemy neither expects nor desires him to do," stated Custer. Lieutenant Godfrey, who knew where the villages stood, rode with Custer at the head of the column of fours in the advance. Ben Clark recalled how the force was arrayed: "The regiment was drawn up in close marching order. Three hundred yards ahead of the advance guard of one troop were the scouts. A quarter of a mile in the rear of the advance guard was another troop, close behind which were the captives on ponies. Then came the main body of the troops, the wagon train and the rear guard."[30]

During the advance, flankers went out along the side of the Washita to guard against surprise attacks from the woods and to keep watch for Elliott's men. (The soldiers passed by Elliott's dead obliviously, for their bodies lay beyond view in the growing dusk on the south side of the river.) Initially, the Indians rode forward to make repeated feints against the soldiers. From his ambulance, the wounded Barnitz saw "painted aboriginees [sic], bedecked with war-bonnets, as they made desperate charges, in efforts to stampede the mules." But the troops effectively countered these thrusts, dismounting and kneeling as they delivered their rounds against the warriors. Finally, believing that the soldiers were about to assault their camps in the same manner as they had

Black Kettle's, and perhaps afraid that shots directed against the column might hit the prisoners, most of the Indians on the hills quickly dispersed down the valley to their homes. Then, under cover of darkness, after slowly passing several miles down the valley but at a point well short of actually sighting the camps, Custer pulled in his skirmishers and quickly took the back trail, leading his command past the battlefield and northwestwardly up the Washita in a forced march to reach the wagon train.[31] The troops hurried on for perhaps a dozen miles until 2:00 A.M., when, in apparent security, they halted to rest, Custer sending Captain West's squadron forward to find and support the train. The Osages took the occasion to fire several volleys over their scalp collection, ostensibly to rid the area of the spirits of the slain. Resuming the push at dawn on the twenty-eighth, the troops joined the wagon train at about ten o'clock. Stopping but briefly while the teams were harnessed, Custer continued his withdrawal to the northeast until early afternoon, crossing the Canadian and probably halting somewhere in the vicinity of upper Hackberry Creek. No Indians were seen on the return march. At this well-picketed camp, the men pitched tents, unsaddled their weary mounts, and downed their first substantive meals in almost two days. From here, after querying his officers for data about Indian casualties, Custer dispatched California Joe Milner and Jack Corbin to General Sheridan, bearing the first word of his regiment's attack on, and the destruction of, the Cheyenne village.[32]

The Indian perspective of the Washita attack generally parallels that of the soldiers and helps round out the knowledge of the event. Most of the Cheyenne narratives describe what happened to individuals when they came under fire from the troops and how they dealt with the emergency circumstances that confronted them. Following Black Kettle's return from his meeting with Hazen, a number of people in the village, including the chief's wife, urged that the camp move, and according to one source, some of the youngsters were removed to Old Whirlwind's camp downstream. But the majority of village occupants remained where they were. At dawn on the twenty-seventh, some of the people got news of the soldiers' approach. Moving Behind, who was fourteen years old at the time, remembered people calling to others to wake up, that the soldiers were coming. But as they did so the assault commenced. "At that instant," said Moving Behind, "the soldiers let out terrible yells, and there was a burst of gunfire from them." The young girl joined her aunt, Corn Stalk Woman, outside her lodge. She could see the people racing about frantically and noted, "Black Kettle and his wife were last seen when they rode off on a horse." Another Cheyenne woman, who was about sixteen years old at the time, recalled that a man named Double Wolf was supposed to be watching at night but fell asleep. When the commotion started, he was expected to raise a white blanket flag but instead fired his weapon; Double Wolf was one of the first killed in the charge. The Cheyenne woman remembered that pandemonium then erupted: "We all ran out of our tepees and tried to run out through the narrow entrance. We saw white men in front of us motioning us to go back. Then the battle began. I don't know which side started shooting first. I fell on my face in the snow and could hear nothing but guns. At last the shooting stopped, and the next thing I knew a soldier punched me with his gun and motioned to me to get up. There were several other women lying close to me. Men, women, and children lay dead everywhere. I saw many of the warriors lying dead with their guns in their hands."[33]

Regarding Black Kettle's death, the chief was warned of the imminent danger by a woman running through the camp. He fired a shot from his rifle to awaken the people still sleeping, then reached for the pony tethered at his lodge. A man named Bearmeat Face described the chief and his wife, Ar-no-ho-wok (Woman Here After, according to Bent, but also translated as Medicine Woman Later), mounting an iron-gray horse, "but the horse was badly frightened by the great firing and the morning excitement" so much that they could not get away quickly. The couple tried to make it to the ford to cross to the north side, but soldiers were already storming through the brush near the stream. Then the horse they were riding was shot in the right hind leg, and Black Kettle and his wife were killed. The chief was hit in the stomach, and another shot struck him in the back between the shoulder blades. They fell in the water, the horse struggling to reach the far bank, where it died. Bearmeat Face fled and joined a young woman escaping with her baby, then helped conduct other noncombatants to safety.[34]

The men grabbed their weapons, dashing out of the lodges to meet the soldiers' onrush. Some tore around trying to find places to mount a defense. Moving Behind told how one man, Statue, astride his horse berated the leaders for leaving the women and children behind as they ran. Many of the noncombatants panicked, running every which way and screaming and crying as the yelling soldiers charged through them. Some, however, remained in the tipis as the troops raced around outside, hoping they would be safe there. Numbers of people finally ran to the Washita and jumped in the freezing water, seeking protection from the bullets under the banks of the river. Some tried to wade downstream, but the soldiers found them and shot many in the water.[35] In the chaos Moving Behind joined her aunt in getting through and south of the camp and seeking refuge in the tall grasses there. She later described her escape:

> Many Indians were killed during the fight. The air was full of smoke from gunfire, and it was almost impossible to flee, because bullets were flying everywhere. However, somehow we ran and kept running to find a hiding place. As we ran, we could see the red fire of the shots. We got near a hill, and there we saw a steep path, where an old road used to be. There was red grass along the path, and although the ponies had eaten some of it, it was still high enough for us to hide. In this grass we lay flat, our hearts beating fast; and we were afraid to move. It was now bright daylight. It frightened us to listen to the noise and the cries of the wounded. When the noise seemed to quiet down, and we believed the battle was about to end, we raised our heads high enough to see what was going on. We saw a dark figure lying near a hill, and later we learned it was the body of a woman with child. The woman's body had been cut open by the soldiers.[36]

During the opening charge, Cranky Man came out of his lodge on the west of the camp. He lifted his rifle and fired, hitting a soldier, possibly an officer. Then Cranky Man stood in front of his lodge, firing at the soldiers until their bullets felled him. Two others, Red Shin and Medicine Elk, also met the charging troopers in the village, firing at them until the soldiers forced them to flee into the woods and bushes, where the two continued shooting at the troopers racing about the camp. Elsewhere, dismounted soldiers closed in on groups of men and boys congregated behind fallen trees and the river bank, killing some and forcing others from their cover before shooting them as well. Many of these warriors joined others in the stream as they tried desperately to hold off the attackers. Women and children sought the protection of the banks too, including that offered by the large piece of collapsed earth on the north side of the stream. There, as the people fell at the hands of the troopers, one woman, in a helpless rage, stood up with her baby, held it out in an outstretched arm, and with the other drew a knife and fatally stabbed the infant—erroneously believed by the soldiers to be a white child. She then plunged the blade into her own chest in suicide.[37]

Afraid for their lives, other women in the camp broke and ran to the southeast. The Osages, who had already killed and mutilated some of the women and children, rode after them, grabbing limbs from trees and brush with which to beat their quarry back into the village. Yet some people managed to escape. Three of them, Big Man, Magpie, and Pushing Bear, were in the western part of the village when the soldiers struck. They ran farther west, then south, finally encountering the troops of Myers's battalion, who shot at them, slightly wounding Magpie, who kept moving. Somehow Big Man became separated from the others. Magpie and Pushing Bear remained to the south, finally heading toward a ridge in that direction that would protect them; a lone horseman spied them and closed in. The soldier swung his saber at the youth, who ducked and then shot his assailant with a pistol. Magpie and Pushing Bear mounted the horse and rode away. A group of troopers spotted them and briefly rode toward the two Cheyennes, but their attention was shortly diverted to a group of women and children who were running to the east. Pursuing them, the soldier party—which was headed by Major Elliott—came upon and killed an old Cheyenne man and a youth named Crazy, then continued their pursuit of the party of women and children.[38]

Cheyenne accounts of the demise of Elliott and his party are vital to any determination of what happened to these soldiers after they left the area of the village and pursued the women and children east. The Cheyennes they were trying to overtake included She Wolf (also known as Packer); Little Rock; Trailing the Enemy (a Kiowa); Little Beaver, the twelve-year-old son of Wolf Looking Back; three unidentified children; three women (two of them White Buffalo Woman and her sister); and two very young men, Blind Bear and Hawk. All were a considerable distance east of the camp and were crossing open ground when the troopers discovered them and started their pursuit. The two young men began running to draw the soldiers away from the women and children. But the soldiers went immediately to the women and children, pausing for a few moments before most of them started after Blind Bear and Hawk, now far ahead. Sergeant Major Walter Kennedy remained to escort the women and children back to the village. As he did so, Little Beaver attempted to pull a revolver on him but was foiled and surrendered the weapon. White Buffalo Woman devised a ruse to slow the party, binding the bleeding feet of the children while allowing a rescue party from the downriver camps to approach. As Kennedy and the party moved west toward the village, a few warriors fell in between them and Elliott's group. These were four Arapahos from Little Raven's downriver camp—Little Chief, Tossing Up, Kiowa, and Lone Killer—appearing suddenly from the trees near the river on Kennedy's right. Kennedy fired at the men, then bolted away on his horse, attempting to get another round into his carbine, while the women and children broke away and ran for the river. The Arapahos soon overtook the sergeant major, however, counting coup on him and finally pulling him from his mount and killing him.[39]

Meantime, Elliott and the rest of his volunteer party had overtaken and killed Blind Bear and Hawk at a point beyond present Sergeant Major Creek, then started after another group of more than twenty women and children emerging from the timber near the river to trek across the open terrain.[40] Little Rock, She Wolf, and Trailing the Enemy accompanied the noncombatants and had protected their flight from the village. As Elliott's men engaged the three tribesmen, Little Rock received a bullet in the head, killing him. Retrieving Little Rock's gun, the other two followed the women and children, firing on the soldiers as opportunity allowed. Presently, the Indians gained the river again and dropped down behind the bank, Trailing the Enemy appearing occasionally to level gunfire at Elliott's troopers. Suddenly, a large number of warriors appeared, riding toward the soldiers from downriver. Upstream, the four Arapahos who had dispatched Kennedy, now joined by five more—Left Hand, White Bear, Black Bull, Yellow Horse, and Two Wings—also converged on the scene. These nine men quickly moved up and posted themselves to prevent Elliott's retreat to the village while driving the soldiers back from the river into open country. Then the Arapaho warriors charged the troopers, who had dismounted to fire at them, encircling them and shooting at them; neither side scored any hits. As the warriors charged again, some of the army horses broke away. The troopers then advanced on foot toward the Indians, firing volleys at them; still, none of the warriors were struck.

Gradually, the number of warriors increased, with the arrival of Cheyennes, Kiowas, Arapahos, and Kiowa-Apaches from the down-river camps, many cutting directly across the sweeping north loop of the Washita to reach the action. Before long, Elliott's party was pressed back farther in the direction of where Kennedy had been killed.[41] All of the army horses had by now been killed or stampeded away. Shortly, Elliott and his soldiers sought protection in the tall grass growing along the east side of Sergeant Major Creek, where it makes a sharp bend before continuing east to enter the Washita.[42] Here, approximately one and a half miles east of Black Kettle's village, the troopers lay down in the grass in a circle, facing and firing at the warriors all around them. Some of the men raised their carbines overhead to fire blindly without exposing themselves. From near the head of the ravine, a Cheyenne named Man Riding on a Cloud (Touching the Sky) gathered some other warriors and began shooting into Elliott's position at close range, hitting some of the men. At this the mounted warriors moved closer. Roman Nose Thunder, a Cheyenne youth, swept in on horseback, racing his mount directly through the cluster of soldiers, touching one and claiming first coup, though he was wounded in the effort. An Arapaho, Tobacco, is also credited with having scored the first coup, but he was killed as he rushed through the group. Simultaneously, more warriors were approaching the troopers by moving up the ravine on their hands and knees, but before they succeeded in their mission, more mounted warriors rushed the men. All of the men with Elliott perished within minutes.

In 1905 George Bent described the soldiers' last moments as recalled by participants:

> When Elliott seen he was surrounded he turned all his horses loose and got into hollow with his men among tall grass. The Indians say . . . they could only see smoke from their guns when they shot. Soldiers were lying down in high grass. Indians got all around them and very close. The Indians soon found out that Elliott's men were firing wild so they closed in on them. Before the soldiers could get up from lying down they had them all killed. The Indians say to this day they do not know who counted "coes" [*sic*, coups] on Maj Elliott and Liet [*sic*] Hamilton as they all jumped on them same time. Roman Nose Thunder . . . first counted "coe" on soldier (private). He was very first to run in on them. Then the big crowd jumped on them.[43]

Several Indians received wounds during this latter fighting, but only one, Single Coyote, an Arapaho, was mortally injured.[44] The fight reportedly lasted about two hours, with Big Mouth, an Arapaho, leading the final attack. Following the killing of Major Elliott and his troopers, the tribesmen, including the women who had earlier hidden behind the river bank, stripped and mutilated the bodies.[45]

The victorious warriors belonged to the same bands as those seen by Lieutenant Godfrey during his withdrawal along the north side of the river, before which he had seen one or more of the camps. Warriors approached Godfrey's platoon from Little Raven's village and began shooting at his men. As the retirement proceeded ridge to ridge, both sets of belligerents heard the roar of musketry south of them across the Washita, most likely from the attack then occurring on Elliott's men. The warriors facing Godfrey eventually pulled back, joining those who were ascending the hills above Black Kettle's camp, from which they harried Custer's troopers late in the afternoon. Several hundred men gathered to participate in the fighting, many wearing war bonnets and carrying lances and coup sticks. They came from the villages of Little Raven, Medicine Arrows, and Old Whirlwind, having raced forward upon learning of the attack against Black Kettle from Cheyenne refugees of the assault straggling into their camps. The warriors opened a sporadic attack against the troops, managing to capture the overcoats and haversacks left by the men of West's and Hamilton's battalions and Cooke's sharpshooters at the time Bell's wagons penetrated their cordon in their race to join Custer. Later these same Indians made repeated feints against army skirmishers positioned around the camp. They taunted the soldiers, waving some of the overcoats and haversacks, trying to entice them to come out, but the men did not respond. Instead, the warriors watched in exasperation as the soldiers looted the tipis of dried buffalo meat, flour, tobacco, richly ornamented clothing, sacred shields, robes and hides, bows and arrows, and weapons and ammunition, among other things. They saw the soldiers pull down the lodges, heap them into many piles, and then set it all afire. The warriors, incensed at the loss happening before them, shot at the soldiers, but the troops responded forcefully and drove the Indian observers beyond carbine range. Late in the day, the troops destroyed the pony herd, delivering a final indignity to the distantly watching tribesmen. Afterward, the soldiers arranged themselves in marching order and struck out as if to attack the lower villages, causing the warriors on the hills to disperse to their camps.[46]

Moving Behind and her aunt, Corn Stalk Woman, still hidden in the grass south of the village, watched and waited as the ponies ran by, many of them wounded and moaning loudly "just like human beings" as the soldiers drove them to the killing place. "The snow on the whole bend of the river was made red with blood," recalled another woman. Later, they watched as the regiment pulled away across the Washita, headed toward the lower camps. The women then mounted and went to the spot near the river where Black Kettle and his wife had fallen. They saw the bodies of the chief and his wife submerged beneath the surface, along with that of the horse they had been riding. Some of the men dragged the Indians' bodies to the shore and placed them on a blanket. The party then moved on, encountering the corpses of other dead tribesmen. "We would stop and look at the bodies, and mention their names," recalled Moving Behind.[47]

Official army casualty figures for the Washita engagement, filed in January 1869 after determination of Elliott's fate had been made, listed two officers (Elliott and Captain Hamilton) and eighteen enlisted men (seventeen with Elliott) killed, and three officers (Barnitz, Lieutenant Thomas W. Custer, and Lieutenant March) and twelve enlisted men wounded. Two of the wounded enlisted men subsequently died of their injuries, making a final total of twenty killed and thirteen wounded. (Two of the dead enlisted men were brothers, Carson D. J. Myers and John Myers, both of Company M and killed with Elliott.)[48] Some especially light casualties were customarily not formally reported during the Indian campaigns, so the true number of wounded likely exceeded the official figure.[49] On the field much was made over the popular Hamilton's death; borne to the hospital area by a guard of honor, his body was viewed by many of the officers and men who felt his loss personally. The captain's remains were removed to Camp Supply, where on December 4, 1868, a full military funeral ensued, with Sheridan; Custer; Lieutenants Crosby, Cooke, Hale, and Thomas Custer; and Captain William M. Beebe Jr. serving as pallbearers. Hamilton was temporarily buried at Camp Supply. On January 21, 1869, his remains were sent to Fort Dodge, Kansas, arriving there on the twenty-fourth. From there they were forwarded for burial in the family plot in Poughkeepsie, New York.[50] Meantime, the supposedly fatally wounded Barnitz improved. Dr. Lippincott, on first examination, thought that the captain's intestines had been injured from the Cheyenne bullet and that Barnitz would die. On December 8 at Camp Supply, Lippincott operated and removed a mass of tissue from the wound. Barnitz eventually recovered.[51]

Losses among the approximately 250 Cheyennes at the Washita are more difficult to ascertain. Custer reported 103 warriors killed and fifty-three women and children taken prisoner. The former figure, however, was based on what appears to be the pooled recollections of his subalterns, provided after the column stopped on the afternoon of November 28, 1868, following their withdrawal. Custer later revised the figure upward, claiming that "the Indians admit a loss of 140 killed, besides a heavy loss of wounded. This, with the Indian prisoners we have in our possession, makes the entire loss of the Indians in killed, wounded, and missing not far from 300." Custer's figures were inflated, and the specific sources of his information remain unknown. Evidently, no accurate field count of Indian casualties occurred. As might be expected, the best estimates must come from the people who suffered the losses, yet even these do not agree. Custer's prisoners later reported that thirteen men, besides two Sioux and an Arapaho, had been killed at the Washita, but evidently they gave no figure for noncombatant losses. Months later, Special Agent Vincent Colyer and Colonel Grierson learned from several of the Cheyennes, including Little Robe, Minimic (Bald Eagle), Gray Eyes, and Red Moon, that thirteen men, sixteen women, and nine children died at the Washita, a seemingly plausible figure in keeping with what the prisoners said. Similarly, Magpie and Little Beaver claimed that 12 warriors died in the fighting whose names they knew, though possibly two or three more were also killed, along with many women and children.[52]

These accounts compare well with casualty figures researched by George Bent. In 1913 Bent provided the names of eleven Cheyenne men who died in the attack, adding to this twelve women (two of whom were Sioux) and six children for a total of twenty-nine people killed. Later he added two Arapaho men as fatalities and dropped one child, bringing his total to thirty killed. In an apparent final revision in 1916, he listed thirteen men killed. Assuming that his figure for noncombatant fatalities did not change, Bent's final list of killed at the Washita totals twenty-nine, a number that does not appear unreasonable.[53] Given this likely figure, the number of wounded Cheyennes fleeing Black Kettle's camp probably at least doubled this total and likely stood at somewhere around sixty. This figure is based on a presumption, common though not universal during the Indian wars, that the number of wounded exceeded the number of fatalities in combat, especially where large numbers of noncombatants were involved, as in surprise army attacks on villages. This presumption lies in knowledge of the remarkable ability of Indians to survive extremely severe wounds that might be considered fatal in other populations, as well as the likelihood that many, if not most, of the bullets fired by the soldiers struck nonvital parts of their targets if they did not miss altogether. Ben Clark estimated "the Cheyenne loss at seventy-five warriors and fully as many women and children killed. The number of wounded was never known."[54]

Beyond the dead and wounded among the Cheyennes, there were the losses represented in the people taken captive during the engagement. When Custer marched his command away from the Washita village, fifty-three women and children accompanied him, eight of whom were wounded, and others were sick. Each waking day and each night en route to Camp Supply, the women, who knew nothing of their ultimate fate, sang their dirges. One morning Lieutenant Godfrey was responsible for moving the prisoners along. One of them asked permission to leave the column temporarily, and Godfrey obliged. After a lengthy absence, during which the lieutenant feared that the young woman might have run off, she reappeared, galloping forward on horseback to present herself and her newly born child to the relieved officer. "Instead of losing a prisoner, I had gained one," remembered Godfrey. The captives remained with Custer's command until after they reached Camp Supply. Eventually, they were transferred to Fort Hays, where a stockade had been prepared for them.[55]

For his initial report to Sheridan late on the twenty-eighth, Custer had seemingly prepared more precise figures itemizing the village contents than he had respecting Indian casualties.

We captured in good condition eight hundred and seventy-five horses, ponies, and mules; two hundred and forty-one saddles, some of very fine and costly workmanship; five hundred and seventy-three buffalo robes, three hundred and ninety buffalo skins for lodges, one hundred and sixty untanned robes, two hundred and ten axes, one hundred and forty hatchets, thirty-five revolvers, forty-seven rifles, five hundred and thirty-five pounds of powder, one thousand and fifty pounds of lead, four hundred arrows and arrow-heads, seventy-five spears, ninety bullet molds, thirty-five bows and quivers, twelve shields, three hundred pounds of bullets, seven hundred and seventy-five lariats, nine hundred and forty buckskin saddle bags, four hundred and seventy blankets, ninety-three coats, seven hundred pounds of tobacco. In addition, we captured all their winter supply of dried buffalo meat; all their meal, flour, and other provisions; and, in fact, everything they possessed; even driving the warriors from the village with little or no clothing. We destroyed everything of value to the Indians, and have now in our possession, as prisoners of war, fifty-three squaws and their children.[56]

Inexplicably, Custer additionally stated: "we also secured two white children held captive by the Indians. One white woman who was in their possession was murdered by her captors the moment we attacked."[57]

For the several wounded soldiers, the jolting ride north was difficult in the extreme. "During the whole time I could not eat one morsel of anything," wrote Captain Barnitz, "and for every spoonful of water that I drank I vomited up two." After dispatching Milner and Corbin with news of the fight, Custer on the twenty-ninth continued toward Camp Supply, marching twenty-two miles and probably moving down Bogy Creek to gain Wolf Creek, where the troops and their caravan bivouacked about ten miles from Sheridan's headquarters.[58] Next day, November 30, specially arrayed for the general's review, the command entered the post in triumph, having fulfilled his orders to the letter.

One of only two photographs of Black Kettle, both of which were taken during the meeting at Camp Weld, Colorado Territory, in 1864. This picture shows the Southern Cheyenne peace chief holding a pipe and flanked by other Cheyenne and Arapaho leaders scarcely two months before the Sand Creek Massacre. *First row, left to right*: Neva, Black Kettle, Bull Bear, and White Antelope (Cheyenne); *back row, left to right*: Heap of Buffalo, Notanee (Arapaho), and Bosse (Cheyenne). Courtesy Western History Department, Denver Public Library.

B-4496

Major General Philip H. Sheridan masterminded the 1868 winter campaign against the southern plains tribes. It was under his administration at either the department and division levels that most of the subsequent Indian campaigns in the trans-Mississippi West took place. Photo taken about 1865. Courtesy Little Bighorn Battlefield National Monument, National Park Service.

Lieutenant Colonel George A. Custer poses bearded and buckskin outfitted for campaign duty in an image likely taken at Fort Cobb or Fort Sill in early 1869. Courtesy Little Bighorn Battlefield National Monument, National Park Service.

Captain Frederick W. Benteen (shown here in 1871), although a brave officer, remains a controversial figure in the history of the Seventh Cavalry; there is probably truth in the notion that his presence contributed to apparent divisiveness within the unit through the Little Bighorn engagement. Courtesy Little Bighorn Battlefield National Monument, National Park Service.

First Lieutenant Thomas W. Custer was the brother of the lieutenant colonel commanding the Seventh Cavalry. In this photo taken around 1872, he sports the two Medals of Honor awarded him for his service at Namozine Church and Sayler's Creek, Virginia, during the closing days of the Civil War. In the Washita encounter, Custer received a bullet wound in his right hand. Courtesy Little Bighorn Battlefield National Monument, National Park Service.

Captain George W. Yates commanded Company F at the Washita. Shown here in an 1867 pose for a Leavenworth, Kansas, photographer, Yates died with his troopers at the Little Bighorn in 1876. Fort Yates, Dakota Territory, was named for him two years later. Courtesy Little Bighorn Battlefield National Monument, National Park Service.

Captain Louis M. Hamilton, 1866, grandson of former Treasury secretary Alexander Hamilton, used family influence to gain appointment in the regular army. Highly regarded, nonetheless, by the officers and men of the Seventh Cavalry, Hamilton fell mortally wounded while leading Company A in the opening assault on Black Kettle's village. Courtesy Little Bighorn Battlefield National Monument, National Park Service.

First Lieutenant Edward S. Godfrey (Company K), Second Lieutenant Francis H. Gibson (Company A), and Second Lieutenant Edward Law (Company K) posed for this image at Leavenworth, Kansas, in 1867. Godfrey and Gibson each rendered important accounts of the Washita action. Courtesy Little Bighorn Battlefield National Monument, National Park Service.

New Yorker and First Lieutenant Owen Hale of Company M, Seventh Cavalry, purportedly overheard Major Joel Elliott's "brevet or a coffin" remark prior to the destruction of that officer's detachment at the Washita. Hale, shown here as a captain in 1869, was himself killed less than a decade later during the Nez Perce War. Courtesy Little Bighorn Battlefield National Monument, National Park Service.

Captain Albert Barnitz, Company G, gravely wounded at the Washita, provided invaluable information about the attack through his diary and in his letters to his wife, Jennie, pictured here. This photo was taken at Fort Leavenworth in 1868. Courtesy Little Bighorn Battlefield National Monument, National Park Service.

The army recruited Osage scouts for service in Custer's movement to the Washita. They posed for this photo, probably taken at Camp "Sandy" Forsyth near Fort Dodge, Indian Territory, in October 1868. Courtesy Little Bighorn Battlefield National Monument, National Park Service.

Moses "California Joe" Milner (seen here in 1869) had a propensity for liquor, which prompted his speedy replacement as chief of scouts on the campaign to the Washita. He was murdered by a bushwhacker near Camp Robinson, Nebraska, in October 1876. Courtesy Little Bighorn Battlefield National Monument, National Park Service.

Captain William Thompson's battalion, delayed while negotiating broken and heavily wooded terrain in the darkness, was late on the attack, thereby permitting many Indians to flee the village. Photo taken about 1872. Courtesy Little Bighorn Battlefield National Monument, National Park Service.

Battle of the Washita, as interpreted by James E. Taylor in 1878, depicts the soldiers' opening assault on Black Kettle's Cheyenne village. Interestingly, the artist's brother, Private Richard L. S. Taylor, who rode with Thompson's battalion at the Washita, is portrayed here as the central figure in the attack. Courtesy Little Bighorn Battlefield National Monument, National Park Service.

Major Joel Elliott was but twenty-nine when he died fighting at the Washita.
A brave and intelligent leader of Quaker family origins, he had commanded
the Seventh Cavalry during Custer's court-martial suspension. Photo taken
about 1867. Courtesy Little Bighorn Battlefield National Monument, National
Park Service.

Sergeant Major Walter Kennedy, twenty-seven years old when killed at the Washita, was a native of Clarksburg, Virginia (later West Virginia), and had enlisted in the regular army in 1866 at Philadelphia. He stood a bit over five feet, eight inches tall and had gray eyes and dark hair. This picture shows Kennedy as a Confederate officer during the Civil War. Courtesy National Anthropological Archives, Smithsonian Institution.

Heroic Death of Walter Kennedy is a fanciful 1874 depiction of the sergeant major's demise at the Washita by artist James E. Taylor. Courtesy National Anthropological Archives, Smithsonian Institution.

Canadian-born Assistant Surgeon (First Lieutenant) Henry Lippincott accompanied Custer's regiment to the Washita. He later examined the dead from Elliott's engagement and provided a detailed inventory of their condition. Courtesy Little Bighorn Battlefield National Monument, National Park Service.

Cheyenne women and children captured at the Washita as photographed in December 1868 at Fort Dodge, Kansas. Courtesy Little Bighorn Battlefield National Monument, National Park Service.

Cheyenne prisoners Fat Bear, Big Head, and Dull Knife (Lean Face) were captured by Custer near the Sweetwater River in Texas in March 1869 and held pending the release of two white women. This image was taken at Camp Supply in 1869. Courtesy Little Bighorn Battlefield National Monument, National Park Service.

The Seventh Cavalry monument of rock and horse skulls (as seen in 1891) was erected near the Washita River, likely at the village site, by First Lieutenant Hugh L. Scott. The engraved stone at top currently reposes in the museum of Washita Battlefield National Historic Site, Oklahoma. Courtesy Little Bighorn Battlefield National Monument, National Park Service.

This 1891 view shows the Washita encounter site. The "x" in the foreground designates the area where Elliott's force was believed to have been killed, while the arrow above the trees represents the location of Black Kettle's village to the west. Courtesy Little Bighorn Battlefield National Monument, National Park Service.

"Black Kettle Tree," just left of center, designated the supposed location near the river (as of 1891) of Chief Black Kettle's lodge at the time of the army assault. Courtesy Little Bighorn Battlefield National Monument, National Park Service.

8

END RESULTS

Custer had received Sheridan's congratulatory message by the time his command reached Camp Supply. Borne south by California Joe Milner, Jack Corbin, and one other scout, it had reached the column along with a package of dispatches and other mail as the troops approached Wolf Creek. The colonel drew his soldiers up in line and read the contents of General Field Orders No. 6, by which the department commander complimented the men's "energy and rapidity" in seeking out the Indians in severe weather conditions and thanked Custer "for the efficient and gallant services rendered, which have characterized the opening of the campaign against hostile Indians south of the Arkansas." From Wolf Creek, Custer sent word to Sheridan of his proximity and received, in return, notification of the general's desire to review the troops on their approach to Camp Supply. The triumphal march was a spectacle to behold. According to Lieutenant Godfrey, the Osage scouts, arrayed in their splendor, singing war songs, and occasionally firing their weapons, preceded the white scouts, who in turn preceded the blanketed prisoners. The band, playing "Garry Owen," followed, and then came Lieutenant Cooke's sharpshooting "Corps d'Elite" and the remainder of the Seventh Cavalry, arranged in column of platoons. The wagon train brought up the rear. The procession briefly spooked the post horses, but they were soon controlled. As the victorious column passed Sheridan, the troopers raised their sabers in a precision salute; the general doffed his hat in return.[1]

Following the celebration, Sheridan and his staff listened as the Seventh's officers described the battle. Then they reviewed the evidence from the village indicating that the Indians had taken part in the Kansas raids, and the general evinced concern over the fate of Major Elliott and his men. Indeed, the presumed loss of Elliott and his party was viewed as the sole immediate defect in the Washita operation. The matter soon became one of nagging controversy and would not disappear; aspects of it would haunt the regiment, as well as perceptions of Custer's leadership, for years to come. On December 4 Captain Hamilton's remains, "attired in the full uniform of a captain," were placed in a coffin made of pine boards and buried in a solemn ceremony on the banks of Beaver River. Those of two enlisted men killed and of one who died from wounds were also interred.[2]

With the return of the troops, Sheridan lost no time in preparing for more action, as was suggested in his congratulatory order. His efforts focused on continuing to pressure the Cheyennes, Arapahos, and other tribes in the wake of the Washita attack. He had already wired General Sherman the news of Custer's strike against Black Kettle, whose band "committed the first depredation on the Saline and Solomon rivers in Kansas." From the prisoners he learned of the composition of the other camps along the Washita and that the Indians would likely go into Fort Cobb seeking peace. He learned that three white women were among the people who had camped below Black Kettle's village. Sheridan hoped that the tardy Kansas troops under Colonel Crawford would soon be in condition to move out. "If we can get one or two more good blows there will be no more Indian troubles in my Department." The general settled on December 7 as the date to resume operations, which would allow men and horses to rest and the refurbishment of supply trains for Camp Supply and the expedition with provisions from Fort Dodge. Ammunition and thirty days' rations would be required for the Seventh Cavalry and the Nineteenth Kansas for a march to the Wichita Mountains and back.[3]

While these preparations ensued, Sherman wired his congratulations to Fort Hays to be delivered to Sheridan. He regarded Custer's success "as decisive and conclusive. I have no doubt [that] by Christmas he will have all these Indians begging for their lives, when he can turn them over to the management of General Hazen, after having executed every Indian who began this war." Soon Secretary of War John M. Schofield added his appreciation too. Sherman believed that the defeated Cheyennes, along with the Arapahos, Kiowas, and Comanches, would now congregate seeking relief with Hazen at Fort Cobb, and he wrote General Augur, "I think the same process may have to be applied to the Powder River Sioux." Although Schofield asked that the names of deserving officers and men be forwarded for attention, Custer maintained he could not comply "for the gratifying reason that every officer and man belonging to the expedition had performed his full part" in the campaign. While there was no immediate individual recognition for officers or men following the Washita engagement, Custer deemed the performances there of Lieutenants Robbins and Smith of sufficient merit to drop misconduct charges pending against them.[4]

But the overall effusiveness of the military hierarchy's response to the Washita news was soon neutralized somewhat by criticism emanating from other quarters of the country as specifics of Custer's attack filtered through the media in the weeks that followed. In his memoirs Custer claimed to have predicted the reaction no matter the outcome: "If we failed to engage and whip the Indians—labor as we might to accomplish this—the people in the West, particularly along and near the frontier, those who had been victims of the assaults made by Indians, would denounce us in unmeasured terms as being inefficient or lukewarm in the performance of our duty; whereas if we should find and punish the Indians as they deserved, a wail would rise up from the horrified humanitarians throughout the country, and we would be accused of attacking and killing friendly and defenseless Indians." The principal reproach came from Commissioner of Indian Affairs Nathaniel G. Taylor, his Indian agents, and those politicians who sided with them, a consortium facetiously tagged the "Indian Ring." Taylor and his ally, Colonel Samuel Tappan, who had served with him in the 1867 commission negotiating the Medicine Lodge Treaty, believed that Black Kettle's camp had been friendly, and that Custer's attack amounted to a repetition of the Sand Creek carnage. Members of the Senate Committee on Indian Affairs were similarly outraged. Through Taylor, Tappan complained that the attack would promote general warfare throughout the West, that the volunteers sent to support the regulars should be withdrawn, and that the war policy should be curtailed. Agent Edward Wynkoop, in the East on leave of absence at the time of the Washita engagement, abruptly resigned his position, protesting too that Custer's strike was but a repeat of Chivington's unwarranted butchery of Black Kettle's people. Also, members of the Cherokee, Choctaw, and Creek tribes—the so-called Civilized Tribes, regional neighbors of the Cheyennes—protested the Washita affair as "a brutal massacre of friendly Indians" and appealed through Commissioner Taylor for a "fair and thorough investigation."[5]

Over the next few weeks, Sherman mustered all of his considerable resources to meet the verbal assault. "We need not be disturbed," he wrote, "by the clamorous of the peace men who have succeeded in making little capital out of the punishment inflicted on the Cheyennes which they so richly merited and deserved." The general used the same arguments he had made to justify opening the campaign against the southern tribesmen, effectually stretching reality to show that Black Kettle's people had been the prime instigators of the violence the preceding summer and that Custer's punishment of them was fully warranted. Although he averred that "Black Kettle himself did not wish to be at war," the chief had "lost all control over his young warriors," a position that, while to some degree true, failed to identify the prominent role of the Dog Soldiers and the other bands' military society members in the depredations along the Saline and Solomon rivers. There were also complaints that U.S. troops had violated the reservation lands established for the Cheyennes and Arapahos. "This is a falsehood," responded Sheridan. "The reservation extends but 30 miles up the Washita from Fort Cobb. The battle took place 120 miles up the river. It is also alleged the band were friendly. No one could make such an assertion who had any regard for truth. The young men of this band [*sic*, Black Kettle's village] commenced the war." The Indian Ring, chimed the *Army and Navy Journal*, fortunately was small and included in its membership only "a few place-holders, a few philanthropists, and a few plunderers. . . . Its nucleus is the Indian Bureau, its strength the horde of Indian agents, contractors, and peddlers."[6] And further, opined the *Journal* editor: "We are told that Black Kettle's band was friendly, and, accordingly, that Custer is a second Chivington. That is not the fact. Black Kettle himself has not of late been engaged personally in the hostilities. . . . But his camp has been a rendezvous for young warriors, who start from it as a 'base,' and return to it with booty. We have the word of such officers as Sherman, Sheridan, Hazen, [and] Custer for these facts. If it be true, in the popular sense, that 'the receiver is as bad as the thief,' Black Kettle suffered a just fate." Even

Colonel Hazen at Fort Cobb toed the company line and weighed in on the chief's war complicity. "In his talk with me, . . . Black Kettle stated that many of his men were then on the war path, and that their people did not want peace with the [white] people above the Arkansas."[7]

Despite the army's policy of blaming all of the Cheyennes for the offenses of some, there was an outpouring of sympathy for Black Kettle personally, owing to his past friendship and the tribulations that he as a peace chief had weathered, first because of Sand Creek and now because of Washita. Many people, civilian and military, had for years recognized such commitment in him and strongly mourned his passing. Thomas Murphy of the Central Indian Superintendency called him "one of the best and truest friends the whites have ever had among the Indians of the plains." Of the chief, Murphy wrote Taylor: "When he ascertained that some of the young men of his tribe [village] had committed the atrocities upon the Solomon and Saline in August last, . . . so great was his grief he tore his hair and his clothes, and naturally supposing that the whites would wreak their vengeance upon all Indians that might chance to fall in their way, . . . he went south to avoid the impending trouble." Murphy believed that the conflict with the Indians could have been avoided had prescribed treaty appropriations been forthcoming. Even retired brigadier general William S. Harney called the fallen chief "as good a friend of the United States as I am." And Albert G. Boone, Indian agent for the Upper Arkansas Agency, lamented that Black Kettle "was a good man; he was my friend; he was murdered." The debate over the attack continued for months, with the western white population endorsing the military activity but calling on the army to do more. Reflecting a common imperative for conquest, the position was expressed in the statement of one frontiersman: "If this war should be abated one jot, in recognizing less rights than we claimed in the beginning it will have to be fought over again, or we must relinquish to the Indian the Pacific Railroads, all the gold mines of the mountains, the towns and settlements, the farms of the Plains, with all their improvements, and the white man forever quit the country."[8]

Following the destruction of Black Kettle's village and the withdrawal of the soldiers, the people who had escaped returned to the site with the downriver villagers to bury relatives and friends and to retrieve whatever could be salvaged. The Cheyenne named Magpie stated that the day after the attack, he and several women pulled Black Kettle's body from the Washita and carried it to a sandy knoll, where the women debated over the place to inter the remains. Another Cheyenne later claimed that the chief's body was not recovered until several days had passed, during which time wolves had partly devoured it; the remains were placed in the fork of a tree. Following the visit to the destroyed village, the Cheyennes started southwest into the Texas Panhandle. The Arapahos accompanied them, as did the Kiowas who had been at the Washita and some of the Comanches. On the Sweetwater, Chief Medicine Arrows convened a council with the Arapaho, Kiowa, and Comanche leaders over what to do next. Relatives of the Washita captives had urged the chiefs not to strike back in revenge raids for fear that their people would be harmed by the soldiers. The chiefs agreed, yet they would fight the soldiers and their Indian allies from the north. They wished peace with the troops at Fort Cobb and sought the aid of the tribes at that agency to help subsist the Sweetwater bands with food and supplies. Most of the Kiowas and Comanches subsequently moved back to the Washita camps above Fort Cobb.[9]

Much official interest focused on the disposition of the "auxiliary tribes"—the Kiowas, Comanches, and Kiowa-Apaches—in the wake of the Washita engagement. The Arapahos were already guilty by association through their longstanding historical relationship with the Cheyennes; it was more or less understood that they would receive the same treatment as their close friends under the War Department's policy of holding all the people accountable for the sins of the few. But the status of the other tribes was not as clear. Those tribes had professed their friendship for the government during frequent visits for rations at Fort Cobb. But now word circulated that those people not only had a presence in the fighting but also had aided and abetted Black Kettle's Cheyennes throughout their ordeal. Reportedly, when the stricken villagers moved south after Custer's attack, some of the Kiowas of Satanta and Satank traveled with them, and bands of Comanches had camped near the Cheyennes along the north fork of the Red River below the Antelope Hills. These developments suggested that some elements of the tribes were coalescing into a united front to face down any military forces that might come after them. So-called friendly elements of the Kiowas, Comanches, and Kiowa-Apaches maintained their camps at the Washita and gravitated down the river in the direction of Fort Cobb. By December 2, five days after the Washita engagement, there were reported in camp at the mouth of Sweetwater Creek 150 lodges of Cheyennes, 180 of Arapahos, 80 of Kiowas, and 75 of Comanches—

approximately 485 lodges in all. These now constituted the coalition that concerned the military authorities.[10]

News of the Washita attack dominated events around Fort Cobb in the days following the action, and the Indians already camped near that place, anticipating an army strike upon them too, moved closer to the agency. "This fight has decidedly stirred up the Indians who were encamped along the Washita between this point and the scene of battle," reported Captain Alvord at Cobb. One of the earliest Indian accounts of the action alluded to what was probably the killing of Major Elliott and his men. Alvord presented the particulars as derived from his scouts sent up the Washita:

> When the Cheyenne camp was surprised at dawn, a few of the fleetest runners escaped and endeavored to gain the other camps. These were followed by a squad of eighteen soldiers mounted upon gray horses, and as an Indian lagged in the race, he was overtaken and killed. Finally, a few of the leading young Indians reached another camp, and the 18 soldiers following were then surrounded and all killed—their horses being captured. There were one or two officers in this party. The warriors of the Cheyennes & Arrapahoes then gathering, returned to the village of Black Kettle, which they found destroyed, all the men killed, and the troops engaged in shooting a large number of ponies which they had collected in the neighborhood. Then and there, the main battle began, and lasted all day Friday, both parties holding their ground at night. . . . Saturday morning the troops commenced falling back, Indians following and attacking the rear and flanks, till at 10 o'clock the former reached their wagons on the Canadian, when the fighting ceased.[11]

Alvord reported that but one band of Kiowas—guests of the Arapahos—had witnessed part of the engagement and had participated in killing a shaved-head Osage scout (though according to the records, no Osages were killed). But a few Comanches were "neutral spectators"; one was killed by a long shot as he looked on, and his loss caused bitterness among his people.[12]

Considerations about the attitude of the Kiowas and Comanches regarding the Cheyennes and Arapahos were paramount as Sheridan prepared his force for a second venture south. The Cheyennes mourned not only the loss of so many of their people killed in Custer's attack but also of the prisoners who were led away from the Washita. The fifty-three women and children, initially terrified at their situation, fully expected to be executed by the soldiers. Despite the fact that some bore serious injuries, all eschewed the wagons and ambulances and rode their ponies into Camp Supply. Fearing the worst was about to happen to them, several of the women broached the matter to an interpreter, who quickly set their minds at ease. The prisoners received treatment for their wounds at the post hospital before most of them were escorted in late December to a log stockade at Fort Hays. Three of the captives— Mahwissa, sister of Black Kettle; Monahseetah, or Meotzi, daughter of Little Rock; and an unidentified Sioux woman—returned south with Sheridan and Custer as potential intermediaries with the Cheyennes on the second leg of the campaign.[13] Subsequent histories of the 1868 campaign, along with biographies of Custer, have weighed the notion that the colonel and some other officers of the Seventh Cavalry took sexual liberties with the women prisoners and that Custer maintained a relatively long-term liaison with Monahseetah. There appears to be credible evidence, both in Cheyenne oral history and in the written reminiscences of witnesses—both rendered altogether exclusive of knowledge of the other—that would thereby tend to validate the assertions. Ben Clark told Walter M. Camp: "many of the squaws captured at Washita were used by the officers. . . . Romero was put in charge of them and on the march Romero would send squaws around to the officers' tents every night. [Clark] says Custer picked out a fine looking one and had her in his tent every night." This statement is more or less confirmed by Frederick Benteen, who in 1896 asserted that Custer selected Monahseetah/Meotzi from among the women prisoners and cohabited with her "during the winter and spring of 1868 and '69" until his wife arrived in the summer of 1869. Although Benteen's assertions regarding Custer are not always to be trusted, his statements nonetheless conform entirely to those of the reliable Ben Clark and thus cannot be ignored.[14]

The renewed offensive against the tribes got underway on Thursday, December 7, a cold but sunny day. "We started on another raid, south in the same direction as before," wrote Private Harvey. "I do not know where we will fetch up at." The immediate objective was, in fact, Fort Cobb. Sheridan and his staff would accompany and direct much of this campaign, though Custer was in nominal command. As a follow up to the Washita, the general intended to attack any tribesmen he met en route and then at Fort Cobb make demands of any "Ring leaders" present there.[15] Equipped with sufficient forage and rations (thirty days' worth) brought down from Fort Dodge, and his animals being in satisfactory condition to set out anew, Custer departed at 10:00 A.M., despite a snowstorm the previous night that laid down eight inches of drifting white cover. The command, totaling nearly seventeen hundred men, consisted of eleven companies of the Seventh Cavalry, one of the Tenth, and ten of the Nineteenth Kansas Volunteer Cavalry under Colonel Crawford, with thirty or so white, Osage, and Kaw Indian scouts.[16] Three companies of the Third Infantry, one of the Fifth, and one of the Thirty-eighth stayed behind to garrison and continue building Camp Supply, under the command of a Captain Page of the Third. Three hundred six-mule wagons loaded with provisions went along, guarded front and rear by the cavalry and infantry, respectively. The command traveled about a dozen miles, crossed Wolf Creek, and bivouacked on the plain along the south bank. Already, many of the wagon teams played out, and more were hurriedly forwarded from Camp Supply to take their place.

At 6:00 A.M. on the eighth, the command was again in motion south, its wagons arrayed in four columns, guarded on either flank by the horse and foot troops and in van and rear by mounted squadrons. Far in front rode flankers, whose purpose was to reconnoiter for Indians. During the march, the convoy passed through lands dominated on one side by assorted gravelly hummocks and on the other by thickets of dwarfed oak trees. After passing thirty miles, the troops camped along Hackberry Creek amid increasing evidence of the presence of Indians in the area. On the third day out, a terrific "norther" enveloped the soldiers and substantially impeded the wagons' advance. That night, with temperatures hovering near eighteen degrees below zero, they settled in along the Canadian River at a place with bad water and little timber. "The camp on the Canadian," wrote Randolph Keim, "will long be remembered by all who participated in the campaign of 1868–69. The wintry blast swept mercilessly through the valley, demolishing tents and extinguishing the few fires built against the intense cold. The night was intolerably dark. The troopers unable to keep warm, could be heard through the long hours tramping up and down, within the limits of the camp, afraid to lie down for fear of freezing to death. The animals without covering or protection from the wind suffered intensely. All night shivering at the picket-rope the poor brutes uttered melancholy moans, but it was beyond the power of man to alleviate their sufferings. At headquarters it was no better. Fires were out, tents were either down or flapping in the wind."[17] The following day went much the same. The troops forded the river in below-zero temperatures, and the wind continued its barrage unabated. The crossing was difficult and took five hours, with many animals falling or becoming otherwise hurt in the icy bottom. Back up on the plain, the column proceeded slowly downstream to the east until late in the day, as the Antelope Hills loomed ahead. Finally, at 4:00 P.M., December 10, the men made camp along the north side of the Washita River, a scant five or so miles below the ashes of Black Kettle's destroyed village. Sheridan, desirous of seeing the field of the encounter, directed that the column lay over the next day while a party proceeded to the village site to look for the remains of Elliott and his men.

The next morning the group, consisting of Sheridan and Custer, several staff and other officers, and newspaper correspondent Keim, started away, accompanied by an escort composed of detachments of each of the Seventh's companies under Captain Yates and Lieutenants Custer and John F. Weston.[18] Their advance was preceded by several of the Indian scouts. The party traced the north side of the Washita. After one and a half hours, they approached the river from the northeast, along the route Elliott and his battalion had taken in preparation for the initial charge. Then they crossed the stream. Custer described the scene with some apparent exaggeration:

> The bodies of nearly all the warriors killed in the fight had been concealed or removed, while those of the squaws and children who had been slain in the excitement and confusion of the first charge, as well as in self-defence, were wrapped in blankets and bound with lariats, preparatory to removal and burial. Many of the Indian dogs were still found in the vicinity lately occupied by the lodges of their owners; they probably subsisting on the bodies of the ponies that had been killed and then covered several acres of ground near by. As 10 days had elapsed since the battle, and scores of Indian bodies still remained unburied or unconcealed, some idea may be had of the precipitate haste with which the Indians had abandoned that section of the country.[19]

Entering the desolate ruins of the village, the group rousted thousands of noisy ravens and crows, which took flight or scattered at the approach. Wolves watched from a distance, pondering the movements of the soldiers. "We found the evidences of the late engagement much as we had left them," recalled Custer. On examining the site, the party found the blanket-wrapped remains of a warrior; then others appeared, finally numbering thirty bodies, many of which had been similarly prepared. "Some were laid in the branches of trees," wrote Keim, "while others were deposited under protections made of bushes." Custer observed that the large number of corpses proved "that the enemy's loss in killed warriors far exceeded the number (103) first reported by me." At the village site they saw the charred remnants of the Cheyennes' homes. Nearby, stated an officer of the Nineteenth Kansas, "were the carcasses of between four and five hundred poneys [sic] captured from the Indian and killed by Custer's order."[20] Sheridan and an escort mounted a ridge from which they obtained an overview of the field. From there, Custer explained how the engagement had unfolded. Then he and Sheridan, in company with Lieutenant Owen Hale and a small body of soldiers, rode downstream along the south side of the river, approximating Elliott's route away from the village. They were shortly followed by the remaining members of the party.

Proceeding down the river, the men ascended another rise to view the country, then started downstream again. Some one hundred yards away, they encountered the body of a white man, "perfectly naked, and covered with arrow and bullet holes." It was one of Elliott's men, likely Sergeant Major Walter Kennedy. The party marked the location of the body, then continued east, passing over a small ravine (possibly the trace of modern Sergeant Major Creek). Soon more objects appeared in the grass about two hundred yards beyond the ravine, encouraging the riders to hurry forward. There, within a space of fifteen yards, lay the naked bodies of sixteen men, all, wrote Keim, "frozen as solidly as stone." The bodies of several cavalry mounts lay nearby. Many cartridge shells littered the ground around the corpses, evidence of the hard fighting that had occurred. All of the soldiers had been mutilated in accordance with tribal customs. They lay face down.[21]

Custer studied the scene and later drew conclusions about what had happened to Major Elliott and his men:

At a short distance, here and there, from the spot where the bodies lay, could be seen the carcasses of some of the horses of the party, which had been, probably, killed early in the fight. Seeing the hopelessness of breaking through the lines which surrounded them, and which undoubtedly numbered more than one hundred (100) to one (1), Elliott dismounted his men, tied their horses together, and prepared to sell their lives as dearly as possible. It may not be improper to add that in describing, as far as possible, the details of Elliott's fight, I rely not only upon a critical and personal examination of the ground and attendant circumstances, but am sustained by the statements of Indian chiefs and warriors who witnessed and participated in the fight.[22]

Near the corpses of Elliott and his men, the group found several of Indians, presumed killed by the soldiers. Having determined the fate of Custer's missing component, Sheridan and his party started back to camp, and soon after they passed through some of the hastily abandoned villages of the downstream Arapahos, Cheyennes, and other tribes. These were littered with kettles, pots, rifles, untanned robes, lodge poles, and hundreds of other items, and Sheridan issued orders to destroy it all. Soon fires consumed the abandoned dunnage, and smoke could be seen rising along several miles of the Washita. As a detachment of soldiers scoured the ground near an abandoned Indian encampment downstream, the men came upon the remains of a white woman and child. The bodies were taken to the army camp and examined. That of the woman bore two bullet holes in the back of the head, which had also been scalped and crushed, seemingly by a hatchet. That of the child, a boy, bore only a bruise on the face, the possible result of having been flung against a tree. They were subsequently identified as Clara Blinn and her two-year-old child, Willie, who had been taken from the wagon train along the Arkansas River near Fort Lyon the preceding October, reportedly by Kiowas under Satanta. Through the intervention of a trader named William "Dutch Bill" Griffenstein and an intermediary, Blinn had managed to get word of her and her son's plight to Fort Cobb in a poignant, desperate letter written November 7 in which she stated that they were with the Cheyennes and expressed her fear of being traded by the Indians into slavery in Mexico. "For our sakes, do all you can [for us] and god will bless you," she concluded.

Mrs. Blinn's body, reported Keim, "was dressed in the ordinary garments of a white woman; on the feet were a pair of leather gaiters, comparatively new. Upon the breast was found a piece of corn-cake, and the position of the hands indicated that woman was eating when she, unexpectedly, received the fatal blow."[23]

The remains of Blinn, her son, and Major Elliott were transported to the main camp to be conveyed ultimately to Fort Arbuckle for burial.[24] Wagons were promptly dispatched under Lieutenant Hale to retrieve the other dead and return them to camp; they arrived back at 9:00 P.M. A trench had meantime been dug "on the crest of a beautiful knoll, overlooking the valley of the Washita," and there, by torchlight, Elliott's men were interred. "Several men from each of the companies, to which the deceased soldiers belonged, were present to identify the remains." Dr. Lippincott examined the bodies and detailed his findings as follows:

Major Joel H. Elliott—two bullet holes in head; one in left cheek; right hand cut off; left foot almost cut off; * * * deep gash in right groin; deep gashes in calves of both legs; little finger of left hand cut off, and throat cut.

Sergeant-major Walter Kennedy—bullet hole in right temple; head partly cut off; seventeen bullet holes in back, and two in legs.

Corporal Harry Mercer, troop E—bullet hole in right axilla; one in region of heart; three in back; eight arrow wounds in back; right ear cut off; head scalped and skull fractured; deep gashes in both legs, and throat cut.

Corporal Thomas Christie, troop E—bullet hole in head; right foot cut off; bullet hole in abdomen, and throat cut.

Corporal William Carrick, troop H—bullet hole in right parietal bone; both feet cut off; throat cut; left arm broken.

Private Eugene Clover, troop H—head cut off; arrow wound in right side; both legs terribly mutilated.

Private William Milligan [Mulligan?], troop H—bullet hole in left side of head; deep gashes in right leg; * * left arm deeply gashed; head scalped, and throat cut.

Corporal James F. Williams, troop I—bullet hole in back; head and both arms cut off; many and deep gashes in back.

* * * * * * * *

Private Thomas Dooney, troop I—arrow hole in region of stomach; thorax cut open; head cut off, and right shoulder cut by a tomahawk.

Farrier Thomas Fitzpatrick, troop M—scalped; two arrow and several bullet holes in back; throat cut.

Private Ferdinand Lineback, troop M—bullet hole in left parietal bone; head scalped and arm broken; * * throat cut.

Private John Meyers [Myers], troop M—several bullet holes in head; scalped; skull extensively fractured; several arrow and bullet holes in back; deep gashes in face; throat cut.

Private Carsten [Carson] D. J. Meyers [Myers], troop M— several bullet holes in head; scalped; 19 bullet holes in body; * * throat cut.

Private Cal. Sharpe, troop M—two bullet holes in right side; throat cut; one bullet hole in left side of head; one arrow hole in left side; * * left arm broken.

Unknown—head cut off; body partially destroyed by wolves.

Unknown—head and right hand cut off; three bullet and nine arrow holes in back.

    * * * * * * * * * *

Unknown—scalped; skull fractured; 6 bullet and 13 arrow holes in back; three bullet holes in chest.[25]

By midnight, the dead, wrapped in blankets, had been placed in the trench and covered over. There was no service.[26]

On December 12, five days after leaving Camp Supply, Sheridan's column proceeded down the Washita, passing over the ground of the hastily abandoned camps on the Indian trail toward Fort Cobb. Scouts with the command decreed that the Cheyennes and Arapahos had gone off toward the southwest. Progress was slow, the debilitated animals failing rapidly, with "horses and mules killed every day as they are too poor and weak to travel." Over the next several days, the troops fought blizzards, deep snows, and subzero temperatures as they made their way southeast, and pioneer units worked constantly to clear the way for the wagons. "Creek banks had to be dug down to make crossings for the wagon trains," remembered one veteran. On Friday, December 15, warriors appeared in the distance. "We saw twenty Indians today but could not catch them," observed Harvey. "They ran very fast and got away." More appeared the following day, and on the seventeenth word arrived from Colonel Hazen announcing to Sheridan and Custer that all the Indians in the vicinity of his agency were friendly. Soon after, a party of Kiowas, including the leaders Satanta and Lone Wolf, asserting their peaceful disposition, approached the column and conferred with Custer and other officers. Enticed by the promise of rations at Fort Cobb, these people had removed themselves from the proximity of the Cheyennes and Arapahos and had ventured toward the agency. Sheridan believed that these Indians had been involved at the Washita but, because of Hazen's promise of protection to them, felt constrained not to attack them. Yet Custer believed that the Kiowas and Comanches had admittedly participated in the Washita engagement by attacking his troops after the village had been captured.[27] Moreover, the bodies of Blinn and her child had reportedly been found in the abandoned camp attributed to Satanta's Kiowas.[28] Now the Kiowas "were only deterred from hostile acts by discovering our strength to be far greater than they had imagined." Thus, wary of the Indians' overtures, Custer permitted the leaders and their people to accompany the troops to Fort Cobb. As more and more of the panicked Indians gradually drew away from the command, however, ostensibly to help their families come in, the officers suspected that they were trying to flee. To forestall this, the soldiers arrested Lone Wolf and Satanta. The next day, when the Indians had still not appeared, Sheridan threatened to hang the chiefs, an alarm that brought most, if not all, of the people to assemble near Fort Cobb. The chiefs remained imprisoned for two months pending the surrender of the remaining Kiowas.[29]

Meanwhile, as Custer dealt first with the Cheyennes at the Washita and then went with Sheridan in pursuit of them and the other tribes in the following weeks, the remaining wings of Sheridan's grand strategy had also been activated. These columns were to contain the tribesmen while pressing them toward the Sheridan-Custer force. The troops sent by Colonel George W. Getty were the first afield, six companies of the Third Cavalry and four of the Thirty-seventh Infantry, augmented by four mountain howitzers, all under the command of Major Andrew W. Evans, left Fort Bascom, New Mexico Territory, on November 18. Two weeks later, on December 2, Major Eugene A. Carr departed Fort Lyon, Colorado Territory, in command of seven companies of the Fifth Cavalry, four of the Tenth, and one of the Seventh in his movement. The columns together totaled approximately 650 soldiers.

Despite their intent, the movements of Evans's and Carr's commands were of little overall consequence. On a snowy and blustery Christmas Day, 1868, more than a month after leaving Fort Bascom, Evans's cavalrymen discovered a village of Comanches at Soldier Spring, along the North Fork of Red River near the west end of the Wichita Mountains in present southwestern Oklahoma, unleashed the howitzers, and quickly captured it. The Comanches, with Kiowa assistance, feebly countered the strike, but the soldiers succeeded in destroying the Indians' property and meat supply. The people fled, but Evans, his command plagued with fatigued animals, did not pursue. His casualties numbered but three men wounded, one mortally, while the tribes were estimated to have suffered as many as thirty casualties. Most of the Indians eventually came in to Fort Cobb or journeyed to Fort Bascom to surrender. Evans reprovisioned his troops near Fort Cobb and occupied a depot at the Canadian River 185 miles from Bascom until late January 1869 before returning to New Mexico. Carr's undertaking, meantime, was fraught with bad luck and worse weather from the beginning. A command under Captain William H. Penrose had departed Fort Lyon in November 1868 to establish a base camp along the North Canadian. Penrose contended with terrible snowstorms, his horses and mules froze, and he was forced to destroy scores more animals in the course of his mission, which was additionally jeopardized by failing rations and forage. Major Carr ventured south into Indian Territory to rendezvous with Penrose but encountered the same severe conditions before the two joined forces at a base camp along Palo Duro Creek on December 21. Then the soldiers headed south, contacted Evans's depot—even crossing his line of march—and continued probing the Canadian drainage before conditions dictated their return to Palo Duro without success. Believing that the other components of Sheridan's offensive had concluded their involvement, Carr in mid-February 1869 directed his command back to Fort Lyon. Three men perished, two from exposure, during the Carr-Penrose operation.[30]

Although Sheridan described Evans's assault on the Comanche village as "the final blow to the backbone of the Indian rebellion," the statement rang with hyperbole. All in all, the campaigning of Evans and Carr, while keeping the tribes to the south anxious and moving, had but a residual effect on events well underway with the Sheridan-Custer column. By the end of December 1868, thousands of Indians of various tribes, both traditionally sedentary peoples as well as members of the groups targeted by the army, all fearing attack in the wake of the Washita encounter, had descended on the Fort Cobb agency, then garrisoned by only three companies of the Tenth Cavalry and one of the Sixth Infantry. "There is no fort here," remarked one man, "only a large warehouse and quarters for probably one or two companies." So many people and their animals camping in the constricted area depleted the winter grass. Sheridan's own force added to the congestion, its wasted horses and fatigued soldiers enervated by the conditions around them. Several hundred of the played-out beasts were shot. Supplies for the command had to be hauled in overland from Fort Arbuckle to the southeast. Furthermore, heavy rains now deluged the region, turning the ground around Fort Cobb into a quagmire. The troops were miserable. Wrote Harvey: "I am afraid our camp will overflow before it stops raining. We are all wet and our blankets are damp." In early January 1869 Sheridan settled on a new site for the agency thirty miles south, near the eastern foot of the Wichita range where Medicine Bluff Creek entered Cache Creek, a location selected previously by Colonel Benjamin H. Grierson. Grierson's cavalrymen began building a six-company cavalry post, dubbed Camp Wichita. Sheridan later named it Fort Sill to honor Brigadier General Joshua W. Sill, a West Point classmate killed at Stone's River, Tennessee, during the Civil War.[31]

With the relocation of the Kiowas, most of the Comanches, and the other tribes at the new agency, Sheridan turned his attention to the Cheyennes and Arapahos, still smarting over the Washita encounter and secluded beyond the Wichita Mountains to the west.[32] While still at Fort Cobb, Custer employed Black Kettle's sister, Mahwissa, and a Kiowa-Apache named Iron Shirt as emissaries to determine the whereabouts and condition of the Cheyennes. Although Mahwissa subsequently stayed with her people, through her efforts several of the chiefs, including Little Robe of the Cheyennes and Yellow Bear of the Arapahos, agreed to a council. They disclosed to Sheridan the impoverished condition of the people, many of whom now favored surrendering. Speaking bluntly, the general explained that if they did not come in and stay peacefully, his soldiers would "fight the thing out." The chiefs assented, but Sheridan warned them that none of the prisoners taken at the Washita would be returned until *all* of the Cheyennes and Arapahos came in. He also broached the subject of the two remaining white women held by the Indians, pointedly telling Little Robe that the captives must be delivered.

Guided by Little Robe and Yellow Bear, in late January Custer moved out of Fort Sill with a body of forty cavalrymen, mostly Lieutenant Cooke's sharpshooters. They encircled the nearby Wichitas and convinced sixty lodges of Little Raven's Arapahos to move from Mulberry Creek, in the Texas Panhandle, into Fort Sill, where stood the relocated camps of Kiowas, Comanches, and Kiowa-Apaches. Custer described Little Raven's people as being in pitiful condition, with both people and animals hungry and naked. The major objective, however, remained the transient Cheyennes, who had moved into the Texas Panhandle and were reportedly migrating toward the Llano Estacado, or Staked Plains. By early February, the Cheyenne camps targeted by the army were estimated to number approximately two hundred tipis with between one thousand and fourteen hundred people traveling together.[33]

In early March Custer set out with eleven companies of the Seventh Cavalry and ten of the Nineteenth Kansas, guided by white and Osage scouts, his mission to find the Cheyennes and "administer to them such treatment as past conduct and existing circumstances demanded."[34] Many of the volunteer troops, dismounted because of their jaded animals and unaccustomed to being infantry, nonetheless "made a pretty fair stagger at it," recollected one Kansan. This movement was driven immediately by knowledge that the winter season was nearly ended and by concern that with the greening of springtime and consequent strengthening of the Indians' ponies, the army's advantage over the tribes would be lost. Sheridan, subsequently promoted to divisional commander upon Sherman's promotion to general following Ulysses S. Grant's inauguration as president on March 4, shortly left the expedition and returned to Camp Supply and stations east. Colonel Crawford also resigned his commission in February, turning command of the Kansas troops over to his lieutenant colonel, Horace L. Moore. Thus provided, Custer moved southwest from Fort Sill, tracing the southern edge of the Wichita Mountains to reach the North Fork of Red River. His command suffered severely in transit, and on March 6 Custer sent four hundred enfeebled regulars and volunteers, along with part of their wagon train, east to a supply depot at the Washita River a mile below the field of the November 27 fight. Four days later these troops reached the depot to find Captain Inman's train from Camp Supply.[35]

Custer and his remaining eight hundred men, their own condition bordering on desperate, kept moving west to the Salt Fork, then pursued a trail northeast to Gypsum Creek. On March 8 the command rousted a small camp of Cheyennes before continuing west and south. Three days later the Osages found a slight trail, and the column headed northeast in pursuit amid increasing signs of Indians nearby. "No bugle calls or discharges of fire arms were permitted," reported Custer. On the afternoon of March 15, beset by scant forage and rations and with his men living on butchered mule meat, the troops came upon a village of Cheyennes under Medicine Arrows along Sweetwater Creek. Learning that the camp harbored the two captive white women and fearful that an attack might bring on their deaths, Custer advanced with an escort to council with Medicine Arrows and other headmen, who had indicated a desire to parley. "Never before or since," he explained, "have we seen so favorable an opportunity for administering well-merited punishment to one of the strongest and most troublesome of the hostile tribes."[36] He learned, moreover, that other camps of Cheyennes stretched along the Sweetwater for miles, altogether totaling some 260 lodges, many of them occupied by Dog Soldiers. While his command gradually deployed at either end of the camp, the colonel smoked a ceremonial pipe and explained his mission. At the conclusion of the meeting, the chief purportedly emptied ashes from the pipe bowl onto Custer's boots in a gesture ensuring his future bad luck, a vignette that later found its way into Cheyenne folklore regarding the officer's relationship with the tribe.[37] The captives were Anna Belle Brewster Morgan and Sarah Catherine White, the former a twenty-four-year-old farmer's bride taken from the Solomon settlements in September 1868, the latter an eighteen year old from the Republican River valley, where she had been captured the previous August in an attack that killed her father.

The colonel determined to secure the women's release. His decision to watch and wait elicited complaints from some of the Kansas troops, who wanted to attack the village. During an assembly hosted by the Cheyennes later that day, seemingly contrived to distract the officers while the villagers, doubtless frightened in the wake of the Washita attack, abandoned their lodges and cleared out, Custer's men seized four Cheyennes, three of whom were Dog Soldiers. The offense caused instant commotion among the tribesmen, and an immediate crisis loomed. One of the captured men was shortly sent forward, bearing demands respecting the release of the women and the removal of the Cheyennes to Camp Supply. The next day Little Robe and some followers appeared from a village downstream and consulted over the situation, but they left only with Custer's ultimatum that the Indians release the women without condition. On the seventeenth the command moved southeast toward the downstream camps. After continued uneasy negotiations, Custer, instituting the strategy imposed in dealing with the Kiowas, announced that the remaining hostages—Big Head, Dull Knife (also known as Lean Face), and Fat Bear—would be hanged at sunset March 19 if the captives had not appeared.[38] "I knew," recorded Custer, "when the question was forced upon them as to whether they preferred to deliver up the white girls to us or to force by their refusal the execution of the three chiefs, their decision would be in favor of their people." This intimidation brought results; before the deadline, the Cheyennes handed over the women, emaciated and swathed in stitched-together flour sacks, leggings, and moccasins. "I never saw such heart-broken, hopeless expressions on the face of another human being," remarked a white scout who was present. Morgan's brother, Daniel A. Brewster, had accompanied Custer from Fort Sill and was there to witness her release to the Kansas officers.[39] The troops moved back to their former camp near the site of Medicine Arrows's deserted village, which they then plundered. Custer retained the hostage chiefs and extracted assurances that the Cheyenne villages would go in to Camp Supply. Pressed for time by his failing animals and insufficient rations, the colonel took the three hostages with him when he started to the Washita field depot, known as Camp Inman, on March 21. His worn and hungry soldiers, many now afoot, barely made it back to the depot, passing by "the bones of the ponies killed at the destruction of Black Kettle's camp" to arrive there during the night of the twenty-third. "We have penetrated every haunt frequented by the five tribes which were lately hostile," Custer penned Sheridan. "We now know their accustomed routes and hiding places. We have taught the Indians that they are safe from us at no place and at no season, and . . . that the white man can endure the inclemencies of winter better than the Indian."[40]

With Captain Inman's train accompanying, the soldiers reached Camp Supply on March 28. The troops passed through Fort Dodge four days later and gained Fort Hays on April 7. Eleven days later the Kansas volunteers, now discharged, entrained east for their homes. By early April, most of the Arapahos and some of the Cheyennes had come in to Fort Sill. The Dog Soldiers refused to yield, however, and moved north to the Republican River country, where in July 1869 they were mostly wiped out in battle with Colonel Carr's Fifth Cavalry at Summit Springs, Colorado Territory. By that time, the Washita prisoners had been returned to their people. Little Robe, Eagle's Head, Medicine Arrows, and Buffalo Head and their followers had all come into Camp Supply, and remaining bands continued to straggle in over the ensuing months. The expedition against the southern tribes, particularly the Southern Cheyennes and Arapahos, was at an end, and Sheridan's strategy of striking the tribes during the winter had brought seemingly resounding success. On August 10, 1869, in an executive order, President Grant declared a new reservation for the Cheyennes and Arapahos in the western part of Indian Territory in lieu of that designated for them in the Medicine Lodge Treaty.[41] Yet the peace would prove fleeting, for policies forged during the Grant administration by the mid-1870s spilled over into even broader warfare with the tribes of the Great Plains, a final struggle in which the Cheyennes and the other southern tribesmen would again be major players.[42]

9

CONTROVERSIES

The attack on Black Kettle's village along the Washita once again devastated the Southern Cheyennes. It was the second time in four years—almost to the day—that this particular camp, regardless of its size, had felt the brunt of full-scale military assault. At Sand Creek the Colorado volunteers had swept down to visit upon the people a particularly heinous tragedy. At the Washita the U.S. regulars' assault seemed in many ways similar, resurrecting and punctuating among the Cheyennes the grievous wound of the earlier attack. Black Kettle, the leading proponent and spokesman for peace among his entire tribe, was struck down and silenced forever at Washita, an action that reverberated for years within Cheyenne society while clouding the issue of peace in the near and distant future. Other wars with the Cheyennes would come and go during the next decade before they all succumbed to the reality of reservation status. The days of freedom were gone forever.

The Washita action compounded existing difficulties within the Southern Cheyenne infrastructure originally wrought by Sand Creek. Besides the deaths of Black Kettle and Little Rock, other headmen and leading warriors fell, along with the women and children killed in Custer's assault, and the effects of these losses among the families during the following weeks and months were profound. Mostly likely, the survivors of Black Kettle's village—already greatly diminished in size—dispersed to other bands and camps, including those of Medicine Arrows and Little Robe; as an independent community, Black Kettle's village ceased to exist. In addition to the loss of lives, as well as to those women and children taken prisoner by the soldiers, there was much material destruction registered at the Washita, including the ponies and the lodges and their contents. Winter was already a difficult experience, and the forfeiture of so many material goods complicated the difficulty of surviving in frigid temperatures, though this problem likely found temporary relief as the village refugees joined relatives and friends in the other camps.[1]

One of the later pretexts on which Custer and General Sheridan hung their defense of Washita concerned captive whites presumably found in Black Kettle's village. In his official report of the encounter, dated November 28, 1868, Custer stated: "we . . . secured two white children, held captive by the Indians. One white woman who was in their possession was murdered by her captors the moment we attacked. A white boy held captive, about 10 years old, when about to be rescued, was brutally murdered by a squaw, who ripped out his entrails with a knife." In transmitting this report forward, Sheridan repeated the essence of Custer's remarks in his dispatch to General Sherman of November 29: "Two white children were recaptured; one white woman and one boy 10 years old were brutally murdered by the Indian women when the attack commenced." But following Custer's return to Camp Supply, he and Sheridan must have conferred at length and likely concluded that the statement could not be even reasonably justified. By then, however, the reports had gone forward, bound for public consumption. Custer's references to the recapture of two white children and to the murder of a white woman at the commencement of the attack remain a mystery, possibly the result of miscommunication either during or in the hurried aftermath of the fighting. Certainly, if two white children had been retrieved and presumably accompanied the column returning to Camp Supply, Custer must have seen them. The folly of his statement, therefore, must have been apparent by the time he reached that post. While no formal correction to the public record, so far as is known, was ever made, both Custer's and Sheridan's subsequent descriptions of the Washita action mention neither the rescue of the children nor the murdered white woman, suggesting that these events, in fact, never happened.[2]

The second part of Custer's comment—that regarding the white boy who had been "brutally murdered by a squaw, who ripped out his entrails with a knife"—enjoyed a longer run, possibly because several military participants either witnessed such an incident during the encounter or had learned of it conversationally shortly afterward.[3] But even this seems not to have occurred as described. In 1904 Ben Clark, Custer's chief of scouts, in an interview spoke of witnessing the episode: "I saw a Cheyenne squaw . . . kill her child with a butcher knife and then stabbed [sic] herself. Several of the soldiers thought she had murdered a white child. Some Cheyenne babies were almost as fair as white children, and one of the soldiers poked his carbine over the [river]bank and shot her through the head. In relating this incident in the history of the battle, Custer made the mistake of saying that this woman killed a captive white child." Clark later confirmed his statement in another interview, this with historian Walter M. Camp in 1910, thereby effectually dispelling this prevailing myth of the Washita.[4]

Besides these unsubstantiated references to whites in Black Kettle's village, some postaction accounts confusingly promoted the belief that Clara Blinn and her child were present there at the time of the engagement.[5] Nearly all of these insinuate that the Blinns' remains were found in or near Black Kettle's village. Contemporary accounts, however, place the discovery of their bodies downstream from the scene of Custer's attack, removed even from the area of Elliott's action, with most reporting that they were found in the vicinity of the former Kiowa village.[6] While it is possible that some exchange had been implemented with the Kiowas that ultimately placed the Blinns in that village, documentary evidence strongly suggests that they were with the Cheyennes, though most likely not with Black Kettle's people. If they had been in Black Kettle's village at the time of Custer's attack, they would have been found there, dead or alive. But that they were present in one or another village of Cheyennes there can be little doubt. Clara Blinn stated as much in her pleading letter of November 7, while Captain Alvord's Indian scouts placed her and her son with the Cheyennes as early as November 15 and as late as five days before the attack. Moreover, the Blinns were reported to be in "the large main camp" of the Cheyennes and Arapahos. This assemblage—moving separately from Black Kettle's village—included the camps of Medicine Arrows, Little Robe, Old Whirlwind, and other chiefs and undoubtedly also included

the captives Sarah C. White and Anna Belle Morgan.[7] An evaluation
of the available evidence thus indicates that there were *no* whites in
Black Kettle's village at the time of the army assault.

Nor is there evidence to support the notion that Black Kettle was
personally to blame for the events that precipitated the attack. Whatever the role the young men of his village played in the eastern Kansas
raids during the summer and early autumn of 1868, the incidents
reflected instilled behavioral tenets of Cheyenne society that were
beyond Black Kettle's—much less anybody else's—power to modify and
thus prevent. That the chief moved his people south of the Arkansas to
be beyond complicity in the Kansas events testifies strongly to his personal resolve to avoid conflict if at all possible and was consistent with
his historical behavior. Unfortunately for Black Kettle and his people,
the army hierarchy neither fathomed the sociocultural dynamics of
Plains Indian societies nor chose to discriminate between guilty and
innocent parties in its condemnation and prosecution for the Kansas
raids. Because of this blanket indictment, Black Kettle and his followers
consequently suffered for the sins of probably few of his people. As
stated, in accordance with the Medicine Lodge Treaty, the Indians had
a right to be along the Washita, south of their prescribed reservation.
That Custer ironically stumbled onto Black Kettle's village—detached
as it was from the downriver camps—was pure chance, but in light of
Sand Creek, it represented something of a cruel twist in the vicissitudes
of fortune.

Neither in his report nor in his later memoir did Custer explain
finding evidence implicating Black Kettle and his people in the Kansas
raids. That enumeration appeared first in General Sheridan's communication of January 1, 1869, in which he referred to "mules taken from
[Captain] Carpenter's train, mail matter carried by our murdered couriers, [and] photographs stolen from the scenes of outrages on the Solomon
and Saline" as being found in Black Kettle's village. He further stated,
"I have their own illustrated history, found in their captured camps,
showing the different fights or murders this band was engaged in; the
trains attacked, the hay parties attacked about Fort Wallace; the
women, citizens, and soldiers killed." The general elaborated on these
finds in his annual report of November 1, 1869: "We found in Black
Kettle's village photographs and daguerreotypes, clothing, and bedding,
from the houses of the persons massacred on the Solomon and Saline.
The mail which I had sent by the expressmen, Nat Marshal and Bill

Davis, from Bluff Creek to Fort Dodge, who were murdered and mutilated, was likewise found; also a large blank book, with Indian illustrations of the different fights which Black Kettle's band had been engaged
in, especially about Fort Wallace and on the line of the Denver stages;
showing when the fight had been with the colored troops—when with
white; also, when trains had been captured and women killed in wagons." Sheridan's remarks offered a strong indictment of Black Kettle's
people. Most intriguing of the items he mentioned was the ledger book
with illustrations testifying to the conniving complicity of the chief's
followers in the raids. A careful reading of the general's initial reference
to this document, wherein he stated that it had surfaced "in their captured *camps*" suggests that this evidence, with which he promoted
Black Kettle's guilt, was found, in fact, among the vestiges of the downriver sites. Otherwise, this incriminating chronicle would most certainly have been seized upon much earlier as a device with which to
further validate Custer's attack.[8]

For the Seventh Cavalry, the Washita encounter generated considerable enduring trauma, mostly resulting from the debate arising
within the regiment over whether Custer consciously and purposefully
abandoned Major Elliott and his men to their fate. While heretofore
latent seeds of dissension perhaps dated back to the unit's organization
in 1866, following Washita, the searing fissures suddenly rushed front
and center. Their impetus lay in the publication of an anonymous
letter, later claimed by Captain Benteen to have been written by himself, bluntly asserting that Elliott's force had gone to their deaths having
first been forsaken by Custer, then, in the colonel's desperation to save
his command from the downriver villagers, being abandoned by him
altogether. "Surely some search will be made for our missing comrades," mocked Benteen's piece, before concluding, "No, they are forgotten." The captain, no friend of Custer, had mailed the missive from
Fort Cobb to a friend on December 22, 1868. Custer learned of its publication upon returning to Camp Supply in late March 1869, sparking
a sharp verbal confrontation between the two officers after Benteen
admitted to its authorship.[9] Most accounts suggest that Custer remained
unaware of Elliott's whereabouts until long after the major and his seventeen volunteers had departed downstream in pursuit of the fleeing
party of Cheyennes. As stated, when Lieutenant Godfrey reported the
additional villages downstream and the sounds of shooting he had heard
during his movement in that direction, Custer initially dismissed the

latter information, believing that a squad under Captain Myers operating downstream would have reported it earlier. As second in command, Elliott was a significant fixture in the command hierarchy, and his whereabouts on the field would have been important knowledge in the wake of the opening assault. Similarly, Sergeant Major Walter M. Kennedy was the senior enlisted man in the regiment. But apparently their disappearance was obscured in the onrush of succeeding events. By the time Elliott's absence was noted, the lateness of the hour and the need to extricate his command from its position preempted Custer's rapt effort to search longer for the detachment, by then presumed dead, and recover the bodies, though flankers kept watch for signs of the missing party during the downstream march. While it is difficult to ascertain what more Custer could have done under the circumstances, Sheridan was not satisfied with his subordinate's feeble explanation of Elliott's disappearance.[10] The incident, seemingly aggravated by Benteen's offensive letter, became a hot topic of conversation within the regiment, leading to untold speculation and supposedly producing factionalism among the officers. It has since been viewed as having aggravated discord and partisanship so strong in the unit as to influence the personal and professional interrelationships to the degree of affecting the Seventh's performance in subsequent campaigns up to and including the Little Bighorn River eight years hence.[11]

The most enduring controversy emanating from the Washita is whether the action should be classified as a battle or a massacre. Nearly everyone who has heard of Custer's attack on Black Kettle's Cheyennes holds an opinion about its proper nomenclature. Yet any substantive discussion must have established at the outset the structure of authoritative definitions regarding what the terms mean. According to one well-known dictionary, "battle" describes "a general encounter between armies" that is usually "a general and prolonged combat." A prominent military dictionary of the late nineteenth century presents much the same meaning but further identifies an "offensive battle," in which "an army seeks the enemy and attacks him wherever he is to be found."[12] *The American Heritage College Dictionary* describes "massacre" as "the act or an instance of cruel, indiscriminate killing of a large number of human beings," while the military dictionary defines it as "the killing of human beings by indiscriminate slaughter, murder of numbers with cruelty or atrocity, or contrary to the usages of civilized people; coldblooded destruction of life; butchery; carnage."[13]

Granted these semantic parameters, the action on the Washita must be viewed on the grounds of whether the events that occurred on November 27, 1868, were of sufficient form and magnitude to classify them one way or the other. Given the War Department's mandate that all Cheyennes were guilty for the sins of the few in regard to the Kansas raids, there is no question that Custer succeeded in this purpose by attacking Black Kettle's village. His instructions from his superiors had been "to destroy their villages and ponies; to kill or hang all warriors, and bring back all women and children."[14] In effect, Custer had carried out an offensive strike against one village. But whether it was truly an "offensive battle" remains murky, for that term's definition assumes that the enemy is an opposing army and not a village containing large numbers of noncombatants.

Certainly, for the tribesmen who experienced the early morning attacks on their homes and families, wherein bullets from the charging forces ripped through the lodges, every army assault must have seemed like a massacre.[15] For Black Kettle's Cheyennes, ever skittish following Chivington's butchery at Sand Creek—an encounter that embodied every characteristic of that word—Custer's attack must have seemed especially brutal, in many ways a figurative exclamation point to the earlier carnage and a sequel that in their troubled existence they had anticipated for a long time. Yet Washita exhibited aspects that—by definition—were significantly different from what happened at Sand Creek. Most notably, it was not an indiscriminate slaughter. While there exists substantial evidence that some noncombatants were killed by soldiers in the course of the confusion and excitement of the initial charge, some of these deaths likely could not have been avoided, given the nature of the army's warfare methodology. "In the excitement of the fight, as well as in self-defense," explained Custer, "some of the squaws and a few children were killed and wounded." And Lieutenant Godfrey remembered that, during the charge, the assailants made no effort "to prevent hitting women." Despite such losses, the troops evidently took some measures to protect the women and children. Custer claimed to have earlier enjoined his men "to prevent the killing of any but the fighting strength of the village," and soon after the initial charge, he directed that Captain Myers's action in chasing a group of women and children be halted and that they be taken to a designated lodge to be kept there under guard. He later sent Romero to assure other women and children who had remained in their lodges during the attack that they would not be harmed. By most accounts, however, many of the women who fell in the attack were victims of the Osage scouts, traditional enemies of the Cheyennes. The directions to the troops to protect women and children and to take them prisoner, however, did not extend to the men, and as Ben Clark pointed out, *all* warriors who lay wounded in the village—presumably no matter the extent of their injuries—were summarily executed by the soldiers in a very discriminating manner. At least fifty-three women and children taken captive at the Washita served as assurance against attack from the downriver peoples during Custer's extrication of his command from the scene late on November 27. They accompanied the column to Camp Supply and later to Fort Hays, where they were incarcerated in a stockade. Certain of them, including Black Kettle's sister, played key roles in inducing the surrenders that followed. The fact that during the course of the fighting, attempts were made to save and protect these women and children, and that they were thereafter taken north as prisoners and became the subject of manuscript and photographic documentation of their status, necessarily disqualifies Washita as a "massacre" under that term's definition as "indiscriminate, merciless killing" and "indiscriminate slaughter."[16]

Yet at least one act often associated with massacres—including that at Sand Creek—occurred at the Washita. In the various accounts of the action, there appear several references to instances of scalping— the practice whereby part of the hair-bearing flesh on a human head is cut or torn from its victim as a token of revenge or of victory. Clearly, the society that the army represented generally viewed scalping as a form of mutilation. But it is documented that at the Washita, the Osage scouts took scalps from the Cheyennes they killed during the attack. That these acts occurred there can be no doubt, and its repetition on the field was evidently sanctioned because scalping represented ingrained cultural behavior on the part of the Osages (as it also did among the Cheyennes), was thereby condoned as an aspect of intertribal warfare, and any attempt by the troops to curtail its practice among their Indian allies would have offended them. Indeed, one account described an extreme case where an Osage scout killed a Cheyenne and completely beheaded the body. The Osages seem to have been particularly severe in their treatment of Cheyenne women, reportedly beating them with switches as they tried to run away and then scalping and otherwise mutilating those they killed. Beyond these incidents, there occurred occasional scalpings (at least two) by members of Custer's command, though the practice among the soldiers that day appears to have been infrequent.[17]

Without question, the occurrence of these offenses helped color the Washita encounter and contributed to it qualities reminiscent of a full-fledged massacre. But more than anything, the army's own Indian-fighting tactics bolstered that perception, especially as the concept of "offensive battle" became transposed on the frontier to embrace not surprise attacks upon otherwise prepared adversaries, but dawn attacks on enclaves normally containing a high percentage of sleeping non-combatants. Such procedures comprised the army's modus operandi of the Indian wars period. This kind of engagement, which in the West preceded the Civil War (and was therefore perhaps a coincidental precursor of the "total war" strategy later enacted by Grant, Sherman, and Sheridan), often resulted in the deaths of women, children, and the elderly. This fact, while accepted among the officer corps to varying degrees, did not change the existing definition of "battle." The army justified these mission-oriented tactics as imperative to controlling highly mobile, belligerent native populations with the long-range objective of protecting U.S. citizens on the frontier. Clearly, the tactic accommodated a prevalent and none-too-subtle perception of Indians as inferior beings from less significant and more expendable cultures ultimately destined for oblivion.[18] Clearly too, the very nature of this combat methodology, embracing as it did a theory of conscienceless total destruction of men and resources, in practice often balanced hazardously on the precipice of "massacre" and accordingly promoted—and continues to promote—its frequent correlation with that term. For the Cheyennes at the Washita in 1868, with the specter of the Sand Creek Massacre ever at hand, Custer's force delivered the quintessential example of this ruthless and remorseless form of warfare.[19]

Although the techniques applied at Washita—complete surprise at daybreak, the squeezing off of escape routes, and the rapid isolation of the pony herd to ruin mobility—would be more or less emulated, with varying results, against other tribes in the West over the next decade, the engagement itself appears to have had no long-term resounding influence on the military institution. Indeed, the controversies generated by Custer's attack seem to have nullified any positive publicity that the army might otherwise have expected in view of such recent episodes as Fetterman's defeat by Sioux in 1866 and Hancock's failed summer expedition of 1867. While Sheridan initiated a winter campaign against the Cheyennes, the concept had been applied earlier, including by Brigadier General James H. Carleton and Colonel Christopher Carson against the Navahos in 1863–64 and Colonel Patrick E. Connor against the Northwestern Shoshones in 1863. Dawn attacks on Indian villages had also happened before Washita, all with deadly consequences—witness Colonel William S. Harney's strike against Lakotas at Blue Water Creek, Nebraska Territory, in 1855; Connor's above-mentioned assault on Shoshones at Bear River, Idaho Territory, in January 1863; and Chivington's onslaught of Black Kettle's Cheyennes at Sand Creek in November 1864. The "dawn attack" scenario, no doubt influenced to some degree by what happened at Washita in 1868 and rationalized as "battle" partly as a result of that encounter, played out time and again over subsequent years, not only on the plains but also in the Southwest and Northwest. Cavalry troops (rarely infantry) in single or multiple columns stormed into sleeping camps in all seasons at such places as Marias River, Montana Territory (1870); McClellan Creek, Texas (1872); Turret Peak, Arizona Territory (1873); Palo Duro Canyon, Texas (1874); Powder River, Montana Territory (1876); Slim Buttes, Dakota Territory (1876); Red Fork of Powder River, Wyoming Territory (1876); and Clear Creek, Idaho Territory (1877), among others. Occasionally, such as at Big Hole, Montana Territory (1877); Bear's Paw Mountains, Montana Territory (1877); and Little Bighorn, Montana Territory (1876), the villages managed to turn back their assailants, and the engagements evolved into full-fledged contests of duration and substance—indeed, real battles. Further, at the Little Bighorn, Custer appears to have at least initially contemplated an assault on the Lakota and Cheyenne encampment using tactics reminiscent of those he employed at the Washita eight years earlier.[20]

Despite the controversies that emanated from the attack, Custer's reputation as an Indian fighter—considered the best in the U.S. Army, at least momentarily by the public—was sealed in the aftermath of Washita. His abysmal performance on the plains in 1867 under Hancock, which had ended with his court-martial and suspension from rank and command, was largely expunged by the bold strike against Black Kettle, and he thrived in the limelight it afforded for the next several years. In fact, considering that Washita was his only *major* encounter preceding Little Bighorn, Custer managed a certain mileage from that single event, as evidenced in his memoir, which appeared serially under the title "Life on the Plains" in *The Galaxy* between 1872 and 1874, antedating its book appearance as *My Life on the Plains* in the latter year. Washita sustained his reputation and kept him visible until his next contests, extended skirmishes with Lakota tribesmen along the Yellowstone River in Montana nearly five years later in 1873. After that, the only other time Custer engaged Indians was at the Little Bighorn. In terms of numbers of engagements with Indian warriors, Custer, in fact, pales in comparison with Colonel Nelson A. Miles and Brigadier General George Crook, both of whom had more-extensive experience—not to mention success—leading troops after Indians and combating them in the field. In essence, Custer's claim to fame rested on two engagements—the controversial Washita and the even more controversial Little Bighorn. While he basked in the afterglow of the former, his death at the latter permanently negated for him any personal aftereffects. Instead, it delivered him immortality.

Of course, Little Bighorn marked the last time Custer fought the Cheyennes. Although most of the Cheyenne people in Montana in the summer of 1876 belonged to the northern branch of the tribe, there were some southerners who had been at Washita and in Indian Territory and Texas during his subsequent campaign in 1868–69. After the fighting at Little Bighorn had ended and women and children poured onto the field to strip and plunder the soldiers' bodies, two Southern Cheyenne women reportedly recognized Custer's naked corpse and knelt tentatively beside it. Recalling his council along the Sweetwater with Medicine Arrows, Keeper of the *Maahotse*, or Sacred Arrows, wherein the Keeper emptied ashes from a ceremonial pipe over the officer's boots to ensure his bad fortune should he ever again threaten the Cheyennes, the women at Little Bighorn pushed the tip of a sewing awl deep into each of his ears so that he would hear better in the afterlife. Decades later, another Southern Cheyenne woman who was present at both Washita and Little Bighorn pondered if she had seen Custer at the latter place and, as she rode among the dead that afternoon, if her pony had kicked dirt upon his body.[21]

Appendix A

MONUMENTS AND RESOURCES OF THE WASHITA ENCOUNTER SITE

L ess than five years after the attack on Black Kettle's village, a surveyor going over the ground of Section 12, Township 13 North, Range 23 West, saw evidence of the struggle there, including "the bones of mules and ponies and skulls of men." During the following decades, the country gradually filled up as the Cheyennes and Arapahos relinquished through lease and allotment parts of their reservation granted them by executive order in 1869.[1] Twenty-three years after the attack, a U.S. Army officer stationed with the Seventh Cavalry at Fort Sill visited the site. All that then remained identifiable on the ground was an old cottonwood tree reportedly blazed by the Cheyennes near the spot in the stream where Black Kettle had fallen. Concerned that the location of the engagement would likely be lost and forgotten as settlement increased in Roger Mills County, First Lieutenant Hugh L. Scott determined to raise a marker to commemorate the action. For three days in January 1891, he and his escort, aided by a military ambulance, searched the vicinity for large rocks suitable for a monument. Scott then commissioned one of his party, Sergeant Thomas Clancy, a former stone mason, to inscribe a large, flat, red sandstone slab with the inscription "7th CAV," followed by "Nov. 27, 1868." The stone pile, surmounted by the carved slab, was built on the south side of the Washita at the site of Black Kettle's village. A number of horse skulls collected from the spot where, in 1868, the soldiers had killed the Cheyenne ponies were placed around the foot of the marker. Fearing that an influx of settlement would harm both the marker and Black Kettle's tree, Scott wrote to area newspapers to urge residents to protect them.

Scott's makeshift monument to his regiment, occasionally knocked over by floodwaters or cattle and then rebuilt, remained more or less intact until the early twentieth century, when the bottomland became increasingly used for grazing.[2] Some time after 1902, landowners dismantled the marker and moved the sandstone slab to a "little red hill"— the Custer observation knoll, in fact—south of the former village location. By then too, many of the horse bones, including the skulls from the base of the monument, had been removed by local residents for sale to a Texas fertilizer company. Black Kettle's tree likely died or was removed during this period. Occasional visitors to the area chipped pieces from the rock for souvenirs. By 1910, Mrs. W. T. Bonner, wife of the owner of the land encompassing the village site, had organized a ladies' group in Cheyenne, Oklahoma, for the purpose of erecting a permanent memorial. Eight years later, however, historian Joseph B. Thoburn of the Oklahoma Historical Society notified then Major General Hugh Scott that his sandstone marker, though weathered and evidently lying flat on the surface, still graced the site. "If we succeed in having a permanent marker placed there within the next few years, as I hope we may, that stone, which you had inscribed and placed as a temporary marker, should be brought here and preserved in the collections of this society." Thoburn was interested in unveiling and dedicating a permanent commemorative marker at the Washita site during observance of its fiftieth anniversary, and Brigadier General Edward S. Godfrey, who had participated in the engagement and now long retired, indicated a desire to make a "pilgrimage" to the site, though he did not, finally, attend. During the 1920s, Sheriff James M. Lester removed the inscribed stone of Scott's monument to the corridor of the courthouse in Cheyenne to preserve it.[3]

In the autumn of 1930, two aged Cheyennes, Magpie and Little Beaver, visited the site and pointed out places significant in the action, including that of the village. At the pony kill area, hundreds of bones still could be seen. That November, during a Thanksgiving ceremony coinciding with the sixty-second anniversary of the event, the remains of a warrior killed defending his home and family, uncovered in 1914 during a railroad excavation project, were buried north of the highway and south of where Black Kettle's village had stood, and the citizens of Cheyenne dedicated a memorial to all of the Indian people killed at the Washita. During the ceremony, Chief Magpie, who had been wounded in the army attack, spoke charitably to a throng numbering in the thousands, telling them that "he forgave Gen. Custer for the part he had in the Battle of the Washita, and that he prayed God to forgive Custer." Early in 1933, through the efforts of the Platonic Club of Cheyenne, a red granite marker with the words "Custer's Battle, November 27, 1868," was erected near the grave.[4]

Yet another marker was erected in 1956—a brick-based monument, raised north of State Route 47A, overlooking the site and funded by popular subscription, on which was depicted the date of the Washita engagement together with a map of Oklahoma. This structure was temporary, however, for it was removed in the 1960s. In 1958 the Black Kettle Museum was built by the State of Oklahoma, and as the centennial of the Washita engagement approached, the site became the focal point for more observances. On April 17, 1962, the Oklahoma Industrial and Development Board placed a large granite interpretive panel near State Route 47A that briefly told the story of Custer's attack on the Cheyenne encampment. The next year, the state acquired three acres encompassing this marker and established an overlook park. On October 22, 1965, Secretary of the Interior Stewart Udall unveiled a plaque designating the scene of the Washita engagement as a National Historic Landmark. All of this activity culminated three years later, at a ceremony commemorating the one hundredth anniversary, when Indian remains found in 1934 during excavation work for a bridge were consigned to eternity in a flag circle near the county courthouse and the Black Kettle Museum in Cheyenne. The inscription on the granite plaque reads: "The unknown who lies here is in commemoration of Chief Black Kettle and the Cheyenne tribal members who lost their lives in the Battle of the Washita." In 1983 the National Historic Landmark boundaries were approved, and in 1996, following an agreement between the federal government and the State of Oklahoma, the Washita encounter site, encompassing a core area of 320 acres, became a unit of the national park system.[5]

The efforts to memorialize in stone the army attack on Black Kettle's village, as well as to learn particulars of the event from Indian participants, represent the importance of the event in American history, not only as it reflected the immediate state of Cheyenne-army relations in 1868 but also as it affected the Cheyenne people and the course of their long-term relationship with the U.S. government during the years and decades that followed. Historically, Washita is significant as representing the ultimate manifestation of culture conflict resulting from the failure of intercultural diplomacy and the treaty system. It further embodies the optimum example of the military strategy of the winter offensive in dealing with the plains tribes, affording perhaps the preeminent illustration of all post–Civil War army-Indian combat, wherein execution of the tactic of encirclement and early morning assault became a hallmark.

The land itself promotes the interpretation of not only its significance but also many of the terrain features that contributed to the event, allowing visitors to achieve a broader and richer comprehension of what happened.[6] The 1996 enabling legislation called on the National Park Service "to protect and preserve the national historic site, including the topographic features important to the battle site, artifacts and other physical remains of the battle, and the visual scene as closely as possible as it was at the time of the battle." The following properties, regardless of their location within or without the park service tract (or, for some, of their tangible existence), possess degrees of historical value (and in some cases integrity) sufficient to sustain the interpretation and future development plans of Washita Battlefield National Historic Site. (See map 3 for the relative location of each site, denoted by its number.)

1. Black Kettle's Village

The village, numbering fifty-one lodges (a few of which were not Cheyenne) and including as many as 250 people, was on the south side of the stream and for the most part situated in a northward jutting loop of the Washita. All of the area of the village is presently incorporated within the boundary of Washita Battlefield National Historic Site, though the configuration of the river at this point has drastically changed since the early 1900s. Ben Clark, the former chief scout accompanying the troops in 1868, visited the scene on several occasions. In 1899 he described the village site as "an admirable camping place in a big bend of the river, on a level stretch of ground." In 1904 he returned to point out to a news correspondent various features connected with the engagement. By then, much of the timber along the river had been felled. Respecting the village site, the correspondent wrote: "Where Black Kettle's village stood is now a meadow. The land has never been plowed, as the Washita rises and overflows it every spring. The Washita flows from the west against an almost perpendicular bank which marks the break of the high prairie on the south as it descends suddenly to the level floor of the river valley. Then the river turns northward for about a thousand yards and turns again to the wall-like embankment of the prairie. Surrounded on two sides by this gooseneck bend of the river and flanked on the south by the higher ground, is a tract of about twenty-five acres, the old Indian camp ground."[7]

Fortunately, through the efforts of Oklahoma historian Fred S. Barde, who recorded the course of the stream in the north half of Section 12 before major rechanneling projects altered it, the appearance of the loop, and thus the historic scene, can be approximated with some degree of accuracy. Barde's map, possibly derived with the assistance of Ben Clark, indicates that "gun cartridges & bangles [decorative cone-shaped tinklers used as Cheyenne clothing ornaments]" had been found in the southern part of the loop.[8] The area remained largely undeveloped as late as 1910, when Walter M. Camp, who visited the site with Clark, wrote that the Washita "flows in precisely the same channel that it did in 1868. . . . The identical ground on which the village of Black Kettle stood has not been ploughed up yet." Clark reported that the village was in the northeast quarter, Section 12, Township 13 N, Range 24 W. "The river bends sharply to the north and from the bluff where the horses were shot, out to the bend, the area is about 30 acres. The village was in the northwest corner of the bend." Without doubt, the channeling project, which occurred between 1910 and 1930, along with ongoing relic collecting and increased agricultural activity, caused the loss of other artifacts in the Washita bottom that would likely have further confirmed the precise location of Black Kettle's village.[9]

2. SITE OF BLACK KETTLE'S LODGE

The chief's tipi stood near the river in the western part of the village, apparently slightly west of the major loop, in a smaller bend somewhere in what is now the bottom half of the northwest quarter of Section 12. A few other tipis were located there too, but most had been raised in the north-jutting encircling bend. A giant cottonwood tree grew nearby. Reportedly, only one lodge stood farther west, that of Big

Man, who was related to Black Kettle and who was the father of Magpie, who years later provided Cheyenne perspectives of the attack. Subsequently, the large cottonwood tree was used to designate the site of Black Kettle's tipi.[10]

3. Observation Ridge

The spot from which the Osage scouts Little Beaver and Hard Rope discovered Black Kettle's village during the night of November 26–27 is on rising ground in the northeast quarter of Section 2, Township 13 North, Range 24 West, about one mile northwest of the village site. Custer and his officers, said Clark, "lay on this very spot and spied out the village and the lay of the land."[11]

4. Army Preattack Staging Area

In 1904 Clark stood on the property of a man named Kirtley and, pointing northwest, told an interviewer, "there is where the troops came down from the divide and in that cotton field is where the men dismounted." The site is in the southwest of the northeast quarter of Section 2. In 1910 A. G. Smith owned the property, and Clark told Camp, "the command was halted on the ground right north of this barn." Then the troops evidently moved lower down to a tract owned in 1910 by Frank Turner. "It is on flat ground lower than the barn & north of barn."[12]

5. Custer's Attack Route

Custer and his four companies (A, C, D, and K), besides the scouts, sharpshooters, and regimental band, attacked from the northwest. Lieutenant Godfrey later claimed: "Custer's immediate command . . . moved into place facing nearly east. . . . Following the General [Custer], the command marched over the crest of the ridge and advanced some distance to another lower ridge." Based on knowledge of Custer's position during the night of November 26–27, the route of his assault toward the village likely followed a broad swath leading down to the river through Sections 2 and 1. From all accounts, Lieutenant William Cooke's sharpshooters approached along a course to the left of Custer's main command and fairly fronted on the Cheyennes at the northernmost part of the river bend after the attack opened. Barde learned that as the assault commenced, Custer crossed the stream at the northwest corner of the loop where two big cottonwood trees were standing in about 1900. As the troops fanned out in the village, he continued his diagonal to the southeast, passing through the tumult to ascend a knoll to the south.[13]

6. THOMPSON'S ATTACK ROUTE

Custer directed Captain William Thompson, commanding a squadron composed of Companies B and F, to march to the west and then in a broad circular movement to turn south and cross the Washita, keeping his men beneath the hills, and coordinate with Major Elliott's battalion in closing on the village on horseback from the opposite side while keeping the people from fleeing south before Custer's charge. The precise route of Thompson's command after leaving the high ground is unknown, but it was seemingly circuitous and likely occupied several miles. Of all the squadrons, Thompson's had the longest distance to cover, and consequently his soldiers were not altogether in position when the attack began, thereby leaving open a route of escape for many of the Indians fleeing the village.[14] It is likely that Thompson's men passed through parts of Sections 2, 3, 10, 11, 15, and 14 in making their approach.

7. MYERS'S ATTACK ROUTE

Captain Edward Myers and Companies E and I moved down from the heights some three-quarters of a mile west and south of Custer's squadron. Myers crossed the Washita, passing east through the woods toward the village. On signal, he was to attack from the west while preventing the people from escaping in that direction. Rather than join in the assault, however, Myers played more of a containment role.[15] His squadron possibly passed through parts of Sections 2, 3, 10, and 11 in their advance.

8. ELLIOTT'S ATTACK ROUTE

Major Joel Elliott's column of Companies G, H, and M departed the staging area, passing northeast behind knolls and ridges, then south to the river, to gain a position east of the village on either side of the Washita "and then [to] move up the stream to the attack at the proper time." His force began its assault from that direction when the engagement opened at dawn.[16] Presumably, the squadron traversed parts of Sections 2, 1, 6, and 7 in gaining its appointed place of attack.

9. SUGAR LOAF BUTTE

This prominent landmark, a "very steep conical hill" named by Captain Albert Barnitz, stands about one-half mile north of the village site, in the northwest quarter of Section 1. Following Custer's disposition of his troops, Major Elliott commanded the battalion that would strike the village from the east. From their vantage on Sugar Loaf, which they encountered as they led their troops into position, Barnitz and Elliott reconnoitered the village during the night of November 26–27. After descending the butte, the officers led their troops down a draw, or "canyon," east of Sugar Loaf toward Black Kettle's lodges preparatory to opening the assault at daybreak.[17]

10. CUSTER'S KNOLL

Custer ascended a knoll following the opening charge into the village. From this vantage, he monitored the unfolding action and made dispositions and adjustments through his aides. Presumably, he did not remain on the knoll for the duration of the engagement but came and went as appropriate. The position probably assumed more value as an observation post after Custer learned that other Indian villages lay downstream. There are three knolls in the immediate area. The one that Custer used was also the one, according to Ben Clark in both 1904 and 1910, to which the slab marker stone, originally erected near the river by Lieutenant Scott, had been removed. Barde's map shows the location of this "stone on mound" near the lower center of the northwest quarter of Section 12. The knoll, slightly northwest of the present overlook, was identified by the daughter of a local landowner as being the site of Scott's relocated stone and thus probably represents Custer's position. The north side of the knoll was torn away during construction of the adjoining railroad grade.[18]

11. Hamilton Death Site

Captain Louis Hamilton and his squadron, composed of Companies A and C, rode on the left of Custer's line in the advance from the high ground northwest of the village. Hamilton personally rode close to Custer. Most accounts indicate that the captain was one of the first, if not *the* first, man killed in the assault and that he was shot among the undergrowth bordering the stream.[19] Based on the apparent location of the channel in 1868, Hamilton likely fell in the northeast part of the northwest quarter of Section 12 just before or immediately after fording the stream during the charge into the village.

12. Barnitz Rock Circle

A circle of large stones designates the spot where Captain Barnitz, severely wounded in the fighting southeast of the village, dismounted and collapsed to await death. Instead, he was found and taken to obtain help from the doctors, who pronounced his wound mortal. Barnitz survived. The location of the rock circle, while not precisely known, is believed to be in the southeast quarter of Section 12.[20] It is possible that the rocks have since been removed for use in building foundations for area farmhouses and outbuildings.

13. Cheyenne Stand Areas

Ben Clark designated two places where the Indians made forceful stands against the soldiers. One was behind a large piece of fallen embankment opposite the northernmost part of the village loop, where the river had ground into the north bank and, through time, forced a large piece to collapse into the bed. Here a number of people held out against the troops until Cooke's sharpshooters ended their resistance. It was also here that the Cheyenne woman killed her child and then herself. This site is believed to have been near the north-central portion of the northern half of Section 12. The other major stand area was evidently downstream, near where the loop of the river ended and the channel straightened out in its eastward course. Here a number of warriors took shelter in a ravine until the sharpshooters found them and killed them all. This action is believed to have taken place beneath the high embankment near the center of the northeast quarter of Section 12.[21]

14. Magpie's Escape Route

The Cheyenne youth Magpie, along with some others, managed to flee the western part of the village during the attack, running west and south before troops saw them and fired. Wounded, Magpie continued toward a ridge to the south and there engaged and shot a solitary soldier, perhaps Captain Barnitz, before eluding pursuit. Years later, an aged Magpie pointed out the place where he hid in the grass following the initial assault on the village.[22] It is in the area of the southwest quarter of Section 12.

15. Twin Knolls

Many of the women and children trying to escape the army attack fled in the direction of these two buttes, which rise from the prairie about one-half mile south of the village site. Here they encountered Captain Myers's squadron, which began to pursue them, "killing them without mercy," according to Ben Clark. The scout brought Custer's attention to the matter, and "he ordered me to stop the slaughter, which I did." The captives were ushered back to the village and placed under guard in one or more tipis. From the top of the northernmost knoll, the girl Moving Behind witnessed much of the action around the village.[23] The knolls are located at the approximate center of the bottom half of Section 12, southwest of the present observation area.

16. Godfrey's Advance Downstream

As he rounded up ponies from the village, Lieutenant Edward S. Godfrey led a party of soldiers across the Washita to its north bank, then headed east, pursuing a group of dismounted Indians he had spotted. After several miles, Godfrey mounted a rise from which he could see the tipis of the downriver camps. Warriors then confronted him, and the lieutenant began an organized withdrawal in which his small detachment skirmished with the advancing tribesmen. Godfrey reported his sighting to Custer, telling him also of having heard firing on the south bank of the river and that it might have come from Major Elliott, who had earlier gone in that direction.[24] While his exact route remains unknown, Godfrey's movement extended for perhaps three miles downstream and northeast from the village and likely passed through parts of Section 12, Township 13 North, Range 24 West; Sections 6 and 5, Township 13 North, Range 23 West; and Section 32, Township 14 North, Range 23 West.

17. Areas Where Warriors from Downriver Villages Assembled

Warriors from the several downriver camps of Cheyennes, Arapahos, Kiowas, and Comanches gradually occupied the hills on the north and south sides of the Washita, and squads of troopers were eventually dispatched to engage these tribesmen in long-range shooting. On the north side of the stream, warriors appeared all along the crests of the distant hills and must have occupied appropriate points in Sections 2, 1, and 6; some advanced as far as the ridges in Section 2 to capture the greatcoats and equipment left there by the soldiers before the attack. Custer later directed Lieutenant Matthew Berry to dislodge the Indians from this area.[25] Presumably, warriors also occupied parts of Sections 11 and 12, Township 13 North, Range 24 West, and Section 7, Township 13 North, Range 23 West, south of the river.

18. Possible Skirmish Line Site Southeast of Village

One area that conforms well with records of known skirmishing that occurred as Custer's troops returned fire on the warriors from the downriver camps is that located in the southeast quadrant, northeast quarter of Section 12. Numerous expended Spencer cartridge cases were found during archeological examination of a ridge at that location, about four hundred to five hundred yards northeast of the present overlook.[26]

19. Elliott's Departure Point

At some point midmorning, following the charge on the village, Major Elliott, accompanied by Sergeant Major Walter Kennedy, surveyed the country from a hill east of Custer's Knoll. From here, he spotted through his field glasses a number of Cheyenne men and boys hiding in the woods below and called out for volunteers to join him in attacking these people. Fifteen soldiers joined him and took up the chase downstream. The knoll on which Elliott and Kennedy stood was pointed out by Ben Clark in later years.[27] It is believed to be southeast of the command knoll in the northeast quarter of Section 12, just northeast of the present overlook.

20. ROUTE OF BELL'S ADVANCE

Following the departure of the regiment on the evening of November 26, First Lieutenant James Bell continued on the trail with his two wagons and four ambulances. He forded the Washita several times in his advance. When the shooting got underway, Bell crossed his train to the north bank at a place approximately one and one-half miles upstream from the village and ascended the high ground where the troops had earlier waited to attack. By the time he reached the place where the overcoats had been left, warriors from downstream had appeared. Unable to retrieve all of the garments and equipment, Bell and his escort raced the train forward through the cordon of Indians and down the slope to ford the stream and deliver new supplies of ammunition to the command.[28] In passing down the heights north of the river, Bell presumably maneuvered his train through the south half of Section 2 and the north half of Section 12 to gain the village area.

21. PONY-KILL SITE

Late in the day Custer determined to kill as many as 875 ponies and mules that had been rounded up. Not only would they delay his withdrawal from the proximity of the downriver villages if he took them with him, but they would remain an enticing prize as well for warriors who might follow the command. Moreover, the killing of the beasts would further devastate the Cheyennes and cripple their future mobility. With this in mind, the soldiers drove the animals to a point below a high bluff southeast of the village. The Osage scouts received some, while others were spared to serve as mounts for the women and children prisoners. The rest were "bunched against the steep bank," reported Clark, and four companies of cavalry shot them to death. "The hostiles who were gathered on the hills witnessed their destruction and with shrill cries derided the soldiers as cowards and dared them to fight."[29] The pony-kill site is in the northeast quarter of Section 12 near an abandoned railroad grade.

22. Sergeant Major Kennedy's Death

Sergeant Major Walter Kennedy rode with Major Elliott's volunteers downstream in pursuit of several warriors, women, and children. As the warriors drew away, Elliott's men followed. Kennedy, however, paused and began escorting the noncombatants back toward the village. Soon he was set upon by several Arapaho warriors from the downriver villages, who approached from the river. As Kennedy tried to escape on his horse, the Arapahos overtook him, knocked him from his saddle, and killed him. The site of Kennedy's struggle probably occurred in the northeast quarter of Section 7, perhaps one mile or so east of the village site and behind the present U.S. Forest Service offices.[30]

23. Deaths of Blind Bear and Hawk

Elliott's party crossed to the east side of Sergeant Major Creek, where they overtook and killed these two warriors as they bravely drew the soldiers away from a group of women and children. The site of their deaths is in the northwest quarter of Section 8, Township 13 North, Range 23 West.[31]

24. Destruction of Major Elliott's Command

Elliott and his sixteen cavalrymen continued the pursuit of the Indians they had initially targeted. In the course of their chase, the soldiers crossed a tributary, since known as Sergeant Major Creek, killed Hawk and Blind Bear, drove the people back behind the bank of the Washita, and then continued to shoot at them until a large force of warriors appeared from downstream. Other warriors blocked any retreat by the troopers toward the village and forced Elliott's command into open terrain back from the Washita. Gradually, more Indians surrounded the troops, and Elliott's men sought refuge in tall grass along the east side of Sergeant Major Creek in a sharp bend of the stream as it angled east and north toward the Washita. (The configuration of Sergeant Major Creek has changed drastically in this area due to its course having been diverted directly north into the Washita.) There the warriors moved ever closer, firing their weapons into the cluster of men, who were by now shooting their own guns wildly at the tribesmen. Some of the Indians raced their horses through the soldiers' position.

Finally, Elliott's party was overwhelmed. Custer apparently knew nothing of this fighting. Late in the day, desirous of extricating his command, he departed without knowing precisely what had happened to Elliott and his men. The scene of this encounter took place in Sections 7 and 8. Indian accounts indicate that the actual battle site is in the eastern edge of Section 7 or the western half of the northwest quarter of Section 8, adjoining on the east the former big bend of Sergeant Major Creek.[32]

25. LOCATIONS OF SCOTT MONUMENT

The marker raised in 1891 by Lieutenant Hugh L. Scott to commemorate the Seventh Cavalry at the Washita originally stood near the river at the village site, which was then designated as "the battlefield." Presumably, the site of the marker was in the center of the north half of Section 12 and likely in the now long-vanished loop of the river where Black Kettle's village stood. Evidently, repeated flooding in the Washita bottom, together with roaming cattle, caused the monument of rocks to collapse, and some time after 1902, the principal slab of red sandstone was moved southeast to Custer's Knoll.[33] During the 1920s, this stone, increasingly weathered, was removed to the courthouse in Cheyenne, Oklahoma, to protect it from further deterioration. The stone is presently housed in the Black Kettle Museum.

Appendix B

Army Casualties at the Washita

Sources for this compilation are: "Special Report. Officers Killed at the Battle of the Washita, I.T., November 27, 1868"; "Special Report. Enlisted Men Killed at the Battle of the Washita, Indian Territory, November 27, 1868"; and "List of Wounded in the 7th U.S. Cavalry under command of Bvt. Maj. Genl Custer, U.S.A., at the Battle of the Washita, Indian Territory, on the 27th day of Novr. 1868," enclosed in Assistant Surgeon George A. Otis to Colonel Charles H. Crane, Assistant Surgeon General, Jan. 16, 1869, RG 94, Records of the Adjutant General's Office, NA; Mangum, "Muster Roll." For further specifics about the nature of the wounds listed below and their treatment, see the above documents.

Killed

Elliott, Joel H.	Major	"Major Elliott was last seen pursuing some Indians about a mile and a half from the Indian Village in which the battle of the Washita was fought. There can be no doubt of his death. Body not recovered."

Hamilton, Louis M.	Captain	"Was killed in action at the battle of the Washita I T, Nov. 27, 1868. Ball entered about five inches below left nipple, and emerged near inferior angle of right scapula. Death was instantaneous."
Kennedy, Walter	Sergeant Major	"Body not recovered."
Cuddy, Charles	Private, B	"Ball entered about an inch above upper lip and a little to the left of nose, passed upwards and backwards and emerged behind and a little above left ear."
Mercer, Harry	Corporal, E	"Body not recovered."
Christie, Thomas	Private, E	"Body not recovered."
McClernan, John	Private, E	"Body not recovered."
Carrick, William	Corporal, H	"Body not recovered."
Clover, Eugene	Private, H	"Body not recovered."
George, John	Private, H	"Body not recovered."
Mulligan, William	Private, H	"Body not recovered."
Williams, James F.	Corporal, I	"Body not recovered."
Downey, Thomas	Private, I	"Body not recovered."
Vanousky, Erwin	Sergeant, M	"Body not recovered."
Fitzpatrick, Thomas	Farrier, M	"Body not recovered."
Lineback, Ferdinand	Private, M	"Body not recovered."
Myers, John	Private, M	"Body not recovered."
Myers, Carson D. J.	Private, M	"Body not recovered."
Sharpe, Cal	Private, M	"Body not recovered."
Stobascus, Frederick	Private, M	"Body not recovered."

Wounded

Barnitz, Albert	Captain	Bullet; abdomen; severe penetrating wound
Custer, Thomas W.	1st Lieutenant	Bullet; right hand; slight glance shot
March, Thomas J.	2d. Lieutenant	Arrow; left hand; slight flesh wound

Eastwood, William	Corporal, A	Bullet; right elbow joint; severe penetrating wound
Gale, Martini	Private, A	Bullet; right arm; slight flesh wound
Delaney, Augustus	Private, B	Bullet; thorax; severe penetrating wound
Zimmer, George	Private, D	Bullet; left arm; compound fracture
Klink, Frederick	Private, E	Bullet; left arm; slight flesh wound
Brown, William	Private, F	Bullet; left arm; slight flesh wound
Martin, August	Saddler, G	Bullet; right forearm; compound fracture
Morrison, Daniel	Private, G	Arrow; right temple; flesh wound
McCasey, Benjamin	Private, H	Arrow; thorax; severe penetrating wound of lung
Morgan, Hugh	Private, I	Bullet; right arm; severe flesh wound
Strahle, Conrad	Private, I	Bullet; left ankle; flesh wound
Murphy, John	Bugler, M	Arrow; thorax; severe flesh wound

Appendix C

Known Village Fatalities at the Washita

Compiled from information contained in Hyde, *Life of George Bent*, 322 (in which Bent accounts for thirteen men killed); Bent to George E. Hyde, August 28, 1913, Bent-Hyde Correspondence, Charles F. Bates Papers, Coe Collection, Beinecke Rare Book and Manuscript Library, Yale University, New Haven, Conn. (in which Bent accounts for eleven men, twelve women, and six children killed); Bent to George Bird Grinnell, October 12, 1913, Ms. 5, Folder 56.2, George Bird Grinnell Collection, Braun Research Library, Southwest Museum, Los Angeles (in which Bent accounts for fourteen men, twelve women, and five children killed); Bent to Walter M. Camp, December 4, 1916, Folder 2, Box 2, Walter M. Camp Papers, Brigham Young University Library, Provo, Utah, microfilm (in which Bent accounts for thirteen men killed); and 88.32, File 216 (temp), Box 15, Washita Massacre, Folder 1; and File 217 (temp), Washita Massacre, Folder 2, John L. Sipes Collection, Archives and Manuscripts Division, Oklahoma Historical Society, Oklahoma City. Some individuals listed below might have had two or more names, so a few entries might be duplicative.

Men Killed

Bad Man
Bear Tail
Bear Tongue
Big Horse
Bitter Man
Black Kettle
Blind Bear
Blue Horse
Buffalo Tongue
Cranky Man
Crazy
Fool Man
Hawk
Heap Timber (Lakota)
Lame Man (Arapaho), or Lame Arapaho
Little Chief
Little Heart
Little Rock
Medicine Walker
Pilaw (Mexican trader from Santa Fe)
Poor Black Elk
Red Bird
Red Teeth
Running Water
Sharp Belly
Single Coyote (Arapaho)
Standing Out, or Sun Bear
Statue
Tall Bear
Tall Hat (Lakota)
Tall Owl
Tall White Man
The Man that Hears the Wolf
Tobacco (Arapaho)

Unidentified Comanche
Unidentified old, retarded man cared for by Crazy
White Bear (Mexican captive)
White Beaver
Wolf Ear
Wolf Looking Back

WOMEN KILLED

Medicine Woman Later
Unidentified Cheyenne women (nine)
Unidentified Lakota women (two)

CHILDREN KILLED

Unidentified children (six)

Appendix D

Other Known Village Occupants (beyond Fatalities)

Adapted from Mangum, "Inside Black Kettle's Village" (which was prepared from various published and manuscript sources); lists in 88.32, File 216 (temp), Box 15, Washita Massacre, Folder 1, John L. Sipes Collection, Archives and Manuscripts Division, Oklahoma Historical Society, Oklahoma City; and Warde, "Final Report on Cooperative Agreement 1443CA125098002 Modification 1, Conduct Oral History Research for Washita Historical Site." (Some names were provided independently, as indicated below.)

Afraid of Beaver
Big Man
Bird Chief (provided by Colleen Cometsevah)
Black Eagle (Kiowa)
Black White Man (provided by Vernon Bull Coming)
Bobtail Bear
Clown
Corn Stalk Woman (female)
Crane
Crow Neck
Cut Arm, or Walks Different (provided by Colleen Cometsevah)
Half Leg

Little Beaver (age twelve)
Little Woman (provided by Alfrich Heap of Birds)
Little Woman Curious (provided by Colleen Cometsevah)
Magpie (wounded)
Mahwissa (sister of Black Kettle)
Man Riding on a Cloud, or Touching the Sky
Medicine Elk Pipe
Monahseetah (female)
Mosaio (female; provided by Colleen Cometsevah)
Moving Behind (female)
Packer
Pushing Bear
Red Shin
Red Bird (provided by Colleen Cometsevah)
Red Dress Woman (wife of Wolf Looking Back)
Roll Down
Roman Nose Thunder (wounded)
Scabby Man
She Wolf
Standing Bird (provided by Colleen Cometsevah)
Trailing the Enemy (Kiowa)
Walking Woman (provided by Lawrence Hart)
Walking Woman Tall Elk (provided by Colleen Cometsevah)
White Buffalo Woman
Wolf Belly Woman

NOTES

ABBREVIATIONS

AAAG	Acting Assistant Adjutant General
AAG	Assistant Adjutant General
BYU	Brigham Young University Library, Provo, Utah.
LC	Manuscripts Division, Library of Congress, Washington, D.C.
NA	National Archives, Washington, D.C.
RG	Record Group

CHAPTER 1. HUMAN BEINGS AND SAND CREEK

1. See the various accounts of the Sand Creek Massacre in the testimony of white participants contained in congressional and military inquiries presented in John M. Carroll, comp., *The Sand Creek Massacre: A Documentary History* (New York: Sol Lewis, 1973), which documents the atrocities committed. For a Cheyenne perspective and a description of weather conditions following the event, see Hyde, *Life of George Bent*, 151–63.

2. Fenneman, *Physiography of Western United States*, 1–11; Thornbury, *Regional Geomorphology*, 287–90; Beck and Haase, *Historical Atlas of the American West*, map 2 ("Geomorphic Provinces"); Webb, *Great Plains*, 3–17.

3. Fenneman, *Physiography of Western United States*, 6 (map); Thornbury, *Regional Geomorphology*, 289–90; Beck and Haase, *Historical Atlas of the American West*, map 1 ("Relief"); Baughman, *Kansas in Maps*, 7; Webb, *Great Plains*, 17–26; Kraenzel, *Great Plains in Transition*, 12–23; Hunt, *Natural Regions of the United States and Canada*, 344–47, 360–61.

4. Kraenzel, *Great Plains in Transition*, 29–34; Webb, *Great Plains*, 27–33; Fenneman, *Physiography of Western United States*, 88–90. For average precipitation in the region, see Beck and Haase, *Historical Atlas of the American West*, map 3 ("Mean Annual Rainfall").

5. Kraenzel, *Great Plains in Transition*, 34–40; Webb, *Great Plains*, 33–44, 52. For factors bearing on the buffalo on the plains, see Hornaday, *Extermination of the American Bison*; Garretson, *American Bison*; and McHugh, *Time of the Buffalo*.

6. This synopsis of prehistoric occupation of the plains is drawn from Wedel, "Great Plains," 193–220; and Wedel, *Prehistoric Man on the Great Plains*. See also Jesse D. Jennings, *Prehistory of North American* (New York: McGraw-Hill, 1974), 265–80; and Webb, *Great Plains*, 52–60.

7. For Cheyenne history and culture, see Powell, *Sweet Medicine*; Moore, *The Cheyenne*; Moore, *Cheyenne Nation*; Berthrong, *Southern Cheyennes*; Grinnell, *Cheyenne Indians*; Powell, *People of the Sacred Mountain*; Stands in Timber and Liberty, *Cheyenne Memories*; and Moore, Liberty, and Straus, "Cheyenne," 863–85. An insightful overview of Northern Cheyenne and Southern Cheyenne history is in Hoxie, *Encyclopedia of North American Indians*, 110–14. For the Dog Soldiers, see Afton, Halaas, Masich, and Ellis, *Cheyenne Dog Soldiers*.

8. Hoxie, *Encyclopedia of North American Indians*, 113; West, *Contested Plains*, 88–89; Kappler, *Indian Affairs*, 2:595; Utley, *Frontiersmen in Blue*, 113–17. For the presence of Cheyennes at Blue Water Creek, see Drum, "Reminiscences of the Indian Fight at Ash Hollow," 151.

9. West, *Contested Plains*, 88–91. The Solomon's Fork encounter is explicated in Chalfant, *Cheyennes and Horse Soldiers*.

10. D. D. Mitchell to Orland Brown, in *Report of the Commissioner of Indian Affairs, 1849–50* (Washington: Government Printing Office, 1850), 132, quoted in West, *Contested Plains*, 92.

11. Berthrong, *Southern Cheyennes*, 148–52; West, *Contested Plains*, 281–82; Grinnell, *Fighting Cheyennes*, 120; Hoig, *Sand Creek Massacre*, 12–17.

12. Utley, *Frontiersmen in Blue*, 281–83; Josephy, *Civil War in the American West*, 292–94; West, *Contested Plains*, 286–87.

13. Roberts, "Sand Creek," 76–108; Utley, *Frontiersmen in Blue*, 284; Grinnell, *Fighting Cheyennes*, 121–29; Josephy, *Civil War in the American West*, 295, 297–98; Berthrong, *Southern Cheyennes*, 155, 158–61, 166–69.

14. Utley, *Frontiersmen in Blue*, 284–85; Josephy, *Civil War in the American West*, 299.

15. Utley, *Frontiersmen in Blue*, 285–87; Berthrong, *Southern Cheyennes*, 176–91; Hoig, *Sand Creek Massacre*, 36–90; West, *Contested Plains*, 289–91; Grinnell, *Fighting Cheyennes*, 131–42. Chivington, Curtis's inspector general, and Evans quoted in Josephy, *Civil War in the American West*, 300, 303.

16. Hoig, *Sand Creek Massacre*, 91–97; Utley, *Frontiersmen in Blue*, 287–89; Josephy, *Civil War in the American West*, 301–4; Berthrong, *Southern Cheyennes*, 193–208; Grinnell, *Fighting Cheyennes*, 155–58. For a participant's view of these broad operations, see Ware, *Indian War of 1864*.

17. Hoig, *Sand Creek Massacre*, 28–107; Utley, *Frontiersmen in Blue*, 290–91; Josephy, *Civil War in the American West*, 305–6; West, *Contested Plains*, 291; Grinnell, *Fighting Cheyennes*, 152–53.

18. Berthrong, *Southern Cheyennes*, 210–13; Utley, *Frontiersmen in Blue*, 291; Hoig, *Sand Creek Massacre*, 110–28; Josephy, *Civil War in the American West*, 306–7 (quotes, 307); West, *Contested Plains*, 295; Grinnell, *Fighting Cheyennes*, 153–54.

19. Utley, *Frontiersmen in Blue*, 292–93; Hoig, *Sand Creek Massacre*, 129–32; Berthrong, *Southern Cheyennes*, 214–15; West, *Contested Plains*, 297–98; Josephy, *Civil War in the American West*, 307–8.

20. Utley, *Frontiersmen in Blue*, 293–94; Hoig, *Sand Creek Massacre*, 135–43; Grinnell, *Fighting Cheyennes*, 159–62; Chivington quoted in testimony by Lieutenant Joseph A. Cramer, cited in Utley, *Frontiersmen in Blue*, 294. For a discussion of the status of Black Kettle's people prior to Chivington's attack on them, see West, *Contested Plains*, 298–300.

21. The locations of the Cheyenne camp components are laid out according to George Bent; see Hyde, *Life of George Bent*, 149. See also Powell, *People of the Sacred Mountain*, 1:299–300.

22. This account of Sand Creek is based upon information in Roberts, "Sand Creek," 421–41; Hoig, *Sand Creek Massacre*, 145–62; Utley, *Frontiersmen in Blue*, 295–96; Josephy, *Civil War in the American West*, 308–11; Powell, *People of the Sacred Mountain*, 1:301–9; Hyde, *Life of George Bent*, 151–56; Grinnell, *Fighting Cheyennes*, 163–73; and Berthrong, *Southern Cheyennes*, 217–22. Chivington's figure is in his report of Dec. 16, 1864, in *War of the Rebellion*, ser. 1, vol. 41, pt. 1, p. 949.

23. Josephy, *Civil War in the American West*, 311–12 (quote); Utley, *Frontiersmen in Blue*, 297 (quote), 309; Hoig, *Sand Creek Massacre*, 163–76 (quote, 166); Roberts, "Sand Creek," 479–521. The three published products of these investigations are: U.S. Senate, *Report of the Joint Committee on the Conduct of the War*; U.S. Senate, *Report of the Joint Special Committee*; and U.S. Senate, *Report of the Secretary of War*.

24. Powell, *People of the Sacred Mountain*, 1:309–10; Roberts, "Sand Creek," 684–91.

CHAPTER 2. WAR OR PEACE ON THE PLAINS

1. For these events, see Utley, *Frontiersmen in Blue*, 300–40; and Roberts, "Sand Creek," 523–66, 686. The quote is from Indian Agent Jesse H. Leavenworth to Brevet Major General John B. Sanborn, Aug. 1, 1865, Entry 769, Vol. 2, RG 393, Records of U.S. Army Continental Commands, Pt. 3, NA, 171.

2. Hyde, *Life of George Bent*, 159–62.

3. This summation of the rise of the Dog Soldiers vis-à-vis the tribal establishment is drawn from Moore, *Cheyenne Nation*, 191–99. See also Berthrong, *Southern Cheyennes*, 224–25, 228. For activities of Cheyenne warriors in attacking white outposts and settlements in the wake of Sand Creek, especially from the Cheyenne perspective, see Afton et al., *Cheyenne Dog Soldiers*.

4. Senate, *Report of the Secretary of War,* 144–45.

5. The complete texts of these treaties appear in Kappler, *Indian Affairs,* 2:594–96, 807–11.

6. Quoted in Berthrong, *Southern Cheyennes,* 242. Proceedings of the treaty council appear in *Report of the Commissioner of Indian Affairs, 1865,* 517–27.

7. Kappler, *Indian Affairs,* 2:887–92; Berthrong, *Southern Cheyennes,* 224–44. During the Little Arkansas councils, treaties were also concluded with the Kiowa Apaches, Kiowas, and Comanches. See Kappler, *Indian Affairs,* 2:891–95.

8. Berthrong, *Southern Cheyennes,* 256–57. For background on Wynkoop, see Isern, "Controversial Career of Edward W. Wynkoop," 1–18; and Wynkoop, *Tall Chief.*

9. Berthrong, *Southern Cheyennes,* 259–60.

10. Ibid., 261–64; Commissioner of Indian Affairs Dennis A. Cooley to Wynkoop, July 25, 1866, in *Report of the Commissioner of Indian Affairs, 1866,* 278–79, cited in ibid., 261; Wynkoop to Cooley, Aug. 11, 1866, in Letters Received, Upper Arkansas Agency, RG 75, Records of the Office of Indian Affairs, NA, quoted in ibid., 261–62.

11. Berthrong, *Southern Cheyennes,* 265–68; Sherman to John Sherman, Dec. 30, 1866, William T. Sherman Papers, Manuscript Division, LC, cited in ibid., 268 (quote); Hancock to Wynkoop, Dec. 17, 1866, in *Reports of Major General Hancock upon Indian Affairs with Accompanying Exhibits,* 14–15, cited in ibid., 268 (quote).

12. Berthrong, *Southern Cheyennes,* 270–72.

13. Utley, *Frontier Regulars,* 115–20. See also Berthrong, *Southern Cheyennes,* 39–47. Personal accounts of Hancock's campaign appear in Hyde, *Life of George Bent,* 255–66; and Custer, *My Life on the Plains,* 23–64.

14. Hyde, *Life of George Bent,* 268–72.

15. Berthrong, *Southern Cheyennes,* 289.

16. Ibid., 290–91.

17. Barnitz and Barnitz, *Life in Custer's Cavalry,* 110.

18. Hyde, *Life of George Bent,* 283–84.

19. *Proceedings of the Great Peace Commission,* 80, 82.

20. Berthrong, *Southern Cheyennes,* 294–97; Jones, *Treaty of Medicine Lodge,* 98. Black Kettle's discomfiture as a peace proponent vis-à-vis other Cheyenne leaders at the proceedings was noticed by some of the reporters present. See ibid., 138–40.

21. Kappler, *Indian Affairs,* 2:985.

22. Ibid., 985. Discussion of provisions is in Berthrong, *Southern Cheyennes,* 297–99; and West, *Contested Plains,* 310.

23. Kappler, *Indian Affairs,* 2:984, 989; Jones, *Treaty of Medicine Lodge,* 165–87, 205–6; Berthrong, *Southern Cheyennes,* 298–99. A contemporary summary of the treaty, along with others negotiated with the plains tribes in 1867–68, appears in *American Annual Cyclopaedia and Register of Important Events of the Year 1868,* 379–80. For a military observer's contemporary view of the events, see Barnitz and Barnitz, *Life in Custer's Cavalry,* 105–16.

24. Barnitz and Barnitz, *Life in Custer's Cavalry*, 115; Berthrong, *Southern Cheyennes*, 299–301.

25. Wynkoop to Murphy, Feb. 1, 1868, in Senate, *Letter of the Secretary of the Interior*, 1–2; Smith to Murphy, Feb. 20, 1868, Box 1, Entry 2601, RG 393, Pt. 1, NA.

26. Murphy to Nathaniel G. Taylor, Feb. 20, 1868, in Senate, *Letter of the Secretary of the Interior*, 3; Wynkoop to Murphy, Feb. 1, 1868, in ibid., 2 (quote).

27. Moore, *The Cheyenne*, 112–13; Hoebel, *The Cheyennes*, 70–72.

CHAPTER 3. SUMMER DEPREDATIONS

1. Major Henry Douglas, Third Infantry, to Colonel Chauncy McKeever, AAG, Department of the Missouri, Jan. 16, 1868, Box 1, Entry 2601, RG 393, Records of U.S. Army Continental Commands, Pt. 1, NA; Captain James W. Walsh to First Lieutenant Richard H. Pratt, Tenth Cavalry, Mar. 12, 1868, Box 4, Entry 2601, ibid.

2. Wynkoop to Murphy, Apr. 10, 1868, in Senate, *Letter of the Secretary of the Interior*, 3–4; Effingham H. Nichols to Secretary of the Interior Orville H. Browning, Apr. 11, 1868, Box 4, Entry 2601, RG 393, Pt. 1; Captain J. Schuyler Crosby to Captain Edwin Butler, Fifth Infantry, May 16, 1868, Entry 2571, ibid. This railroad company was distinct from the Union Pacific Railroad, which built from Omaha to Utah.

3. Thian, *Notes Illustrating the Military Geography of the United States*, 76. Forts Morgan and Sedgwick, Colorado Territory, along with the stage road from Fort Sedgwick to Denver and New Mexico, were made part of the Department of the Platte in 1867. Ibid.

4. For explication of Sheridan and his military philosophy, see Hutton, *Phil Sheridan and His Army*, passim; and Utley, *Frontier Regulars*, 142–43. The roots of the "total war" concept as applied in Indian warfare have been debated, with some historians believing that its antecedents lay in the devastation techniques of Sherman's and Sheridan's armies in the South during the Civil War (see, e.g., Utley, *Cavalier in Buckskin*, 60), while others suggest that it evolved more-or-less naturally from unique postwar frontier army and Indian circumstances and conditions (Wooster, *The Military and United States Indian Policy*, 135–43). For a balanced discussion, see Jamieson, *Crossing the Deadly Ground*, 50–52. The answer probably lies somewhere in between, but it should be noted that army surprise attacks on Indian villages are on record before and during the Civil War.

5. Sheridan's report, Oct. 15, 1868, in *Report of the Secretary of War, 1868*, 16–17.

6. Major Henry Douglas to Captain Samuel L. Barr, AAAG, District of the Upper Arkansas, Mar. 21, 1868, Box 1, Entry 2601, RG 393, Pt. 1; Major Meredith H. Kidd's weekly report of Indian movements, enclosed in (illegible) to AAG, Department of the Missouri, Mar. 25, 1868, Box 4, Entry 2601, ibid.; Douglas to Barr, Mar. 28, 1868, Box 1, Entry 2601, ibid.; Captain Nicholas Nolan to Barr, Apr. 5, 1868, Box 3, Entry 2601, ibid.; Major John E. Yard to Barr,

Apr. 17, 1868, Box 4, Entry 2601, ibid.; Douglas to Barr, Apr. 18, 1868, Box 1, Entry 2601, ibid.; Douglas to Barr, May 5, 1868, ibid.; Lieutenant Colonel Alfred Sully to AAG, Department of the Missouri, July 18, 1868, Box 4, Entry 2601, ibid.

7. James R. Mead to Commander, U.S. Forces, Mouth of Little Arkansas, May 18, 1868, and note from Louis Booth, May 18, 1868, enclosed in Second Lieutenant Elbridge G. Manning, Fifth Infantry, to Captain Mason Howard, May 19, 1868, Box 3, Entry 2601, RG 393, Pt. 1; Manning to Captain Samuel L. Barr, AAAG, District of the Upper Arkansas, May 1, 1868, ibid.; J. W. Douglas to Sheridan, May 23, 1868, Box 1, Entry 2601, ibid.; Brigadier General Alfred Sully, District of the Upper Arkansas, to AAG, Department of the Missouri, May 25, 1868, Box 4, Entry 2601, ibid.

8. Sheridan to AAG, Division of the Missouri, May 17, 1868, Entry 2571, RG 393, Pt. 1, 471; Sheridan to Sully, May 27, 1868, ibid., 469.

9. Major James W. Forsyth, Tenth Cavalry, to AAG, Department of the Missouri, June 9, 1868, Box 3, Entry 2601, RG 393, Pt. 1; Sully to AAG, Department of the Missouri, June 9, 1868, Box 4, Entry 2601, ibid.; Hyde, *Life of George Bent*, 288.

10. Major John E. Yard, Tenth Cavalry, to AAG, District of the Upper Arkansas, July 20, 1868, Box 4, Entry 2601, RG 393, Pt. 1; Sully to AAG, Department of the Missouri, July 18, 1868, ibid.; Sherman to Sheridan, July 7, 1868, Box 3, Entry 2601, ibid.

11. Taylor to Browning, June 24, 1868, in Senate, *Letter of the Secretary of the Interior*, 4–5; Taylor to Murphy, June 25, 1868, in ibid., 5; Wynkoop to Murphy, July 20, 1868, in ibid.

12. Taylor to Murphy, July 23, 1868, in ibid., 6–7; Taylor to Wynkoop, July 23, 1868, in ibid., 7; Wynkoop to Murphy, Aug. 10, 1868, in ibid., 9; Berthrong, *Southern Cheyennes*, 305.

13. Sheridan stated that the party was composed of "about two hundred Cheyennes, four Arapahoes, and twenty Siouxs." "Report of Major General P. H. Sheridan," Sept. 26, 1868, in *Report of the Secretary of War, 1868*, 11 (hereafter referred to as Sheridan's report, Sept. 26, 1868).

14. Major Thomas C. English, Fifth Infantry, to AAG, Department of the Missouri, Aug. 18, 1868, Box 2, Entry 2601, RG 393, Pt. 1; Sully to AAG, Department of the Missouri, Aug. 19, 1868, Box 4, Entry 2601, ibid. For the Saline and Solomon raids, see ibid.; "List of murders, outrages, and depredations committed by Indians from 3rd Aug. to 24th Oct., 1868, officially reported to Headquarters Department of the Missouri, in the field," appended to Sheridan to Sherman, Sept. 26, 1868, Folder 1, Box C-46, Ben Clark Collection, Western History Collections, University of Oklahoma Library, Norman, 3–5; Sheridan's report, Sept. 26, 1868, 13–16; Hyde, *Life of George Bent*, 288–89; Berthrong, *Southern Cheyennes*, 305–6.

15. "Statement of Edmond Guerrier," Feb. 9, 1869, Philip H. Sheridan Papers, Manuscript Division, LC, Roll 76; Wynkoop to Murphy, Sept. 10, 1868, in Senate, *Letter of the Secretary of the Interior*, 16–17. This interpretation for the raiding in Kansas in the summer of 1868 is adapted from a thesis expressed for the Delaware Indians in Weslager, *Delaware Indians* (230) and used in regard to the Northern Cheyenne Indians in Powers, "Northern Cheyenne

Trek through Western Kansas," 10–11, 31–32. Sheridan's quote is from Sheridan to Sherman, Sept. 26, 1868, Folder 1, Box C-46, Clark Collection.

16. "List of murders, outrages, and depredations," 3; Captain William H. Penrose to AAG, District of the Upper Arkansas, Aug. 30, 1868, Entry 2 (Fort Lyon), RG 393, Pt. 5; Major Henry Douglas, Third Infantry, to AAAG, District of the Upper Arkansas, Aug. 20, 1868, copy in Folder 3, Box 120, Walter S. Campbell Collection, Western History Collections, University of Oklahoma Library, Norman; Douglas to AAAG, District of the Upper Arkansas, Aug. 22, 1868, ibid.; Douglas to AAAG, District of the Upper Arkansas, Aug. 24, 1868, ibid.; "Report of Lieutenant General W. T. Sherman," Nov. 1, 1868, in *Report of the Secretary of War, 1868*, 3–5 (hereafter referred to as Sherman's report, 1868); "Tabular statement of murders, outrages, robberies, and depredations committed by Indians in department of the Missouri and Northern Texas in 1868 and 1869 (exclusive of military engagements), and officially reported to headquarters department of the Missouri," in *Report of the Secretary of War, 1869*, 53; Montgomery, "Fort Wallace and Its Relation to the Frontier," 25–26; Hyde, *Life of George Bent*, 295.

17. "Report of an Interview between Colonel E. W. Wynkoop, United States Indian Agent, and Little Rock, a Cheyenne Chief, Held at Fort Larned, Kansas, Aug. 19, 1868, in the Present [*sic*, Presence] of Lieutenant S. M. Robbins, 7th United States Cavalry, John S. Smith, United States Indian Interpreter, and James Morrison, Scout for Indian Agency," in Senate, *Letter of the Secretary of the Interior*, 19–21.

18. Ibid., 21.

19. J. W. McClure and G. D. Houston, to Sherman, Aug. 17, 1868, Box 3, Entry 2601, RG 393, Pt. 1; Crawford to Sheridan, Aug. 19, 1868, Box 2, Entry 2601, ibid.; First Lieutenant Aug. Kaiser, Third Infantry, to First Lieutenant Edward A. Belger, Third Infantry, AAAG, District of the Upper Arkansas, Aug. 24, 1868, ibid.; Sheridan to Sherman, Sept. 26, 1868, Folder 1, Box C-46, Clark Collection; Sheridan's report, Sept. 26, 1868, 12; Hutton, *Phil Sheridan and His Army*, 41, 43; Sheridan to Crawford, quoted in Montgomery, "Fort Wallace and Its Relation to the Frontier," 24–25. Sherman also embraced the view that the outbreak along the Saline and Solomon was inspired by the success of the northern Indians in closing the Bozeman Trail forts in Wyoming. Sherman's report, 1868, 3.

20. Grierson to AAG, Department of the Missouri, July 4, 1868, Box 2, Entry 2601, RG 393, Pt.1; Sully to AAG, Department of the Missouri, July 12, 1868, Box 4, Entry 2601, ibid.; Belger to commanding officers of Fort Hays, Camp End of Track, Detachment Tenth Cavalry, Monument Station, and Fort Wallace, n.d., Entry 2633, ibid.; Belger to commanding officers at Fort Hays, Monument Station, and Camp at End of Track, July 16, 1868, ibid.; Sully to AAG, Department of the Missouri, Aug. 13, 1868, Box 4, Entry 2601, ibid.

21. Sully to Commanding Officer, Fort Wallace, Aug. 12, 1868, Entry 2633, ibid.; Sully to Commanding Officer, Fort Hays, Aug. 12, 1868, ibid.; Sully to AAG, Department of the Missouri, Aug. 13, 1868, Box 4, Entry 2601, ibid.; Sully to Sheridan, Aug. 16, 1868, ibid.; Circular, Headquarters, District of the Upper Arkansas, Aug. 22, 1868, Entry 2633, ibid. Two blockhouses were built, one at Spillman Creek at the forks of the Solomon, the other along the

Republican, each guarded by twenty men of the Thirty-Eighth Infantry. Special Orders No. 121, Headquarters, District of the Upper Arkansas, Aug. 21, 1868, Entry 2633, ibid.; Special Orders No. 123, Headquarters, District of the Upper Arkansas, Aug. 25, 1868, ibid.

22. Belger to First Lieutenant Joseph Hale, Third Infantry, Aug. 24, 1868, ibid.; Belger to Commanding Officer, Fort Dodge, Aug. 24, 1868, ibid.; Belger to Commanding Office, Fort Lyon, Aug. 24, 1868, ibid.; Belger to Commanding Officer, Company C, Tenth Cavalry, Aug. 24, 1868, ibid.; Belger to Elliott, Aug. 24, 1868, ibid.; Belger to Elliott, Aug. 25, 1868, ibid.; Special Orders No. 117, Headquarters, District of the Upper Arkansas, Aug. 12, 1868, ibid.; Special Orders No. 119, Headquarters, District of the Upper Arkansas, Aug. 15, 1868, ibid.; Special Orders No. 121, Headquarters, District of the Upper Arkansas, Aug. 21, 1868, ibid.; Special Orders No. 122, Aug. 22, 1868, ibid.; Special Orders No. 125, Aug. 25, 1868, ibid..

23. Acting Commissioner of Indian Affairs Charles E. Mix to Acting Secretary of the Interior W. T Otto, Sept. 7, 1868, in Senate, *Letter of the Secretary of the Interior*, 8; "Treaty with the Cheyenne and Arapaho, 1867," in Kappler, *Indian Affairs*, 2:988; Mix to Browning, Aug. 22, 1868, in Senate, *Letter of the Secretary of the Interior*, 9–10.

24. Sherman to Browning, Aug. 11, 1868, Box 3, Entry 2601, RG 393, Pt. 1; Appended to Sherman's report, 1868, 340–41; Hutton, *Phil Sheridan and His Army*, 42–43; Heitman, *Historical Register and Dictionary of the United States Army*, 1:517. Although a close friend of Sherman, Hazen became engaged in numerous controversies with other officers during his career and managed to offend elements of the military hierarchy in Washington. Despite this, he eventually became chief signal officer of the army and won promotion to brigadier general. For his biography, see Kroeker, *Great Plains Command*. For Hazen's recollections of his appointment and of some of the surrounding controversies involving his performance, see Hazen, "Some Corrections of 'Life on the Plains,'" *Chronicles of Oklahoma*, 295–318.

25. Douglas to Captain Henry Asbury, Sept. 3, 1868, Department of Missouri, Selected Letters Received, 1878[sic]–1879, Records of the U.S. Army Commands (transcription by General Services Administration, National Archives, 1949, in Folder 3, Box 120, Campbell Collection), p. 188; Douglas to Captain Myles W. Keogh, Seventh Cavalry, Sept. 2, 1868, in ibid., 188–89; General Field Orders No. 1, Headquarters in the Field, District of the Upper Arkansas, Sept. 4, 1868, Entry 2633, RG 393, Pt. 1; Penrose to AAAG, Department of the Missouri, Sept. 10, 1868, Entry 2, Vol. 1 (Fort Lyon, Colorado), RG 393, Pt. 5; Montgomery, "Fort Wallace and Its Relation to the Frontier," 26.

26. Utley, *Frontier Regulars*, 143–44; Leckie, *Military Conquest of the Southern Plains*, 89–90; Wynkoop to Murphy, Sept. 3, 1868, in Senate, *Letter of the Secretary of the Interior*, 17–18; Murphy to Mix, Sept. 29, 1868, in ibid., 15–16.

27. Sheridan's report, Oct. 15, 1868, 349–50; Utley, *Frontier Regulars*, 145–47; Hutton, *Phil Sheridan and His Army*, 45.

CHAPTER 4. MOVEMENTS AND STRATEGIES

1. Sheridan to Governor Samuel J. Crawford, Sept. 10, 1868, Governors' Correspondence—Crawford, Manuscript Division, Kansas State Historical Society, Topeka, as cited in White, "General Sully's Expedition to the North Canadian," 84; Hutton, *Phil Sheridan and His Army*, 49.

2. Special Field Orders No. 4, Headquarters District of the Upper Arkansas (in the field), Sept. 6, 1868, Entry 2633, RG 393, Records of U.S. Army Continental Commands, Pt. 1, NA; Special Field Orders No. 5, Headquarters District of the Upper Arkansas (in the field), Sept. 7, 1868, ibid. Military data on Sully is in Heitman, *Historical Register and Dictionary of the United States Army*, 1:935–36. A brief biography is in Warner, *Generals in Blue*, 488–89. A full-length treatment (though strangely devoid of substantive material regarding his 1868 campaign) is in Sully, *No Tears for the General*. For his earlier Indian campaigns, see Utley, *Frontiersmen in Blue*, 271–80, 308, 322–23, 332–37.

3. Sully to AAG, Department of the Missouri, Sept. 16, 1868, Box 4, Entry 2601, RG 393, Pt. 1; Hyde, *Life of George Bent*, 293, 293 n. 12; Harvey, "Campaigning with Sheridan," 74. A typescript of Harvey's original diary is in Box 6, Edward S. Godfrey Papers, Manuscript Division, LC; Barnitz and Barnitz, *Life in Custer's Cavalry*, 186, 189.

4. Clark to Herbert Myrick, July 15, 1904, Myrick Collection, The Huntington Library, San Marino, Calif. (copy furnished by Bob Rea, Fort Supply Historic Site, Okla.). An alternative account suggests it was Captain Louis M. Hamilton's company that engaged the Indians. James M. Bell account, n.d., Folder 1, Box 2, Field Notes, Topics A–L, Walter M. Camp Manuscripts, Manuscripts Department, Lilly Library, Indiana University, Bloomington (copy, Notebook 4, No. 1, Kenneth Hammer Collection, Little Bighorn Battlefield National Monument, Crow Agency, Mt.).

5. Sully to AAG, Department of the Missouri, Sept. 16, 1868, Box 4, Entry 2601, RG 393, Pt. 1; Harvey, "Campaigning with Sheridan," 74; Bell account. See also the account of Captain Albert Barnitz in Barnitz and Barnitz, *Life in Custer's Cavalry*, 186.

6. Barnitz and Barnitz, *Life in Custer's Cavalry*, 187; *Leavenworth Times and Conservative*, Sept. 24, 1868, as cited in White, "General Sully's Expedition," 89; Sully to AAG, Department of the Missouri, Sept. 16, 1868, Box 4, Entry 2601, RG 393, Pt. 1. See also Harvey, "Campaigning with Sheridan," 75; Bob Rea, conversation with the author, Fort Supply Historic Site, Okla., Dec. 2000. Of this lively action, Barnitz wrote: "I was directed to advance directly through the sand hills, and had forded a stream and gone forward some distance, when 'F' Troop was directed to cross and advance as skirmishers, dismounted. I was moving forward a skirmish line mounted with a platoon in reserve, and had dislodged the Indians from several hills in my front, when they at length, about a hundred of them, occupied a hill on my right, and a little to my rear, and made a stand and succeeded in killing the man [of Company F] . . . , besides inflicting some other damage, until a cross fire from my skirmishers hurried them out of their position." Barnitz and Barnitz, *Life in Custer's Cavalry*, 190.

7. Barnitz and Barnitz, *Life in Custer's Cavalry*, 190. The site of Sully's fight of September 13 is east of the present Fort Supply Lake (a reservoir), about three miles southeast of the present Fort Supply Historic Site. Rea, "Washita Trail," 248–49.

8. Barnitz and Barnitz, *Life in Custer's Cavalry*, 196; Harvey, "Campaigning with Sheridan," 75. Francis M. Gibson, then second lieutenant, Company A, Seventh Cavalry, recalled: "Had our attack been made with as much vigor and determination as the Indians displayed in their resistance, the hills could easily have been taken by the dismounted cavalry, and, leaving the infantry to guard the train, we could have pushed on to their villages, which, we afterwards learned, were but a short distance beyond, and the Washita campaign would in all probability never have been necessary. . . . General Sully for some reason did not consider this plan feasible. . . . We had quite an important victory within easy reach had we chosen to seize it." Gibson, "The Battle of the Washita," ed. Edward S. Luce, in Carroll, *Washita!* 5–6. In fact, the principal concentration of Cheyennes and Arapahos was in the vicinity of the Antelope Hills and the South Canadian, where the people of Black Kettle and Little Raven had been joined by some Lakotas from the north. Powell, *People of the Sacred Mountain*, 1:594.

9. Barnitz and Barnitz, *Life in Custer's Cavalry*, 187–88, 190–91; Sully to AAG, Department of the Missouri, Sept. 16, 1868, Box 4, Entry 2601, RG 393, Pt. 1; Sully to AAG, Department of the Missouri, Sept. 16, 1868, ibid.; Special Field Orders No. 6, Headquarters District of the Upper Arkansas (in the field), Sept. 16, 1868, Entry 2633, ibid.; Special Field Orders No. 7, Headquarters District of the Upper Arkansas (in the field), Sept. 19, 1868, ibid. In addition to the above-cited materials, for Sully's expedition, see "Record of Events of the Seventh Cavalry for the Year 1868," in Carroll, *Washita!* 27–35; Gibson, "Battle of the Washita," 5–6; Sheridan's report, Oct. 15, 1868, in *Report of the Secretary of War, 1868*, 18; Hutton, *Phil Sheridan and His Army*, 48–49; Leckie, *Military Conquest of the Southern Plains*, 81–83; Utley, *Frontier Regulars*, 147; Hoig, *Tribal Wars of the Southern Plains*, 244–47; Berthrong, *Southern Cheyennes*, 318–20.

10. Sherman to Brigadier General Christopher C. Augur, Sept. 28, 1868, Christopher C. Augur Papers, Illinois State Historical Library, Springfield, as cited in White, "General Sully's Expedition," 93; Elliott to Theodore R. Davis, Oct. 31, 1868, Theodore R. Davis Collection, Manuscript Division, Kansas State Historical Society, as cited in ibid., 93 (reproduced in "Sidelights on the Washita Fight," *The Westerners Brand Book* 5 [Dec. 1948]: 57–58); Edward S. Godfrey, "Some Reminiscences, Including an Account of General Sully's Expedition against the Southern Plains Indians," 421–25; White, "General Sully's Expedition," 94–95; Godfrey, "Reminiscences, Including the Washita Battle," 481 (quote).

11. General Field Orders No. 3, Headquarters District of the Upper Arkansas (in the Field), Fort Dodge, Kansas, Sept. 26, 1868, Entry 2633, RG 393, Pt. 1.

12. Sheridan's report, Oct. 15, 1868. Companies of the Tenth Cavalry had been operating regularly out of Fort Wallace, concentrating in the areas of the Smoky Hill and its tributaries, as well as of the Arkansas and its affluents. See

"Tabular Statement of the Marches, Scouts, and Expeditions Made by Detachment 10 U.S. Cavalry," Box 1, Entry 2601, RG 393, Pt. 1.

13. Sheridan's report, Oct. 15, 1868, 350. This engagement, known as the Battle of Beecher's Island, is recounted in context and detail in Monnett, *Battle of Beecher Island*. See also Dixon, *Hero of Beecher Island*. For overviews, see Leckie, *Military Conquest of the Southern Plains*, 75–80; Utley, *Frontier Regulars*, 147–48; Hoig, *Tribal Wars of the Southern Plains*, 248–52; Hutton, *Phil Sheridan and His Army*, 46–48; Berthrong, *Southern Cheyennes*, 311–14; and Brady, *Indian Fights and Fighters*, 72–122.

14. Sherman to Inspector General, Sept. 17, 1868, Box 3, Entry 1601, RG 393, Pt. 1 (quote); Sherman to Sheridan, Sept. 17, 1868, Box 3, Entry 2601, ibid.; Sherman to Sheridan, Sept. 17, 1868, ibid. (quote); Sheridan's report, Oct. 15, 1868; Hutton, *Phil Sheridan and His Army*, 49–50.

15. Sherman to Secretary of War John M. Schofield, Sept. 19, 1868, in Senate, *Letter of the Secretary of the Interior*, 22; Sherman to Schofield, Sept. 26, 1868, in ibid., 22–23; Hazen, "Some Corrections of 'Life on the Plains,'" *Chronicles of Oklahoma*, 300–301; Berthrong, *Southern Cheyennes*, 320–21; Leckie, *Military Conquest of the Southern Plains*, 90–91.

16. Harvey, "Campaigning with Sheridan," 76. For troop dispositions for the remainder of September, see "Record of Events of the Seventh Cavalry for the Year 1868" [particularly that for Company G, Seventh Cavalry], in Carroll, *Washita!* 30–31.

17. Harvey, "Campaigning with Sheridan," 77–78. See also the official report of this attack in Douglas to AAAG, Department of the Missouri, [Fort Hays, Kansas], Oct. 4, 1868, Department of Missouri, Selected Letters Received, 1878[sic]–1879, Records of the U.S. Army Commands (transcription by General Services Administration, National Archives, 1949, in Folder 3, Box 120, Walter S. Campbell Collection, Western History Collections, University of Oklahoma Library, Norman), p. 188.

18. Sherman to Schofield, Oct. 5, 1868, Philip H. Sheridan Papers, Manuscript Division, LC, Roll 80; White, "White Women Captives of Southern Plains Indians," 337–38.

19. Powell, *People of the Sacred Mountain*, 1:594; "List of Murders, Outrages, and Depredations Committed by Indians from 3d Aug. to 24th Oct., 1868, Officially Reported to Headquarters Department of the Missouri, in the Field," appended to Sheridan's report, Sept. 26, 1868, 13–16; Penrose to AAAG, Department of the Missouri, Fort Harker, Kansas, Oct. 15, 1868, Entry 2, Vol. 1 (Fort Lyon), RG 393, Pt. 5; Telegram, Penrose to Sheridan, Oct. 15, 1868, ibid.

20. Sheridan's report, Nov. 1, 1869, in *Report of the Secretary of War, 1869*, 44–45; Sheridan to Sherman, Sept. 28, 1868, Sheridan Papers, Roll 80; Godfrey, "Reminiscences, Including the Washita Battle," 484; Leckie, *Military Conquest of the Southern Plains*, 92–93; Utley, *Frontier Regulars*, 149–50. This plan outline, written long after the fact, reflects what actually occurred. Sheridan originally planned to send Sully, with eleven companies of the Seventh Cavalry and four companies of infantry, toward the Wichita Mountains in southwestern Indian Territory while sending four companies of the Tenth Cavalry and one of infantry to the Antelope Hills. Three companies of cavalry and one of infantry would patrol the stage line west of Fort Wallace. "I think this

arrangement very good, and if the commanders do well there will be much damage done to the Indians." Sheridan to Sherman, Sept. 23, 1868. Sheridan Papers, Roll 80.

21. Sheridan to Crawford, Oct. 9, 1868, Sheridan Papers, Roll 80.

22. Sheridan's report, Oct. 15, 1868, 351. "In compliance with Special Orders No. 19, Ex. 2, Headquarters Department of the Missouri (in the field) dated Fort Hays, Kan. Oct. 4th 1868, Brevet Major General George A. Custer, Lieut. Col. 7th U.S. Cavalry, will, upon receipt of this order, assume command of his regiment in the field." Special Field Orders No. 18, Headquarters District of the Upper Arkansas (in the field), Oct. 17, 1868, Box 3, Entry 2601, RG 393, Pt. 1; "Record of Events of the Seventh Cavalry for the Year 1868," in Carroll, *Washita!* 27–35; Gibson, "Battle of the Washita," 9. Custer's description of the engagement on Oct. 11 is in Custer, *Following the Guidon,* 6–8. Lieutenant Godfrey stated that Sully had requested Custer to take over command of the regiment during the upcoming campaign. "Reminiscences, Including the Washita Battle," 1. In his court-martial, Custer had been found guilty of leaving his command without permission, of illegal conduct in ordering his officers to shoot deserters, of abandoning two of his dead, and of excessively marching his troops. Monaghan, *Custer,* 300–303. For details, see Frost, *Court-Martial of General George Armstrong Custer.*

23. Custer claimed that Sheridan told him concerning the upcoming campaign, "I rely upon you in everything, and shall send you on this expedition without giving you any orders, leaving you to act entirely upon your judgment." Custer to Elizabeth Custer, Oct. 4, 1868, in Custer, *Following the Guidon,* 11–12. Since his death at the Battle of the Little Bighorn in 1876, George A. Custer has become one of the most dominant and controversial figures in American military history. The best biographies are Utley, *Cavalier in Buckskin;* Barnett, *Touched by Fire;* Wert, *Custer;* and Monaghan, *Custer.* Custer's Civil War engagements are especially well chronicled in Urwin, *Custer Victorious.*

24. Barnitz to wife Jennie, Oct. 21, 1868, in Barnitz and Barnitz, *Life in Custer's Cavalry,* 200. See also Barnitz to wife Jennie, Oct. 28, 1868, ibid., 202.

25. Sheridan's report, Oct. 15, 1868, 352; Leckie, *Military Conquest of the Southern Plains,* 84–87; Brady, *Indian Fights and Fighters,* 123–45.

CHAPTER 5. CAMP SUPPLY

1. As late as November 19, unidentified warriors killed a civilian and attempted to stampede cattle and mules near Fort Dodge before being run off by a detachment of Tenth Cavalry. The tribesmen withdrew below the Arkansas after firing the grass on the north side, thereby preventing the soldiers from continuing the pursuit. Captain Andrew Sheridan to AAG, Department of the Missouri, Fort Hays, Nov. 19, 1868, Box 4, Entry 2601, RG 393, Records of U.S. Army Continental Commands, Pt. 1, NA.

2. Custer intimated that the delay had less to do with supplies than it did with purposefully awaiting the proper seasonal changes during which to go after the tribes. "[We planned] to defer our movement against the hostile

tribes until the last traces of the fall season had disappeared, and winter in all its bitter force should be upon us." *My Life on the Plains*, 204–6.

3. Custer to General Sheridan, Oct. 28, 1868, Philip H. Sheridan Papers, Manuscript Division, LC, Roll 3. "The 7th U.S. Cavalry under command of Bvt. Maj. Genl. Geo. A. Custer and the Battalion of Infantry under command of Bvt. Maj. J. H. Page 3rd Infantry will be ready to move on the 9th inst., with these Headquarters, to a point on the north branch of the Canadian River south of here. At this point this column will be joined by the Regiment of Kansas Volunteers under Col. Crawford." General Field Orders No. 6, Headquarters District of the Upper Arkansas, in the field, Nov. 7, 1868, Entry 2633, RG 393, Pt. 1. Winfield Harvey stated that the departure was planned for the tenth. "Campaigning with Sheridan," 82.

4. For histories of the Seventh Regiment, U.S. Cavalry, see E. A. Garlington, "The Seventh Regiment of Cavalry," in *The Army of the United States: Historical Sketches of Staff and Line with Portraits of Generals-in-Chief*, ed. Theophilus F. Rodenbough and William L. Haskin (Governors Island, N.Y.: Military Service Institution of the United States, 1896), 251–67; and Chandler, *Of Garry Owen in Glory*. Regimental strength is calculated from Regimental Returns of the Seventh Cavalry, Nov. 1868, Little Bighorn Battlefield National Monument, Crow Agency, Mont., microfilm. For the composition of the army as a whole during the so-called Indian wars period, see Rickey, *Forty Miles a Day on Beans and Hay*; Foner, *United States Soldier between Two Wars*; and Coffman, *Old Army*.

5. The Seventh received approximately 117 recruits, who were distributed among the companies as follows: A, 17; B, 12; C, 9; D, 15; E, 7; F, 0; G, 13; H, 10; I, 10; K, 12; L (not present), 0; and M, 12. Information compiled from Mangum, "Muster Roll 7th Cavalry."

6. Custer, *My Life on the Plains*, 206–8; Godfrey, "Reminiscences, Including the Washita Battle," 482–83. Other records indicate that the sharpshooter unit numbered but thirty men. Mangum, "Muster Roll 7th Cavalry."

7. Special Field Orders No. 29, Headquarters District of the Upper Arkansas, in the field, Oct. 25, 1868, Entry 2633, RG 393, Pt. 1; Special Field Orders No. 19, Headquarters District of the Upper Arkansas, in the field, Oct. 8, 1868, ibid.; Special Field Orders No. 15, Headquarters District of the Upper Arkansas, in the field, Oct. 4, 1868, ibid.; Custer to General Sheridan, Oct. 28, 1868, Sheridan Papers; Special Field Orders No. 5, Headquarters District of the Upper Arkansas, in the field, Oct. 28, 1868, Entry 2633, RG 393, Pt. 1; General Field Orders No. 2, Headquarters District of the Upper Arkansas, Sept. 25, 1868, ibid.; Special Field Orders No. 33, Headquarters District of the Upper Arkansas, in the field, Nov. 1, 1868, ibid.; Special Field Orders No. 34, Headquarters District of the Upper Arkansas, in the field, Nov. 6, 1868, ibid.; Custer, *My Life on the Plains*, 204, 206; Custer, *Following the Guidon*, 8; Godfrey, "Reminiscences, Including the Washita Battle," 482–83; Leckie, *Military Conquest of the Southern Plains*, 93. This totals twenty-seven wagons, plus seven ambulances for the various units. In all, there were "nearly four hundred army wagons," with the majority designated for hauling materials to build the supply camp as well as carrying provisions for the expedition. Godfrey, "Reminiscences, Including the Washita Battle," 483; Custer, *My Life on the Plains*, 210.

8. Custer to General Sheridan, incomplete, n.d. [late Oct. 1868], Sheridan Papers, Roll 3; Harvey, "Campaigning with Sheridan," 82. In addition, the farriers fashioned two extra horseshoes, precisely fitted to each animal's fore and hind hoofs, to be carried by their riders. Custer, *My Life on the Plains*, 206.

9. Godfrey, "Reminiscences, Including the Washita Battle," 483; Barnitz and Barnitz, *Life in Custer's Cavalry*, 205; Custer, *My Life on the Plains*, 208–9. See also Custer to Elizabeth Custer, Nov. 3, 1868, in Custer, *Following the Guidon*, 14. The "horse color" policy was implemented on November 3. See Harvey, "Campaigning with Sheridan," 81. "Coloring the horses" was not a practice unique to Custer but was a longstanding tradition in the army. Urwin, *United States Cavalry*, 73.

10. Special Field Orders No. 34, Headquarters District of the Upper Arkansas, in the field, Nov. 6, 1868, Entry 2633, RG 393, Pt. 1; *Army and Navy Journal*, Jan. 2, 1869; Custer, *My Life on the Plains*, 209–10; Mathews, *Osages*, 677–78; Leckie, *Military Conquest of the Southern Plains*, 93.

11. For details of this and other campaign clothing and accouterments, see McChristian, *U.S. Army in the West*, 12, 17–19, 20–21, 22, 23, 27–29, 32–33, 36, 69, 130, 132, 141, and passim. See also Scott, "Firearms Identification," passim. Custer perhaps did not acquire the first of his well-known buckskin outfits until the late winter of 1869. Douglas C. McChristian, "Plainsman—or Showman? George A. Custer's Buckskins," *Military Collector and Historian* 52 (spring 2000): 4. A Kansas volunteer, however, wrote in his diary on December 7 that Custer "wears a light colored hat and buckskin suit, the same as the scouts wear, with leather fringe on the seams of arms and legs." Spotts, *Campaigning with Custer*, 72.

12. Ryan, *Ten Years*, 47–48.

13. Francis M. Gibson, "The Battle of the Washita," in Carroll, *Washita!* 9.

14. General Field Orders No. 6, Headquarters District of the Upper Arkansas, in the field, Nov. 7, 1868, Entry 2633, RG 393, Pt. 1; Captain Andrew Sheridan, Third Infantry, to AAG, Department of the Missouri, Nov. 12, 1868, Box 4, Entry 2601, ibid.; *Army and Navy Journal*, Jan. 2, 1869.

15. Harvey, "Campaigning with Sheridan," 83. At the time, officers were usually referred to by virtue of their highest past real or brevet rank. Although Custer's regular grade was lieutenant colonel, he was referred to in the custom of the day as "general," reflecting either his real highest volunteer-army rank of major general or his regular-army brevet rank of major general, both garnered during the Civil War. Beyond quoted material and its use for background information about individuals, in this narrative officers will be referenced by their contemporary regular-army rank.

16. Godfrey, "Reminiscences, Including the Washita Battle," 485. Another member of the expedition remembered: "when the condition of the ground would allow, our wagon train traveled four abreast. The infantry was scattered among the wagons, and the cavalry marched in about six detachments, some of the companies on each side of the train, some as advance guard, and some as rear guard. With the wagons four deep, it, of course, shortened our flank, and rendered the wagon train less exposed to the attacks of Indians." Ryan, *Ten Years*, 46. See also Custer, *My Life on the Plains*, 210–11.

17. Ryan, *Ten Years*, 46–47.

18. General Field Orders No. 7, Headquarters District of the Upper Arkansas, Nov. 12, 1868, Entry 2633, RG 393, Pt. 1.

19. Conversely, Private Harvey noted on the sixteenth: "The buffalo are very scarce; we have killed none on this march yet." "Campaigning with Sheridan," 83.

20. Custer, *My Life on the Plains*, 211–12. Barnitz gave the date of Custer's request as November 19. Barnitz and Barnitz, *Life in Custer's Cavalry*, 207. Harvey makes no mention of the Indian trail in his entries for November 17, 18, or 19. "Campaigning with Sheridan," 83–84. Custer wrote: "Had the Kansas volunteers been here, as was expected, my orders would then have allowed me to follow the back trail of the war party right to their village." Custer, *Following the Guidon*, 16. Details of the march from Camp Sandy Forsyth, November 12–18, are in *New York Herald*, Dec. 12, 1868.

21. General Field Orders No. 8, Headquarters of troops operating south of the Ark's and Dist. Upp. Ark's, in the field, Camp Supply, I.T., Nov. 18, 1868, Entry 2633, RG 393, Pt. 1; *Army and Navy Journal*, Jan. 2, 1869; Special Field Orders No. 38, Headquarters District of the Upper Arkansas, in the field, Nov. 15, 1868, Entry 2633, RG 393, Pt. 1; Custer, *My Life on the Plains*, 212–13; Ryan, *Ten Years*, 46, 47; Gibson, "Battle of the Washita," 9; Godfrey, "Reminiscences, Including the Washita Battle," 485; "Record of Events of the Seventh Cavalry, Company G, Nov. 1868," in Carroll, *Washita!* 32; Barnitz and Barnitz, *Life in Custer's Cavalry*, 206. The site of Camp Supply had been preselected by Sully based on his recollection of the site of his engagement with the Indians on September 13 as well as on the judgments of Major Elliott, Captain Page, and the scout-trader John Smith. Carriker, *Fort Supply*, 13. See also Rea, "Washita Trail," 245.

22. General Field Orders No. 10, Headquarters of troops operating south of the Ark's and Dist. Upp. Ark's, in the field, Camp Supply, I.T., Nov. 18, 1868, Entry 2633, RG 393, Pt. 1; Barnitz and Barnitz, *Life in Custer's Cavalry*, 206–7. For orders detailing work to be performed to facilitate the construction of Camp Supply, see General Field Orders No. 10, Nov. 18, 1868.

23. General Field Orders No. 10, Headquarters of troops operating south of the Ark's and Dist. Upp. Ark's, in the field, Camp Supply, I.T., Nov. 18, 1868, Entry 2633, RG 393, Pt. 1; *New York Herald*, Dec. 26, 1868; Carriker, *Fort Supply*, 12, 17; Barnitz to Joseph B. Thoburn, Nov. 28, 1910, Albert Barnitz Papers (BA-1D), Archives and Manuscripts Division, Oklahoma Historical Society, Oklahoma City; Godfrey, "Reminiscences, Including the Washita Battle," 485; *Harpers Weekly*, Feb. 27, 1869; Gibson, "Battle of the Washita," 10; Barnitz and Barnitz, *Life in Custer's Cavalry*, 207; Rea, "Washita Trail," 245. Captain Barnitz, commenting years later on a drawing of Camp Supply that appeared in *Harpers Weekly* February 27, 1869, recalled that the stockade "consisted of round logs, placed on end, side by side in a trench—their alignment being preserved by scantling 2" × 4" fastened horizontally along the inner side of the structure with wooden pins, driven into augur holes—these strips of scantling affording a bearing for one end of the boards constituting the roofs of buildings—built of small logs or poles, I think—extending around the inner side of the quadrangle, and intended for sheltering our Commissary

stores and quartermasters' supplies, etc.—The troops occupying tents outside the structure and the basement of the *lunettes*—shown in the picture." Barnitz to Thoburn, Jan. 30, 1911, Barnitz Papers (BA-1E); General Field Orders No. 11, Headquarters District of the Upper Arkansas, in the field, Nov. 19, 1868, Entry 2633, RG 393, Pt. 1; Special Field Orders No. 40, Headquarters District of the Upper Arkansas, in the field, Nov. 21, 1868, ibid. The original Camp Supply stood a short distance northeast of where the succeeding and more substantial post quadrangle of Fort Supply was erected in 1870. Rea, "Research."

24. General Field Orders No. 10, Nov. 18, 1868; Harvey, "Campaigning with Sheridan," 84; Godfrey, "Reminiscences, Including the Washita Battle," 487. Sully too held a brevet of major general of volunteers (March 1865), but Custer's own in the volunteers predated it by five months (October 1864). Heitman, *Historical Register and Dictionary of the United States Army*, 1:348, 935–36; Special Field Orders No. 39, Headquarters District of the Upper Arkansas, in the field, Nov. 20, 1868, Entry 2633, RG 393, Pt. 1. Governor Samuel J. Crawford, "Call for State Troops," Oct. 10, 1868, in Crawford, *Kansas in the Sixties*, 426. A roster of officers of the Nineteenth Kansas is in Mills, *Rosters from 7th U.S. Cavalry Campaigns*.

25. General Sheridan's report, Nov. 1, 1869, in *Report of the Secretary of War, 1869*, 45; Captain Andrew Sheridan to AAG, Department of the Missouri, Nov. 15, 1868, Box 4, Entry 2601, RG 393, Pt. 1; Captain Andrew Sheridan to AAG, Department of the Missouri, Nov. 16, 1868, ibid.; General Sheridan to Sherman, Nov. 23, 1868, Sheridan Papers, Roll 80; Godfrey, "Reminiscences, Including the Washita Battle," 485–87; Carriker, *Fort Supply*, 17–18; Hutton, *Phil Sheridan and His Army*, 61–62; Utley, *Cavalier in Buckskin*, 63; Leckie, *Military Conquest of the Southern Plains*, 97; General Sheridan to Sherman, Nov. 29, 1868, William T. Sherman Papers, LC, Roll 13. Sheridan's trip from Fort Hays to Camp Supply is chronicled in Sheridan, *Personal Memoirs*, 2:310–12; and in Keim, *Sheridan's Troopers*, 88–100. Barnitz evinced sympathy for Sully: "I pity Genl. Sully, for I believe that he has tried to hurry forward affairs as fast as possible, whereas his being relieved just now appears to reflect discredit upon him." Barnitz and Barnitz, *Life in Custer's Cavalry*, 213. Accompanying Sully north were Chief District Quartermaster Inman, acting assistant inspector general; Captain Myles W. Keogh; the two companies of the Nineteenth Kansas Volunteer Cavalry; Company K, Fifth Infantry; and 260 supply wagons needing replenishment. This command reported finding en route the remains of two couriers sent by General Sheridan from Bluff Creek to Fort Dodge, killed along Mulberry Creek. Captain Andrew Sheridan to AAG, Department of the Missouri, Nov. 19, 1868, Box 4, Entry 2601, RG 393, Pt. 1; Captain Andrew Sheridan to AAG, Department of the Missouri, Nov. 27, 1868, ibid.; Carriker, *Fort Supply*, 19–20.

26. General Field Orders No. 6, Headquarters District of the Upper Arkansas, in the field, Nov. 7, 1868, Entry 2633, RG 393, Pt. 1. Five days rations for twelve hundred men, to include bacon and hardtack, were sent to Topeka from Fort Leavenworth. Major James W. Forsyth to AAG, Department of the Missouri, Oct. 29, 1868, Box 2, Entry 2601, ibid.

27. This account of the travail of the Nineteenth Kansas in reaching General Sheridan is compiled from the following sources: Schofield to Sherman,

Sept. 15, 1868, Box 3, Entry 2601, RG 393, Pt. 1; Sherman to Schofield, Sept. 17, 1868, ibid.; Crawford to AAG, Department of the Missouri, Nov. 12, 1868, Box 1, Entry 2601, ibid.; David L. Spotts to Godfrey, May 17, 1929, Washita File 2, Box 31, William J. Ghent Papers, Manuscript Division, LC; "Narrative by Josephus Bingaman," Eli S. Ricker Collection, Manuscript Division, Nebraska State Historical Society, Lincoln; Jenness, "Lost in the Snow," 52–57; Moore, "Nineteenth Kansas Cavalry in the Washita Campaign," 353–56; Shirk, "Journal of Private Johnson," 437–50; "A. L. Runyon's Letters," 58–75; and especially White, "Winter Campaigning with Sheridan and Custer," 91–99. The most comprehensive accounts by veterans of the unit are Hadley, "Nineteenth Kansas Cavalry," 431–41; Spotts, *Campaigning with Custer*, 45–64; and Crawford, *Kansas in the Sixties*, 321–24. A complete roster of regimental personnel is in *Roll of the Officers and Enlisted Men of the Third, Fourth, Eighteenth and Nineteenth Kansas Volunteers*, 114–54.

28. Sheridan, *Personal Memoirs*, 2:312.

29. Heitman, *Historical Register and Dictionary of the United States Army*, 1:402; Henry, *Civilian Appointments*, 1:150; Custer, *My Life on the Plains*, 78; Scrapbook, J. E. Taylor File, National Anthropological Archives, Smithsonian Institution, Washington, D.C.; Barnitz and Barnitz, *Life in Custer's Cavalry*, 257–58.

30. Heitman, *Historical Register and Dictionary of the United States Army*, 2:212; *Records of Living Officers*, 182; Carroll and Price, *Roll Call*, 117; Hammer, *Biographies*, 155; Barnitz and Barnitz, *Life in Custer's Cavalry*, 250–51; James M. Bell, interview by Walter M. Camp, n.d., Folder 1, Box 2, Field Notes, Topics A–L Walter M. Camp Manuscripts, Manuscripts Department, Lilly Library, Indiana University, Bloomington. "It always galled Benteen to serve in such low rank as captain after having been a colonel in the war. For this reason, he never took the interest in his company that might have been expected of him." Ibid. A full-length biography of Benteen is Mills, *Harvest of Barren Regrets*.

31. Heitman, *Historical Register and Dictionary of the United States Army*, 2:324; Barnitz and Barnitz, *Life in Custer's Cavalry*, 253; Hammer, *Biographies*, 8.

32. Heitman, *Historical Register and Dictionary of the United States Army*, 2:494, 1:193; Henry, *Civilian Appointments*, 1:156; Barnitz and Barnitz, *Life in Custer's Cavalry*, 262, 3–10; Custer, *My Life on the Plains*, 84.

33. Heitman, *Historical Register and Dictionary of the United States Army*, 1:1020, 460, 487; Barnitz and Barnitz, *Life in Custer's Cavalry*, 280–81, 260–61, 261–62; *Records of Living Officers*, 169; Carroll and Price, *Roll Call*, 61–63, 131; Hammer, *Biographies*, 187–88.

34. Heitman, *Historical Register and Dictionary of the United States Army*, 1:1015, 453, 348; Carroll and Price, *Roll Call*, 162, 130; Hammer, *Biographies*, 91, 155–56, 75; Barnitz and Barnitz, *Life in Custer's Cavalry*, 280, 260, 257.

35. Heitman, *Historical Register and Dictionary of the United States Army*, 1:208, 739, 1065; Carroll and Price, *Roll Call*, 116–17; Hammer, *Biographies*, 91–92, 121; Barnitz and Barnitz, *Life in Custer's Cavalry*, 249–50, 270, 283.

36. Heitman, *Historical Register and Dictionary of the United States Army*, 1:958, 834; Barnitz and Barnitz, *Life in Custer's Cavalry*, 279, 272.

37. Heitman, *Historical Register and Dictionary of the United States Army*, 1:243, 733; Henry, *Civilian Appointments*, 1:140, 172; Barnitz and Barnitz, *Life in Custer's Cavalry*, 251–52, 268–70; Carroll and Price, *Roll Call*, 146–47; Hammer, *Biographies*, 45.

38. Heitman, *Historical Register and Dictionary of the United States Army*, 1:893, 753, 634; Henry, *Civilian Appointments*, 1:181, 91; Hammer, *Biographies*, 45–46, 8; Barnitz and Barnitz, *Life in Custer's Cavalry*, 275–76, 270–71, 267; Carroll and Price, *Roll Call*, 148–49; *Records of Living Officers*, 168.

39. "Report of Persons and Articles employed and hired . . . in the field during the month of November, 1868," Entry 304, RG 92, Records of the Office of the Quartermaster General, NA; *Portrait and Biographical Record of Oklahoma*, 261–62; Thrapp, *Encyclopedia of Frontier Biography*, 1:274–75; Foley, "Walter Camp & Ben Clark," 19; Clark to Dr. E. L. Clark, Sept. 9, 1911, transcribed by Bob Rea from eBay online auction entry, Dec. 21, 1999; *The Daily Oklahoman*, Aug. 2, 1914; Marshall, *Miles Expedition of 1874–1875*, 13–14.

40. Barnitz and Barnitz, *Life in Custer's Cavalry*, 268. A romanticized biography of Moses Milner appears in Milner and Forrest, *California Joe*. For other accounts of Milner, see Custer, *Following the Guidon*, 25–30; and Custer, *My Life on the Plains*, 192–98.

41. Ryan, *Ten Years*, 47; Custer, *My Life on the Plains*, 198.

42. Custer, *My Life on the Plains*, 236–37; John H. Page, "Reminiscences of Indian Wars in Kansas and Indian Territory, 1866 and 1871" n.d. [ca. 1895–98], Old Guard Museum, Fort Myer, Va., 9; *Clinton Times Tribune*, Feb. 19, 1933, as cited in Harrison, "Eyes of the Sleepers," 24 n. 40; "Report of Persons and Articles employed and hired . . . in the field during the month of November, 1868," Entry 304, RG 92; "Descriptive List of Persons and Articles employed and hired. . . ," Entry 304, 1868, ibid. The names on the rolls are at variance with those given in other sources. Other names often given for some of these scouts are Big Wild Cat, Eagle Feather, Tally, Trotter, Wolf, and Little Bear. Shoemaker, "Osage Scouts helped George Armstrong Custer," 10.

43. General Sheridan to Penrose, Oct. 1868, Entry 2, Vol. 1 (Fort Lyon), RG 393, Pt. 5; Burns, *History of the Osage*, 365–67; Custer, *My Life on the Plains*, 209–10; Custer, *Following the Guidon*, 23. For more on the Osages, see Mathews, *Osages*.

CHAPTER 6. CLOSING PROXIMITY

1. Sheridan's report, Nov. 1, 1869, in *Report of the Secretary of War, 1869*; Custer to Elizabeth, Nov. 22, 1868, in Custer, *Following the Guidon*, 16–17. Some time after the subsequent attack on the Indians at the Washita River, a version of Sheridan's orders read: "To proceed south, in the direction of the Antelope hills, thence towards the Washita river, the supposed winter seat of the hostile tribes; to destroy their villages and ponies; to kill or hang all warriors, and bring back all women and children." Quoted in Keim, *Sheridan's*

Troopers, 103. Had Custer received these orders previously, it is doubtful that he could have restrained himself from quoting at least parts of them in his letters to his wife. Furthermore, there was apparently some feeling, among the junior officers at least, that "our exact destination was problematical [and] the location of the hostile villages was purely a matter of conjecture, and . . . our movements seemed to be enveloped in an impenetrable cloud of mystery." Francis M. Gibson, "The Battle of the Washita," in Carroll, *Washita!* 10.

2. Custer, *My Life on the Plains*, 215.

3. *New York Herald*, Dec. 8, 1868; Keim, *Sheridan's Troopers*, 102–3; Harvey, "Campaigning with Sheridan," 184; Gibson, "Battle of the Washita," 11; Godfrey account in *The Daily Oklahoman*, July 14, 1929; "Ten Years with General Custer among the American Indians," *The Newton (Mass.) Circuit,* May 28, 1909, copy in Fred S. Barde Collection, Archives and Manuscripts Division, Oklahoma Historical Society, Oklahoma City. Several years later Custer wrote that reveille came at 4:00 A.M. *My Life on the Plains*, 214.

4. Private Ryan told how during the campaign, some of the bandsmen, disliking the cold, came to believe that if something was wrong with their instruments, they would not have to perform. Some punched holes in their pieces to keep from playing. "Custer got on to the racket," claimed Ryan, "and ordered the men that had anything the matter with their instruments to walk and do the usual fatigue duty while on the trip. . . . After a few days the biggest part of those instruments were brought into service in the band by being patched up with soap and one thing or another, and that ended the business with the Seventh cavalry band." Ryan, "Ten Years," *The Newton (Mass.) Circuit*, May 28, 1909.

5. Thomas Shanley account, *The Daily Oklahoman*, Aug. 2, 1925; Custer, *My Life on the Plains*, 216–18; Godfrey, "Reminiscences, Including the Washita Battle," 487; Gibson, "Battle of the Washita," 11–12; Barnitz and Barnitz, *Life in Custer's Cavalry*, 213; "Record of Events of the Seventh Cavalry, Company G, November, 1868," in Carroll, *Washita!* 32; Rea, "Washita Trail," 248; Harvey, "Campaigning with Sheridan," 85; Charles Brewster, "Battle of the Washita," *The National Tribune*, Aug. 22, 1901. The site of this camp was near the mouth of Boggy Creek. Rea, "Washita Trail," 249. The trail of the Seventh Cavalry is historically delineated on a map by Captain Henry Alvord, "Map of Parts of Kansas, Texas, Colorado, New Mexico and the Indian Territory, with the routes of all columns of U.S. troops operating against hostile Indians in the Department of the Missouri during the winter of 1868–1869," Item Q142, Civil Works Map File, Cartographic Archives Division, RG 77, Records of the Office of the Chief of Engineers, NA, as cited in ibid.

6. Ryan, *Ten Years*, 48–49.

7. *New York Herald*, Dec. 8, 1868; Custer, *My Life on the Plains*, 219–21 (which unaccountably and confusingly has added a day to the events of the march); Edward G. Mathey, "The Washita Campaign and Battle of the Washita," in Carroll, *Washita!* 35–36; Godfrey, "Reminiscences, Including the Washita Battle," 487–88; Gibson, "Battle of the Washita," 12–13; Barnitz and Barnitz, *Life in Custer's Cavalry*, 250–26; "Record of Events of the Seventh Cavalry, Company G, November, 1868," in *Washita!* 32; Rea, "Washita Trail," 249–51. An article in an undated copy of *The Custer County Post-Dispatch*,

entitled "Battle of the Washita," states that the Osages Little Beaver and Hard Rope told Custer that the "usual" crossing place lay twelve to fifteen miles away at a place since known as the Little Robe Crossing.

8. Barnitz and Barnitz, *Life in Custer's Cavalry*, 215; Custer, *My Life on the Plains*, 219–21; Mathey, "Washita Campaign," 35–36; Godfrey, "Reminiscences, Including the Washita Battle," 487–88; Gibson, "Battle of the Washita," 12–13; Rea, "Washita Trail," 253–54; Kraft, *Custer and the Cheyenne*, 40. In his official report Custer wrote that the trail showed evidence of one hundred warriors and was discovered "near the point where the Texas boundary line crosses the Canadian River." *Army and Navy Journal*, Dec. 12, 1868. Captain Barnitz details Elliott's movement, along with the discovery of the trails and camp, in Barnitz and Barnitz, *Life in Custer's Cavalry*, 215–18.

9. James M. Bell interview notes, Folder 1, Box 2, Field Notes, Walter M. Camp Manuscripts, Lilly Library, Indiana University, Bloomington (copy, Notebook 4, No. 1, Kenneth Hammer Collection, Little Bighorn Battlefield National Monument, Crow Agency, Mt.); Custer, *My Life on the Plains*, 225, 227–29; *New York Herald*, Dec. 8, 1868; Brewster, "Battle of the Washita"; Godfrey, "Reminiscences, Including the Washita Battle," 488–89; Gibson, "Battle of the Washita," 14–15; "Record of Events of the Seventh Cavalry, Company G, November, 1868," in *Washita!* 32; Keim, *Sheridan's Troopers*, 108; Dennis Lynch, interview by Walter M. Camp , n.d., Walter M. Camp Papers, BYU (copy, Notebook 9, No. 6, Hammer Collection); Edward S. Godfrey, interview by Walter M. Camp, Mar. 3, 1917, Camp Papers (copy, Notebook 8, No. 36, Hammer Collection); Rea, "Washita Trail," 253–54; Leckie, *Military Conquest of the Southern Plains*, 98–99. Custer's account of Hamilton's switch with Mathey is detailed in Custer to Mrs. Hamilton (mother), Aug. 29, 1869, in "In Memoriam," 365–67.

10. The Canadian is today known as the South Canadian River.

11. Rothman and Associates, "Historic Landscape Conditions," 12, 14, 15. Tree varieties included cottonwood, willow, hackberry, elm, plum, and haw. Bushes bordering the streams included wild plum, wild grape, red and black haw, hickory nut, black walnut, and pecan. Grasses in the area included sideoats grama, little bluestem, sand bluestem, western wheatgrass, buffalo grass, blue joint grass, sand crabgrass, Indian grass, switch grass, and love grass, among other possible species. Other ground cover included prickly pear and yucca. Ibid., 16–20. See also Cowley, *Cultural Landscape Inventory*, 89–90, 105.

12. Custer to AAAG, Department of the Missouri, Dec. 22, 1868, in Senate, *Letter of the Secretary of War*, 69; Powell, *People of the Sacred Mountain*, 1:594, 599; Brill, *Conquest of the Southern Plains*, 132–33. Estimates of the locations of the various tribal bands are in Alvord to Forsyth, Nov. 22, 1868, enclosing "Semi-Weekly Report No. 1. Summary of information relating to Indians," "Reports of Officers in the West and Southwest, 1874–75 [sic]," Military Division of the Missouri Papers, Manuscript Division, U.S. Army Military History Institute, Army War College, Carlisle Barracks, Pa. "Washita" is a Choctaw word meaning "Big Hunt," a reference to the profusion of game in its environs. Brill, *Conquest of the Southern Plains*, 127–28.

13. The village stood in the northeast quarter of Section 12, Township 13 North, Range 24 West, according to Notes, Ben Clark interview by Walter M.

Camp, 1910, Camp Manuscripts. See also "Map of the Washita Battle Ground," Map 3 (township and range), Barde Collection. The course of the stream through the section has changed considerably since 1868, partly for agricultural purposes. See Lees et al., "Archaeology of the Washita Battlefield National Historic Site," 14–15.

14. Powell, *People of the Sacred Mountain*, 1:598–99; Hyde, *Life of George Bent*, 315; Brill, *Conquest of the Southern Plains*, 132–33; Ben Clark, "Custer's Washita Fight," *New York Sun*, May 14, 1899; Rothman and Associates, "Historic Landscape Conditions," 21–22. For some of the individuals known to have been present in the village, see appendixes B and C. In 1909 the village site comprised "a meadow of the farm of G. F. Turner, a merchant of Cheyenne, and as its surface has never been plowed, it has about the same contour as at the time the battle was fought. Each recurrent spring the land is overflowed, and most of the timber present at the time of the contest has been cut down, but enough remains to adequately identify the spot." Hunt, "Subjugation of Black Kettle," 104–5; *The Daily Oklahoman*, July 27, 1930.

15. "Treaty with the Cheyenne and Arapaho, 1867," in Kappler, *Indian Affairs*, 2:985, 988; Watson and Russell, "Battle of the Washita," 50, 54.

16. Basic biographical data for Black Kettle is from Hyde, *Life of George Bent*, 322–24. Bent was married to Black Kettle's niece in 1866, lived with the chief until the early summer of 1868, and knew him well. See also Bent to Joseph B. Thoburn, July 12, Dec. 27, 1911, Jan. 9, 19, 1912, Joseph B. Thoburn Papers, Archives and Manuscripts Division, Oklahoma Historical Society, Oklahoma City. Other sources state that Black Kettle was born in around 1797 and identify his parents as Hawk Stretches Out and Sparrow Hawk Woman and that his siblings were Gentle Horse, Wind Woman, and Stone Teeth. The date of the loss of his wife to the Utes is debatable, with other sources suggesting that it occurred in 1854–55. Item 88.32, Folder 217 (temp.), Box 15, Washita Massacre, Folder 2, John L. Sipes Collection, Archives and Manuscripts Division, Oklahoma Historical Society; Folder 471, George Bird Grinnell Papers, Braun Research Library, Southwest Museum, Los Angeles. Folder 69 of the Grinnell Papers includes "Life of Black Kettle" by Wolf Chief, which states that Black Kettle was elected a chief in 1855 and lead chief of six head chiefs in 1861. Moore, *Cheyenne Nation*, 274, identified Black Kettle's father as Wolf-on-a-Hill, who had married into the southern Suhtai band. Somewhat dated treatments of Black Kettle appear in Thoburn, *Standard History of Oklahoma* 2:864–66; and Gage, "Black Kettle," 244–51. In a piece originally published in the *St. Louis Republican* (December 3, 1868), the chief was viewed as "a man of more than ordinary natural ability." *Army and Navy Journal*, Dec. 12, 1868. For a modern synthesis of biographical data about Black Kettle that differs in some respects from that given above, see Hoig, *Peace Chiefs of the Cheyennes*, 104–21.

17. Berthrong, *Southern Cheyennes*, 320–22. See Alvord's report in Alvord to Forsyth, Nov. 5, 1868, "Reports of Officers in the West and Southwest, 1874–75 [sic]."

18. U.S. Senate, *Record of a Conversation Held Between Colonel and Brevet Major General W. B. Hazen, United States Army, on Special Service, and Chiefs of the Cheyenne and Arapaho Tribes of Indians, at Fort Cobb,*

Indian Territory, Nov. 20, 1868, 40th Cong., 3d sess., 1869, S. Exec. Doc.18, 22–23, as cited in Powell, *People of the Sacred Mountain,* 1:596.

19. Powell, *People of the Sacred Mountain,* 1:596–97; Berthrong, *Southern Cheyennes,* 323–24; Kroeker, *Great Plains Command,* 79–80.

20. Murphy to Taylor, Nov. 15, 1868, in Senate, *Letter of the Secretary of the Interior,* 31–32; Taylor to Browning, Nov. 21, 1868, in ibid., 32–33; Hazen to Sherman, Nov. 22, 1868, Philip H. Sheridan Papers, LC, Roll 76.

21. These scouts had been hired on Sheridan's direction. Alvord to Forsyth, Nov. 21, 1868, "Reports of Officers in the West and Southwest, 1874–75 [*sic*]"; Alvord to Forsyth, Nov. 22, 1868, enclosing "Semi-Weekly Report No. 1. Summary of information relating to Indians," ibid.

22. Alvord to Forsyth, Nov. 26, 1868, enclosing "Summary of Information regarding hostile Indians. 'Semi-Weekly Report No. 2,'" ibid.; Hazen to Major James P. Roy, Nov. 26, 1868, Sheridan Papers, Roll 76.

23. Powell, *People of the Sacred Mountain,* 2:599–600; Brill, *Conquest of the Southern Plains,* 135–36, citing the account of Magpie. According to Brill, a visiting family of Lakotas in Black Kettle's village, upon learning of the reported presence of soldiers in the area, decided to move their lodge downstream to the larger villages the next day. Ibid., 137–38.

24. Powell, *People of the Sacred Mountain,* 2:597–98, citing Grinnell and his Cheyenne informant. George Bent maintained, "this party going to Black Kettle's village has made it appear that Black Kettle's band was hostile, though these Cheyennes were not of his band." Hyde, *Life of George Bent,* 315. Regarding this party's raiding in the Smoky Hill country, see Bent to Hyde, Sept. 2, 1905, Letter 15, Manuscript 54, George Bent Manuscripts, Colorado Historical Society, Denver. Sheridan believed that the trail Custer followed had been made by some Cheyennes and Arapahos who had "brought back three (3) scalps, one (1) of which was the Expressman killed and horribly mutilated just before I had left Fort Dodge,—the mail on his person was found in 'Black Kettle's' camp." Sheridan to AAG, Division of the Missouri, Dec. 3, 1868, Sheridan Papers, Roll 76. On the afternoon of November 26, one of this party, named Crow Neck, returned over the route to retrieve a worn pony he had left to rest the preceding day. Far to the north, the Indian saw what he believed were soldiers, and when he returned to the camp, he told a friend what he had seen. But afraid that others would not believe him, and that Black Kettle might chastise him for being with the raiding party, Crow Neck kept silent. Brill, *Conquest of the Southern Plains,* 136–37.

25. Powell, *People of the Sacred Mountain,* 2:598. Reports that the people in Black Kettle's village stayed up celebrating the return of the war party seemingly are without substance. See ibid., 680 n. 11.

26. Brewster, "Battle of the Washita"; Gibson, "Battle of the Washita," 15. Ben Clark told Camp in 1910 that the fire was actually a rotten log that had been left burning by the Indians. The site of the fire was about six miles above the village. Foley, "Walter Camp & Ben Clark," 19. Clark also said that the approach of the troops along the trail from the northwest put them in the vicinity of where local resident A. G. Smith's barn stood as of 1910. Ibid.

27. One report stated that Custer used a night glass to verify the presence of the herd. *New York Herald,* Dec. 29, 1868.

28. Custer, *My Life on the Plains*, 233. Camp learned that the flat ground on which the troops settled was in 1910 occupied by Frank Turner. Foley, "Walter Camp & Ben Clark," 20. Turner also owned some acreage behind the ridge. Bob Rea, conversation with author, Fort Supply Historic Site, Oklahoma, Dec. 2000. Bell recalled that "the night was cold and the creaking of the wagons and ambulances could be heard for some distance." Bell to Camp, July 28, 1911, Folder 19, Box 1, Camp Papers, microfilm.

29. This tract in 1904 was part of the Kirtley farm, located in "the southwest and southeast of the northeast of Section 2," Township 13 North, Range 24 West. Lees et al., "Archaeology of the Washita Battlefield National Historic Site," 16.

30. *Life in Custer's Cavalry*, 219. One contemporary statement mentioned the presence of fog in the Washita bottom, which, as daylight rose, obscured the trees and lodges in the camp. The fog concealed the troops as they surrounded the encampment. "Medical History of Fort Supply, I.T., 1868–1894," RG 94, Records of the Adjutant General's Office, NA, microfilm. That fog was generally present in area bottomlands at various times in the winter is confirmed in Barnitz's journal entry for November 26. See Barnitz and Barnitz, *Life in Custer's Cavalry*, 215.

31. Beyond the specific references for quoted material, this account of the advance of the cavalry is drawn from Custer to Sheridan, Nov. 28, 1868, "Reports of Officers in the West and Southwest, 1874–75" [hereafter cited as Custer's report, Nov. 28, 1868]; *New York Herald*, Dec. 8, 1868; *New York Daily Tribune*, Dec. 29, 1868; *New York Sun*, May 14, 1899 (containing Ben Clark's account); *Army and Navy Journal*, Dec. 12, 1868; Foley, "Walter Camp & Ben Clark," 19–20; Custer, *My Life on the Plains*, 230–32, 239; Godfrey, "Reminiscences, Including the Washita Battle," 489; Gibson, "Battle of the Washita," 15–16; Barnitz and Barnitz, *Life in Custer's Cavalry*, 218–29; Merington, *The Custer Story*, 220; Brill, *Conquest of the Southern Plains*, 144–48; and Leckie, *Military Conquest of the Southern Plains*, 99–100.

32. For a discussion of the surround, or encirclement, tactic, see Jamison, *Crossing the Deadly Ground*, 43–45.

33. Mangum, "Muster Roll 7th Cavalry"; "In Memoriam," 370–71; *New York Herald*, Dec. 8, 1868; Mills, *Rosters from 7th U.S. Cavalry Campaigns*; Gibson, "Battle of the Washita," 16–17; Brill, *Conquest of the Southern Plains*, 149–50. Custer's report of the engagement indicates a different approach for two of the columns: "Thompson . . . was to attack from the crest north of the village; while the fourth column [which Custer himself accompanied] was to charge the village from the crest overlooking it on the west bank of the Washita." Custer was on the left, or north, side of the river. Custer's report, Nov. 28, 1868.

34. *Life in Custer's Cavalry*, 220; Bell interview notes, Folder 1, Box 2, Field Notes, Camp Manuscripts (copy, Notebook 4, No. 1, Hammer Collection).

35. The rocky draw described by Barnitz does not exist today, possibly having been filled in naturally and/or purposefully since 1868, today constituting more of a ravine. Lees et al., "Archaeology of the Washita Battlefield National Historic Site," 18.

36. Barnitz and Barnitz, *Life in Custer's Cavalry*, 220–25; *New York Herald*, Dec. 29, 1868; Barnitz to Camp, Jan. 12, 1910, Folder 11, Box 1, Camp Papers, microfilm; Barnitz to Camp, Nov. 18, 1910, Folder 14, ibid.; Barnitz, interview by Walter M. Camp, Dec. 5, 1910, Camp Manuscripts; Ryan, *Ten Years*, 51–52; Despain, "Captain Albert Barnitz," 137–38. By his account, Ryan was in Company M at the time of the Washita encounter, though the muster rolls shows him assigned to Company B. Mangum, "Muster Roll 7th Cavalry."

37. "Battle of the Washita," 17. Thompson's command, delayed in its march, likely approached the village through the north part of Section 14 and into the southwest quarter of Section 12. Lees et al., "Archaeology of the Washita Battlefield National Historic Site," 18.

38. William C. Stair Interview notes, Mss. 57, Box 3, Camp Papers, microfilm; Field Notes, Folder 78, Camp Papers (copy, Hammer Collection); Trooper Dennis Lynch said that Tom Custer killed the dog. Ibid., Notebook 9, No. 6, p. 378. Sergeant John Ryan recalled that other dogs were killed too for fear that their barking would arouse the camp. One he mentioned was dispatched with a picket pin through the head (though the animal, amazingly, recovered from the wound). *Ten Years*, 51.

39. Custer's report, Nov. 28, 1868; Custer, *My Life on the Plains*, 234–39; Godfrey, "Reminiscences, Including the Washita Battle," 489–90; Henry Langley account, *Winners of the West*, Dec. 15, 1925; Brewster, "Battle of the Washita,"; Godfrey account in undated newspaper [ca. 1895], W. J. Ghent Papers, Manuscript Division, LC. Ben Clark stated that Custer termed the phenomenon "The Star of the Washita" and said that it forecasted victory. *New York Sun*, May 14, 1899. Modern astronomical calculations indicate that what Custer and his men saw very likely was Mercury, which in its celestial orbit was especially bright on November 27, 1868. Venus, often referred to as the Morning Star, had risen that day more than three hours before sunrise and so was already too far above the horizon to fit the historical description. Data provided by Mort Wegman-French, Jan. 14, 2001, Home Planet software for Windows, Release 3.1, Jan. 2000.

CHAPTER 7. WASHITA

1. Godfrey stated that "the sun came up brightly" before the attack commenced. Field Notes, Notebook 8, Folder 36, Kenneth Hammer Collection, Little Bighorn Battlefield National Monument, Crow Agency, Mt. One man of each company remained with the discarded dunnage with orders to load them in Bell's wagons when they arrived. Godfrey, "Reminiscences, Including the Washita Battle," 490; Godfrey account in undated letter, WA-2, 86.01, File 11, Box 33, Joseph B. Thoburn Collection, Archives and Manuscripts Division, Oklahoma Historical Society, Oklahoma City. Some of the sharpshooters complained and cursed at the directive to remove their overcoats, bringing a rejoinder from Custer to "stop that noise." Dennis Lynch, interview by Walter M. Camp, n.d., Walter M. Camp Papers, BYU (copy, Notebook 9, No.6, Hammer Collection).

2. This low ridge is in the southeast quarter of Section 2. Lees et al., "Archaeology of the Washita Battlefield National Historic Site," 19.

3. Custer's report, Nov. 28, 1868; *New York Herald*, Dec. 8, 1868; Custer, *My Life on the Plains*, 239–40; Mangum, "Muster Roll 7th Cavalry"; *The Daily Oklahoman*, Nov. 23, 1930; Godfrey account in undated newspaper [ca. 1895], William J. Ghent Papers, LC; *Kansas City Star*, Dec. 4, 1904; Godfrey, "Reminiscences, Including the Washita Battle," 490. Godfrey maintained that the shot was fired by an Indian, aroused by the dogs, at a soldier of Elliott's command somewhere on the east end of the camp. Ibid.

4. Godfrey stated that the soldiers, shooting through the lodges, "took no care to prevent hitting women." Edward S. Godfrey, interview by Walter S. Camp, Mar. 3, 1917, Box 3, Camp Papers, microfilm.

5. A soldier who joined the Seventh Cavalry in 1870 maintained that the band's playing "Garry Owen" at the Washita had by then become considered "out of place" and a matter of ridicule and joking among veterans in the regiment. Liddic and Harbaugh, *Camp on Custer*, 36–37. It seems doubtful that the sixteen bandsmen could have played their instruments much while galloping into the village. Ben Clark remembered that "the musicians had little time for music. Their horses became uncontrollable in the rush and rumble of the charge, and a number of the musicians were drawn into the very teeth of the fight." *Kansas City Star*, Dec. 4, 1904. At least one veteran remembered that "the band was stationed at the crossing of the creek" when the attack began. Langley account, *Winners of the West*, Dec. 15, 1925. Barnitz, writing close to the event, said that the band was on a ridge. Barnitz and Barnitz, *Life in Custer's Cavalry*, 225.

6. "In Memoriam," 372–73. Barnitz wrote, "Hamilton was killed near the stream, as I was told, on the left flank of Custer's command—among the trees, or bushes bordering the stream and but a few hundred yards in front of my position occupied by my dismounted men." Barnitz to Walter M. Camp, Nov. 29, 1910, Folder 14, Box 1, Camp Papers, microfilm. Custer indicated that Hamilton fell "as we entered the village." *My Life on the Plains*, 246. Godfrey claimed that Hamilton was the first soldier killed in the engagement. "Notes on Chapter XXII of Colonel Homer W. Wheeler's 'Buffalo Days,'" Accounts Written or Annotated by E. S. Godfrey Sr., Box 16, Godfrey Family Papers Indian Wars, Manuscript Division, U.S. Army Military History Institute, Army War College, Carlisle Barracks, Pa. Captain West's memorial of Hamilton in the *Army and Navy Journal* (January 2, 1869) stated that he "fell dead from his horse, shot by a bullet from a Lancaster rifle in the hands of a savage, who was concealed in his wigwam." Hamilton was struck in the chest. The surgeon's report noted that the "ball entered about five inches below left nipple, and emerged near inferior angle of right scapula. Death was instantaneous." "Special Report. Officers Killed at the Battle of the Washita, Indian Territory, November 27, 1868," RG 94, Records of the Adjutant General's Office, NA. Another account of the engagement said that Hamilton, when hit, "gave one convulsive start" and fell from his horse, "striking on his face, which was from this cause, terribly lacerated and disfigured." *New York Herald*, Dec. 24, 1868. An army shell jacket purportedly worn by Hamilton when he was killed reposes with the Oklahoma Historical Society, donated by Hamilton's brother

in 1908. Oklahoma Historical Society to Allan McLane Hamilton, Aug. 27, 1908, and response, Aug. 27, 1908, Collections Inventory Control Sheet 4339, Archives and Manuscripts Division, Oklahoma Historical Society, Oklahoma City. It seems likely that the damage present in this garment was caused by moths rather than gunfire. See also *Kansas City Times,* Nov. 25, 1908. There is some speculation that Hamilton was killed by his own men and that his death occurred before the Indians had started any return fire, though the surgeon's notation above indicates that the officer was hit in the front, not the back, as he led his men in on the attack. See Brill, *Conquest of the Southern Plains,* 160 n. 1.

7. Godfrey claimed that both Myers and Thompson, befuddled in the approach through the darkness, failed to coordinate their movements for the opening charge. "Reminiscences, Including the Washita Battle," 490–91. The route of the escapees lay east of some mounds or buttes in the eastern half of the southwest quarter of Section 12. Lees et al., "Archaeology of the Washita Battlefield National Historic Site," 20.

8. Edward S. Godfrey, "The Seventh Regiment of United States Cavalry." n.d. [1898?], Box 6, Edward S. Godfrey Papers, LC; Barnitz and Barnitz, *Life in Custer's Cavalry,* 225; George Bent to Samuel Tappan, Mar. 15, 1889, Ms. 617, Samuel Tappan Papers, Colorado Historical Society, Denver; Bent to George E. Hyde, Aug. 1, 1913, Bent-Hyde Correspondence, Coe Collection, Beinecke Rare Book and Manuscript Library, Yale University, New Haven, Conn. The spot where Black Kettle and his wife were killed was identified by two Cheyenne participants, Magpie and Little Beaver, in 1930. See certification sheet, Sept. 19, 1930, U.S. Army Field Artillery and Fort Sill Museum, Fort Sill, Okla. A soldier named Joseph Lemon, Company H, claimed to have killed the chief and taken his Remington revolver and a silver ring, an unlikely assertion since Benteen's company was too far to the east at the opening of the assault, when Black Kettle and his wife apparently died. *Kankakee Sunday Journal,* Feb. 17, 1952.

9. *Kansas City Star,* Dec. 4, 1904; Custer later wrote: "Before engaging in the fight, orders had been given to prevent the killing of any but the fighting strength of the village; but in a struggle of this character it is impossible at all times to discriminate, particularly when, in a hand-to-hand conflict, such as the one the troops were then engaged in, the squaws are as dangerous adversaries as the warriors, while Indian boys between ten and fifteen years of age were found as expert and determined in the use of the pistol and bow and arrow as the older warriors." *My Life on the Plains,* 241.

10. *New York Sun,* May 14, 1899. Clark reported that "the shooting of the women and children was done, but by the twelve Osage Indian scouts." Letter, Aug. 30, 1909, *Overland Monthly,* Nov. 1909. See also Brill, *Conquest of the Southern Plains,* 156–57. But Godfrey remembered that a private named Elihu F. Clear shot and killed a woman during the charge through the camp. Godfrey interview, Mar. 3, 1917, Box 3, Camp Papers, microfilm.

11. Munsall, "7th U.S. Cavalry at the Battle on the Washita," 123; Dennis Lynch, interview by Walter M. Camp, n.d., Camp Papers (copy, Notebook 9, No. 6, Hammer Collection). An untitled diagram map drawn by Ben Clark nearly thirty years later indicates that the tribesmen made two major stands

along the river during the encounter, one at the approximate apex of the bend enclosing most of the lodges, and the other farther downstream, a short distance beyond the bend. Clark map, 1897, Hugh L. Scott Papers, LC. Although unexplained on the map, these were likely the incidents involving the women behind the earthen barricade as well as the seventeen warriors in the depression. Cooke's sharpshooters seemingly engaged both bodies of Cheyennes. For what was apparently the latter incident, see Barnitz and Barnitz, *Life in Custer's Cavalry*, 225.

12. Foley, "Walter Camp & Ben Clark," 22; Custer, *My Life on the Plains*, 244. Clark addressed this apparent policy thus: "As wounded Indians were supposed to or known to fight as long as they could, all of the wounded Indians in this fight were promptly shot to death by the soldiers without discrimination as to appearance of danger, just exactly as Indians would have treated wounded soldiers." Clark did not indicate whether this practice was confined to men or extended also to women, though he accounted for a wounded boy about twelve years old being taken prisoner. "This was the oldest male captured." Foley, "Walter Camp & Ben Clark," 22.

13. Godfrey, "Reminiscences, Including the Washita Battle," 492. The likely promontory mounted by Godfrey in sighting the villages below lies in the northeastern quarter of Section 32, Township 14 North, Range 23 West. Lees et al., "Archaeology of the Washita Battlefield National Historic Site," 22.

14. Barnitz and Barnitz, *Life in Custer's Cavalry*, 225–28. Barnitz's near-fatal encounter, with all of its collateral details, are well documented in the following sources: Barnitz to Thoburn, Nov. 28, 1910, BA-ID Thoburn, .949 86.01, Thoburn Papers; Albert Barnitz, interview by Walter M. Camp, Dec. 5, 1910, Camp Manuscripts, Lilly Library, Indiana University, Bloomington; Godfrey, "Reminiscences, Including the Washita Battle," 492; Barnitz to Camp, Nov. 29, 1910, Box 1, Folder 14, Camp Papers, microfilm; Field Notes, Folder 36S, Camp Papers (copy, Notebook 8, Folder 36, Hammer Collection); Godfrey interview, Mar. 3, 1917, Box 3, Camp Papers, microfilm; John Ryan notes, Field Notes, Unclassified Envelope 130, Camp Papers (copy, Notebook 6, No. 130, Hammer Collection); Despain, "Captain Albert Barnitz," 140–42. Barnitz Creek rises near the modern community of Leedey and runs a north-to-south course east of the encounter site to join the Washita near present Clinton. See Thoburn, "Names of Oklahoma Streams," 59.

15. Clark account, *Kansas City Star*, Dec. 4, 1904. In his 1910 interview with Camp, Clark stated that he had been standing on the same hill with Elliott and Kennedy. Foley, "Walter Camp & Ben Clark," 20.

16. Clark stated that he heard Elliott exclaim, "There's a lot of escaping Indians; come on boys, let's take 'em in." Those who joined the major "did so of their own accord." *New York Sun*, May 14, 1899.

17. Godfrey wrote, "my recollection is that this remark was made to Lieut. Hale." "Notes on Chapter XXII of Colonel Homer W. Wheeler's 'Buffalo Days,'" Godfrey Family Papers Indian Wars. Another source reported: "Gen. Godfrey did not hear it himself but always insisted that officers told him afterwards that Elliott said, 'Here's for a brevet or a coffin.' Godfrey could not remember the officer or officers who made this statement to him, but it was on the day of the engagement." "Battle of Washita, Nov. 27, 1868," Research

Files, 19th Century Army, 1868 Campaign Misc., Collection S-1314, Ser. 3, Bk. 16, Folder 237, Charles F. Bates Papers, Beinecke Rare Book and Manuscript Library, Yale University, New Haven, Conn.

18. *New York Sun*, May 14, 1899; *Kansas City Star*, Dec. 4, 1904; Foley, "Walter Camp & Ben Clark," 20, 22; Custer, *My Life on the Plains*, 246–47; Hunt, "Subjugation of Black Kettle," 106–7. Clark stated: "Elliot [was] killed in SE 1/4 of Sec 5, Township 13 north, Range 23 west. It is 2 1/2 miles straight east of Black Kettles village." Foley, "Walter Camp & Ben Clark," 22.

19. Bell to Camp, July 28, 1911, Folder 19, Box 1, Camp Papers; Barnitz to Joseph B. Thoburn, Oct. 29, 1910, BA-1B Thoburn, 947, 86.01, Thoburn Papers; Godfrey interview, Mar. 3, 1917, Box 3, Camp Papers, microfilm; Camp to Godfrey, Nov. 13, 1919, Godfrey Papers; Lees et al., "Archaeology of the Washita Battlefield National Historic Site," 21. Bell maintained that he did manage to retrieve about one-half of the overcoats. James M. Bell, interview by Walter Camp, n.d., Folder 1, Box 2, Field Notes, Topics A–L, Camp Manuscripts (copy, Notebook 4, No. 1, Hammer Collection). Francis M. Gibson stated that Bell and the train arrived "about an hour after the fight began." "The Battle of the Washita," in Carroll, *Washita!* 18. With Bell was Custer's cook, an Irish woman named Courtenay, who reportedly somehow made coffee on a portable camp stove in one of the ambulances during the frenetic advance to the village. Bell interview notes, Folder 1, Box 2, Field Notes, Camp Manuscripts (copy, Notebook 4, No. 1, Hammer Collection).

20. Clark map, 1897; Ben Clark account, *New York Sun*, May 14, 1899; Foley, "Walter Camp & Ben Clark," 20; Field Correspondence, *New York Herald*, cited in *Mariposa (Calif.) Gazette*, Feb. 12, 1869. The troops' opposition to the warriors' flank attacks may help explain the archeological discovery of numerous expended Spencer cartridge casings on the ridge overlooking the pony-kill site about four hundred to five hundred yards northeast of the present overlook. See Lees et al., "Archaeology of the Washita Battlefield National Historic Site," 48–49; Lees, "Archaeological Evidence," 36–37, 39.

21. Godfrey, "Reminiscences, Including the Washita Battle," 493. For an enumeration of items supposedly found in the village pointing to the Indians' involvement in the Kansas raids, see Sheridan's report, Nov. 11, 1869, in *Report of the Secretary of War, 1869*, 48.

22. John Ryan wrote that when the warriors took position on the other side of the village, Custer placed the women prisoners along that side, causing the warriors to stop firing from that direction. *Ten Years*, 55–56.

23. Custer, *My Life on the Plains*, 257. Referring either to Myer's movement downriver during the engagement or to that officer's search downriver after the fighting, Godfrey remarked, "I learned afterward that he did not go down the valley any distance else he would have discovered Elliott." Godfrey to unknown, n.d., WA-2, File 11 86.01, Box 33, Thoburn Collection.

24. Custer, *My Life on the Plains*, 249.

25. Bell claimed to have advised Custer to destroy the herd. When the colonel demurred for want of ammunition, Bell told him that he had brought twenty thousand rounds with him. Bell interview notes (copy, Notebook 4, No. 1, Hammer Collection). Barnitz very specifically stated that two ponies were selected for each of the women and each officer claimed two ponies.

Barnitz and Barnitz, *Life in Custer's Cavalry*, 228. These latter were probably intended to replace broken-down horses within the companies, as was suggested by Lieutenant Gibson. Gibson, "Battle of the Washita," 18.

26. *New York Sun*, May 14, 1899. Trooper Dennis Lynch claimed that sharpshooters from Company F killed the herd. Camp Papers (copy, Notebook 6, No. 130, Hammer Collection). Likewise, Lieutenant Bell recollected that "Troop F . . . fired volley after volley until all [were] shot down." Bell interview notes (copy, Notebook 4, No. 1, Hammer Collection). Captain Benteen reported that Custer took the opportunity to shoot dogs from the Indian village as well. Letter, *St. Louis Democrat*, as republished in *New York Times*, Feb. 14, 1869, and in Graham, *Custer Myth*, 212. The pony kill took place south of the village and against the face of a sharply rising bluff. The site was identified by a Cheyenne participant, Magpie. "His identification of the location was confirmed by Frank Turner, the pioneer settler . . . , and also by Alvin Moore, an attorney of Cheyenne and member of the Oklahoma senate, whose father once owned the land upon which the battlefield stands. Frank Turner said long after he had staked his claim north of the battlefield he watched freighters load bones of these animals into huge wagons to be taken to Texas and sold for fertilizer." *The Daily Oklahoman*, Nov. 23, 1930. See also William Boyd, interview, "Indian and Pioneer Histories," 1930s Federal Writers' Project, Archives and Manuscripts Division, Oklahoma Historical Society, Oklahoma City, 91:92.

27. Custer, *My Life on the Plains*, 241–43; *New York Herald*, Dec. 24, 1868; Gibson, "Battle of the Washita," 20–21; Hyde, *Life of George Bent*, 317; Powell, *People of the Sacred Mountain*, 1:604–5.

28. *New York Herald*, Dec. 24, 1876; Custer, *My Life on the Plains*, 256–57. Both sources stated that the wounded man was a trumpeter, but official casualty lists indicate that the only bugler (*sic*, trumpeter) wounded was John Murphy of Company M, who received an arrow wound in the thorax. The only possible recipient of the injury described was Private Daniel Morrison, of Company G, who was hit in the right temple and whose injury required a "cold water dressing." "List of Wounded in the 7th U.S. Cavalry under command of Bt Maj Genl Custer USA, at the Battle of the Washita Indian Territory on the 27th day of Nov., 1868," RG 112, Records of the Office of the Surgeon General, NA.

29. Ben Clark account, New York Sun, May 14, 1899; Foley, "Walter Camp & Ben Clark," 20; Hyde, *Life of George Bent*, 317; Grinnell to Camp, Oct. 3, 1916, Box 2, Folder 2, Camp Papers, microfilm; *New York Herald*, Dec. 24, 1868.

30. Custer, *My Life on the Plains*, 249; *New York Sun*, May 14, 1899. Ben Clark maintained that Custer had earlier planned to follow, and presumably engage, the warriors of the downriver villages. Ibid.; Brill, *Conquest of the Southern Plains*, 17 n. 3.

31. Barnitz to Thoburn, Nov. 28, 1910, BA-1D Thoburn, .949 86.01, Thoburn Papers; Rea, "Washita Trail," 256–58. The point on the Washita where Custer presumably turned about was later known as "Custer Bend." "Battle of the Washita," undated clipping [ca. 1915–35] from *The Custer County Post-Dispatch*, Collections, Washita Battlefield National Historic Site,

Cheyenne, Okla. Keim, who was not present, wrote in his dispatch that "after traveling a distance of eight miles the column returned to the scene of the fight." *New York Herald,* Dec. 8, 1868. Custer's plan for extricating his command from the proximity of Black Kettle's village by initially marching toward the downriver camps and then withdrawing under cover of darkness has been credited to his chief of scouts, Ben Clark. Brill, *Conquest of the Southern Plains,* 177–78.

32. *New York Herald,* Dec. 24, 1868; Rea, "Washita Trail," 255–57. Beyond the quoted and explanatory material cited above, this account of the Washita engagement has been constructed from the following sources: *New York Herald,* Dec. 8, 1868; *New York Times,* Dec. 29, 1868; Custer's report, Nov. 28, 1868; Custer, *My Life on the Plains,* 240–61; Custer, *Following the Guidon,* 41–45; Barnitz to Camp, Nov. 29, 1910, Box 1, Folder 14, Camp Papers, microfilm; Clark account, *Kansas City Star,* Dec. 4, 1904; Clark account, *New York Sun,* May 14, 1899; Gibson, "Battle of the Washita," 17–19; Godfrey reminiscence, clipping from an unidentified newspaper, [ca. 1897–98], File 16, Box 24, Ghent Papers; Godfrey interview, Mar. 3, 1917, Box 3, Camp Papers, microfilm; Godfrey, "Reminiscences, Including the Washita Battle," 490–95; Godfrey statements, Field Notes, Camp Papers (Notebook 8, No. 36, Hammer Collection); Ryan, *Ten Years,* 52–58; Charles Brewster, "Battle of the Washita," *The National Tribune,* Aug. 22, 1901; Godfrey, "Notes on Chapter XXII of Colonel Homer W. Wheeler's 'Buffalo Days,'" Godfrey Family Papers Indian Wars; and Hunt, "Subjugation of Black Kettle," 105–6. Thorough secondary accounts appear in Brill, *Conquest of the Southern Plains,* 160–79; Leckie, *Military Conquest of the Southern Plains,* 100–105; and Utley, *Cavalier in Buckskin,* 67–71.

33. Account of Red Bird (Lone Wolf), or Stacy Riggs, in William, *Soul of the Red Man,* 240; Ediger and Hoffman, "Some Reminiscences of the Battle of the Washita," 138–39; Account of Mrs. Lone Wolf, in Puckett and Puckett, *History of Oklahoma,* 99–100.

34. Powell, *People of the Sacred Mountain,* 1:602–3; Brill, *Conquest of the Southern Plains,* 155–56, citing Magpie; account of Bearmeat Face, Jan. 22, 1910, Fred S. Barde Collection, Archives and Manuscripts Division, Oklahoma Historical Society, Oklahoma City; Hyde, *Life of George Bent,* 316–17; Bent to Hyde, Aug. 1, 1913, Bent-Hyde Correspondence.

35. Ediger and Hoffman, "Some Reminiscences of the Battle of the Washita," 139; Powell, *People of the Sacred Mountain,* 1:603–4.

36. Ediger and Hoffman, "Some Reminiscences of the Battle of the Washita," 139.

37. Powell, *People of the Sacred Mountain,* 1:604–6; Hyde, *Life of George Bent,* 317; Clark account, *New York Sun,* May 14, 1899; Clark account, *Kansas City Star,* Dec. 4, 1904. Custer described the incident as involving a "little white boy, a prisoner in the hands of the Indians." *My Life on the Plains,* 243–44.

38. Brill, *Conquest of the Southern Plains,* 161–63; Powell, *People of the Sacred Mountain,* 1:606–7. It has been surmised that the soldier shot by Magpie was Captain Albert Barnitz, though the accounts contain notable differences. See Brill, *Conquest of the Southern Plains,* 303–5.

39. An alternate account of the killing of Kennedy had the warriors coming out the timber from the west as they fled the onslaught in the village. They

rushed the sergeant, and one, a Cheyenne named Bobtail Bear, tomahawked him. George Bent to Robert M. Peck, [ca. 1906–7], in Hadley, "Nineteenth Kansas Cavalry," 444 n. 10.

40. A skeleton unearthed during early-twentieth-century railroad construction work was thought to be that of Hawk, based on ornaments found in the grave and Magpie's reminiscence of the burial spot. The remains were buried south of the village site in 1930. Brill, *Conquest of the Southern Plains*, 307. Two other Indian skeletons that surfaced during construction remained in a deteriorating gunny sack in the basement of the newspaper office until rediscovered in 1987 and buried by the Cheyennes in 1988. See undated clipping, *Sayre Record*, 88.32, File 216 (temp), Box 15, Washita Massacre, Folder 1, John L. Sipes Collection, Archives and Manuscripts Division, Oklahoma Historical Society, Oklahoma City; and clipping from unidentified newspaper, n.d. [ca. late June 1988], ibid.

41. Indians later told army officer Hugh L. Scott: "Elliott and his men could easily have escaped during some little time before [they] were completely surrounded. The Indians at first came up straggling along as they got their mounts and for some time were not strong enough to attack the soldiers. They expected the soldiers to leave, but they did not and held their ground until overwhelmed." Scott, interview by Walter M. Camp, Camp Papers (copy, Notebook 7, No. 4, Hammer Collection).

42. Clark stated that the men tied their horses together before beginning to fight the warriors. *St. Louis Republic*, Jan. 2, 1911.

43. Bent to Hyde, Sept. 11, 1905, Letter 16, Ms. 34, George Bent Manuscripts, Colorado Historical Society, Denver.

44. Hugh Scott learned that an Arapaho named Smokes Road (Tobacco?) also was killed while attacking Elliott's men. Scott to Godfrey, July 2, 1931, Godfrey Papers.

45. This account of the destruction of Elliott's party is drawn from the following sources: Powell, *People of the Sacred Mountain*, 1:607–13, 681–82; Brill, *Conquest of the Southern Plains*, 161–70, 305–6 (containing the accounts of Little Beaver and Left Hand); Grinnell, *Fighting Cheyennes*, 302–5; Hyde, *Life of George Bent*, 318–20; Bent to Peck, [ca. 1906–7], in Hadley, "Nineteenth Kansas Cavalry," 441; account of Red Bird (Lone Wolf), or Stacy Riggs, in Williams, *Soul of the Red Man*, 240–41; Rush, "What Indian Tongues Could Tell," 13, 27–34; *The Daily Oklahoman*, July 27, 1930; Foley, "Walter Camp & Ben Clark," 23; Trenholm, *Arapahoes*, 227, 242; Nye, *Carbine and Lance*, 66–68. A Cheyenne account that places Kennedy's death last is in Puckett and Puckett, *History of Oklahoma*, 102–3. An account that stresses the Kiowas' role in the Elliott affair is Tahan, "Battle of the Washita," 278. Another, less credible, account of Elliott's demise, purportedly given by Little Raven, is in Wright, "Reminiscences of Dodge," 72. According to Clark, the site of Elliott's engagement is in the southeast quarter of Section 5, Township 13 North, Range 23 West. Foley, "Walter Camp & Ben Clark," 22. The Indian accounts strongly suggest that the site is east of the former big bend of Sergeant Major Creek in the area of the extreme eastern edge of Section 7 or the western half of the northwest quarter of Section 8. Lees et al., "Archaeology of the Washita Battlefield National Historic Site," 24–25. But Fred S. Barde placed the site in the

northwestern corner of the southeast quarter of Section 7. See "Map of the Washita Battle Ground," Map 2 (township and range), Barde Collection. In addition, modern Cheyenne perspectives of the Washita attack, many of them as recalled by descendants of participants, appear in Warde, "Final Report on Cooperative Agreement 1443CA125098002 Modification 1, Conduct Oral History Research for Washita Historical Site, Sept. 30, 1999."

46. Powell, *People of the Sacred Mountain*, 1:614–17.

47. Ediger and Hoffman, "Some Reminiscences of the Battle of the Washita," 140–41; Puckett and Puckett, *History of Oklahoma*, 100. Beyond the materials specifically cited above, this account of the Washita encounter from the Indian perspective has been compiled from the following sources: Grinnell, *Fighting Cheyennes*, 300–305; Rush, "What Indian Tongues Could Tell," 11–13, 27–34; *The Daily Oklahoman*, July 27, Nov. 23, 1930; interview with Joe Yellow Eyes, 1937, in "Indian and Pioneer Histories," 1930s Federal Writers' Project, 52:125; interview with Red Bird, 1937, in ibid., 228 (republished in *The Watonga Republican*, May 28, 1997); account of Red Bird (different man from above), *The Watonga Republican*, June 25, 1997; and Nye, *Carbine and Lance*, 64–70. At least one purported Indian account, that of a white captive of the Kiowas, maintained that the warriors were planning to ambush Custer's command as it headed downriver, apparently at some point above the various camps. Tahan, "Battle of the Washita," 280. See also the narrative-compilation presented in Harrison, "Eyes of the Sleepers," 1–24; and John L. Sipes Jr., "Mo-chi, Cheyenne Warrior Woman: The Story of Buffalo Calf Woman," *The St. Francis (Okla.) Herald*, Aug. 30, 1990. Modern oral histories containing Washita-related material include Jess Rowlodge, Arapaho, Mar. 26, 1967, Doris Duke Oral History Collection, Indian Institute, University of Oklahoma, Norman; and Colleen Cometsevah, Southern Cheyenne, Aug. 20, 1999, in Warde, "Final Report on Cooperative Agreement 1443CA125098002 Modification 1, Conduct Oral History Research for Washita Historical Site." See also "Summaries of Interviews," in ibid.

48. "Special Report. Officers Killed at the Battle of the Washita, I.T., November 27, 1868"; "Special Report. Enlisted Men Killed at the Battle of the Washita, Indian Territory, November 27, 1868"; and "List of Wounded in 7th U.S. Cavalry under command of Bvt. Maj. Genl Custer, U.S.A. at the Battle of the Washita, Indian Territory, on the 27th day of Novr. 1868," enclosed in Assistant Surgeon George A. Otis to Colonel Charles H. Crane, Assistant Surgeon General, Jan. 16, 1869, RG 94. See also Custer's report, Nov. 1, 1869, 46; and Gibson, "Battle of the Washita," 25–26. See appendixes A and B for more-complete listings of casualties.

49. For example, Private Henry Langley of Company C claimed to have received two slight wounds "in the left wrist, and in the left leg above the knee," neither of which appeared on the casualty lists. Langley letter, *Winners of the West*, Dec. 15, 1925.

50. See "In Memoriam," 362–86; AAG, Department of the Missouri, to Sherman, Jan. 11, 1868, Philip H. Sheridan Papers, LC, Roll 76; and Barnitz and Barnitz, *Life in Custer's Cavalry*, 243. The resolution appeared in the *New York Herald* and the *Army and Navy Journal* on December 26, 1868. The Camp Supply funeral was described as follows: "The body was carried in an ambulance

[serving] as a hearse and covered with a large American flag. In advance of the ambulance marched Hamilton's squadron commanded by Brevet Lieutenant Colonel T. B. Weir, followed by Captain Hamilton's horse, covered with a mourning sheet, and bearing on the saddle the saber and belt and reversed top boots of the dead soldier." *Kansas City Times,* Nov. 25[?], 1908. A similar account is in the *New York Herald,* Dec. 26, 1868. See also Custer's account of the funeral in Custer, *Following the Guidon,* 45. Of the six pallbearers given above for Hamilton's remains, four subsequently met similar deaths while fighting Indians. But the same issue of the *Kansas City Times* listed the pallbearers as General Sheridan, Colonel Custer, Captain Custer, Beebe, Weir, Crosby, and West.

51. Barnitz's wound was described in detail by his close friend, Lieutenant Godfrey, in a letter of December 5, 1868, to the captain's wife, Jennie: "The ball entered his left side on a line with the left groin and about four inches above the navel; coming out on the left side of the spine cutting the top of his pants. The wound is one that rarely occurs without cutting the intestines, and that was what was at first appeared to be the case." Barnitz and Barnitz, *Life in Custer's Cavalry,* 229. See also the description in *New York Herald,* Dec. 24, 1868. A clinical description of Barnitz's operation is in War Department, Office of the Surgeon General, *Circular No.* 3 (Washington, D.C.: Government Printing Office, 1871), 250–51. The injury forced Barnitz's retirement in 1870. When he died in 1912, doctors discovered that a growth coalescing around the old Washita wound had contributed to his demise; a piece of his overcoat was also found inside his body, driven there by the Cheyenne bullet forty-four years earlier. Barnitz and Barnitz, *Life in Custer's Cavalry,* 243, 247.

52. Custer's report, Nov. 1, 1869, 46; Custer to AAAG, Department of the Missouri, Dec. 22, 1868, in Senate, *Letter of the Secretary of War,* 9; Senate, *Letter of the Secretary of the Interior,* 9; *New York Herald,* Dec. 24, 1868; General Sheridan to AAG, Division of the Missouri, Dec. 3, 1868, in U.S. Senate, *Report of Lt. Col. G. A. Custer, in the Filed, on Washita River, November 28, 1868,* 40th Cong., 3d sess., 1869, S. Exec. Doc. 18, 31; *Report of the Secretary of the Interior, 1869,* 525, 823; Brill, *Conquest of the Southern Plains,* 16 n. 2. Other government officials reported between nine and twenty men killed and between eighteen and forty women and children killed. Berthrong, *Southern Cheyennes,* 328, citing *Report of the Board of Indian Commissioners, Appointed by the President Agreeably to Section Fourth of the Act of Congress Making Appropriations for the Current and Contingent Expenses of the Indian Department for 1869* (Washington, D.C.: Government Printing Office, 1871), 42–43; James S. Morrison to Wynkoop, Dec. 14, 1868, Letters Received, Upper Arkansas Agency, RG 75, Records of the Office of Indian Affairs, NA; Bent to Hyde, Aug. 28, 1913, Bent-Hyde Correspondence.

53. Bent to Hyde, Aug. 28, 1913. Bent-Hyde Correspondence; Bent to Grinnell, Oct. 2, 1913, Ms. 5, Folder 56.2, George Bird Grinnell Collection, Braun Research Library, Southwest Museum, Los Angeles; Bent to Camp, Dec. 4, 1916, Folder 2, Box 2, Camp Papers, microfilm. In the lists accompanying the last two cited letters, the names of several of those killed are not identical. See also Grinnell to Camp, Oct. 3, 1916, Folder 2, Box 2, Camp Papers, microfilm. Cheyenne researcher John L. Sipes compiled a list accounting for

thirty-four named individuals (men and women), one unidentified Comanche, and five unnamed children killed at the Washita. 88.32, File 216 (temp.), Box 15, Washita Massacre, Folder 1, Sipes Collection. See appendix B for a tentative casualty list, based upon the Bent and Sipes enumerations, that accounts for fifty-eight possible Indian fatalities.

54. *New York Sun*, May 14, 1899.

55. Captain Andrew Sheridan, Third Infantry, to AAG, Department of the Missouri, Dec. 14, 1868, Box 4, Entry 2601, RG 393, Records of U.S. Army Continental Commands, Pt. 1, NA; *New York Herald*, Dec. 24, 1868; Godfrey, "Notes on Chapter XXII of Colonel Homer W. Wheeler's 'Buffalo Days,'" Godfrey Family Papers Indian Wars.

56. Custer's report, Nov. 28, 1868.

57. Ibid. The references to the two white children and the white women killed have never been explained, though it is possible that Custer was referencing a six-year-old boy and a fifteen-year-old girl turned over to Lieutenant Colonel Alfred Sully by the Kiowas the preceding summer. See Sully to Sherman, Dec. 10, 1868, William T. Sherman Papers, LC, Roll 13. Furthermore, a later allusion to the prisoners indicated that a badly wounded "Mrs. Crocker" was among them, but this might have been a Cheyenne woman married to a mixed-blood. See J. S. Morrison to Wynkoop, Dec. 14, 1868, cited in Brill, *Conquest of the Southern Plains*, 313–14.

58. Barnitz to wife, Dec. 5, 1868, Barnitz and Barnitz, *Life in Custer's Cavalry*, 235; Rea, "Washita Trail," 257–59.

Chapter 8. End Results

1. Custer, *My Life on the Plains*, 265–67, 268–69; Godfrey, "Reminiscences, Including the Washita Battle," 496. See also Keim, *Sheridan's Troopers*, 121–23; Ryan, *Ten Years*, 60; Spotts, *Campaigning with Custer*, 65–66.

2. Keim, *Sheridan's Troopers*, 125; Custer, *Following the Guidon*, 45; Harvey, "Campaigning with Sheridan," 87. Harvey suggests that the burials occurred on December 3. George H. Shirk, who edited Harvey's diary, identified the enlisted burials as Privates Charles Cuddy and Augustus Delaney, Company B, Seventh Cavalry; and Private Benjamin McKasey, of Company H, who died at Camp Supply on December 1 from wounds received at the Washita. Ibid. The newspaper correspondent Keim, who was present, described Hamilton's funeral:

> The troops formed in the vicinity of the tent in which the body had lain since its arrival at the camp. At two o'clock in the afternoon the roll of muffled drums, the solemn refrain of the band, and the slow step of the pall-bearers, announced that the remains were approaching. The coffin, enveloped in the national colors, was placed in an ambulance. The long line of mourning comrades, in reverse order, broke into column. The squadron of the deceased officer took the advance. Next came the remains, followed by the riderless horse, covered with a morning sheet and [boots and?] spurs reversed. Then the long column of troops and officers, all moving in measured tread towards the grave. . . . The body

was lowered into the cold and solitary grave. The burial service was read by a brother officer, and amid volleys of musketry the earth closed upon its dead. [*Sheridan's Troopers*, 125.]

Oddly, Keim recorded no description of the enlisted men's interment. Hamilton's remains were later disinterred and removed to Fort Dodge for shipment to Poughkeepsie, New York, at the request of the family. AAG, Division of the Missouri, to General Sheridan, Dec. 4, 1868, Entry 2539, Vol. 1, RG 393, Records of U.S. Army Continental Commands, Pt. 1, NA; Sherman to Edward D. Townsend, Dec. 8, 1868, ibid.; Sherman to Townsend, Jan. 9, 1869, ibid. (In 1877, in an addendum to the Hamilton story, Custer's own remains were held in the Hamilton family's vault in Poughkeepsie, pending interment at West Point in October of that year. As Custer's coffin was borne down the Hudson River to its resting place in the Military Academy cemetery, the flag that had once draped Hamilton's bier now covered that of his former commander. Leckie, *Elizabeth Bacon Custer and the Making of a Myth*, 218–19, 358 nn. 27, 28.) The enlisted men do not appear in extant cemetery records for Camp Supply nor are they found in the records of reburials at Fort Leavenworth National Cemetery, Kansas. Reportedly, the first cemetery at Camp Supply washed away in a flood of Beaver River before 1873. Bob Rea, conversation with author, Fort Supply Historic Site, Mar. 23, 2001.

3. Captain Andrew Sheridan to AAG, Department of the Missouri, Dec. 3, 1868, Box 4, Entry 2601, RG 393, Pt. 1; General Sheridan to AAG, Military Division of the Missouri, Dec. 3, 1868, in Senate, *Letter of the Secretary of the Interior*, 44–45; General Sheridan to Sherman, Nov. 29, 1868, Entry 2538, Vol. 1, RG 393, Pt. 1 (quote); Hutton, *Phil Sheridan and His Army*, 70–73. Captain Sheridan requested that "One hundred Thousand Rounds [of] Spencer Carbine Ammunition" be requisitioned for delivery in mid-December by Inman's supply train. Captain Sheridan to AAG, Department of the Missouri, Dec. 12, 1868, Box 4, Entry 2601, RG 393, Pt. 1. There were complaints over the quality of the issued ammunition, likely stemming from its use at the Washita. Adjutant McKeever reported: "General Sheridan states that he has been much embarrassed and crippled in his operations against the hostile Indians by the bad quality of the Spencer Carbine ammunition issued by the Ordnance Department, and that not more than one (1) cartridge out of seven (7) will explode. He thinks this is inexcusable and that the Ordnance Department should be called upon for an explanation." AAG, Department of the Missouri, to Colonel William A. Nichols, Dec. 21, 1868, Entry 2538, Vol. 1, RG 393, Pt. 1.

4. Sherman to General Sheridan, Dec. 2, 1868, Entry 2538, Vol. 1, RG 393, Pt. 1; Schofield to Sherman, Dec. 2, 1868, ibid.; Sherman to Augur, Dec. 4, 1868, ibid.; Custer, *My Life on the Plains*, 271 (quote); Custer to Crosby, Dec. 2, 1868, Box 1, Entry 2601, RG 393, Pt. 1. Years later six officers were cited for gallantry and bravery in the Washita action. They were Colonel Custer; Surgeon Lippincott; Captains Elliott, Hamilton, and Barnitz; and Lieutenants Custer and March. *U.S. Army Gallantry and Meritorious Conduct*, 11.

5. *My Life on the Plains*, 270; Athearn, *Sherman and the Settlement of the West*, 272–73; Sherman to AAG, Dec. 12, 1868, in Senate, *Letter of the Secretary of the Interior*, 36; *New York Herald*, Dec. 24, 1868. Wynkoop's resignation

occurred on November 27 but was coincidental with, and not driven by news of, the Washita engagement. Wynkoop, *Tall Chief*, 30.

6. Sherman to Lieutenant Colonel Chauncey McKeever, Jan. 16, 1869, Entry 2538, Vol. 1, RG 393, Pt. 1; Sherman to AAG, Dec. 12, 1968, ibid.; General Sheridan to AAG, Division of the Missouri, Jan. 1, 1869, in *Army and Navy Journal*, Jan. 23, 1869 (and in Senate, *Letter of the Secretary of the Interior*, 59); *Army and Navy Journal*, Jan. 2, 1869. Sheridan's remarks were technically correct, though in his statement he was referencing the Kiowa and Comanche reserve as specified in the Medicine Lodge accord. In fact, however, the army expedition from Fort Dodge to Camp Supply and south to the Washita River had not penetrated the Cheyenne-Arapaho reservation lands as specified at Medicine Lodge, though it could be said to have invaded the hunting lands below the Arkansas. The route of the Kansas troops in reaching Camp Supply, however, did cross part of the reserve.

7. *Army and Navy Journal*, Jan. 2, 1869; Hazen to Sherman, Dec. 31, 1868, Philip H. Sheridan Papers, LC, Roll 76.

8. Murphy to Taylor, Dec. 4, 1868, in Senate, *Letter of the Secretary of the Interior*, 36–38; *New York Tribune*, Feb. 17, 1877, as cited in Charles H. Whipple to Thoburn, Nov. 5, 1912, 86.01.1038:A, Joseph B. Thoburn Papers, Oklahoma Historical Society, Oklahoma City.; post-Washita letter to the *St. Louis* (Missouri) *Republican*, n.d., quoted in *Army and Navy Journal*, Jan. 30, 1869. See Athearn, *Sherman and the Settlement of the West*, 276–77.

9. Brill, *Conquest of the Southern Plains*, 25, citing Magpie; Powell, *People of the Sacred Mountain*, 2:694–95. In 1934 a skeleton found at the western end of the village area near the spot Magpie had last seen Black Kettle's body bore personal ornaments consistent with those worn by the chief. Brill, *Conquest of the Southern Plains*, 25–26; Edger and Hoffman, "Some Reminiscences," 140 n.

10. "Summary of information regarding hostile Indians. Report of Captain H. E. Alvord," Dec. 7, 1868, Sheridan Papers, Roll 76. Also in "Summary of information regarding hostile Indians. Semi-weekly Report No. 5," Dec. 7, 1868, "Reports of Officers in the West and Southwest, 1874–75 [*sic*]," Military Division of the Missouri Papers, U.S. Army Military History Institute, Army War College, Carlisle, Pa. See also Hazen to Sherman, Dec. 7, 1868 (especially sketch map showing locations of tribes), Sheridan Papers, Roll 76.

11. "Summary of information regarding hostile Indians. Semi-weekly Report No. 4," Dec. 3, 1868, "Reports of Officers in the West and Southwest, 1874–75 [*sic*]," Military Division of the Missouri Papers. A similar account is in Philip McCusky to Murphy, Dec. 3, 1868, in Senate, *Letter of the Secretary of the Interior*, 30. The first notice of the Washita encounter had reached Captain Alvord at Fort Cobb on November 30. "Summary of information regarding hostile Indians. Semi-weekly Report No. 3," Nov. 30, 1868, "Reports of Officers in the West and Southwest, 1874–75 [sic]," Military Division of the Missouri Papers.

12. "Summary of information regarding hostile Indians. Semi-weekly Report No. 4," Dec. 3, 1868, "Reports of Officers in the West and Southwest, 1874–75 [*sic*]," Military Division of the Missouri Papers.

13. *New York Herald*, Dec. 24, 26, 1868; Burkey, *Custer, Come at Once!* 64. Apparently, for a while it was believed by some Cheyennes that Black Kettle's wife had survived and was imprisoned at Fort Hays, for in January 1869, George Bent wrote directly to President Grant requesting her release. Sherman to Townsend, Jan. 28, 1869, Entry 2538, Vol. 1, RG 393, Pt. 1.

14. Foley, "Walter Camp & Ben Clark," 24. See also Powell, *People of the Sacred Mountain*, 2:696, 1327–28 n. 10. Some secondary writers, however, have since elaborated on the basic information without providing supporting evidence for their claims. The most thorough discussion of the prisoners in confinement, as well as of the controversy regarding the women and its borderline fictional aspects, is Burkey, *Custer, Come at Once!* 64–73. Benteen's remarks appear in Benteen to Theodore Goldin, Feb. 17, 1896, in Carroll, *Benteen-Goldin Letters*, 271. Cheyenne references appear in Marquis, *She Watched Custer's Last Battle*, 1; Brill, *Conquest of the Southern Plains*, 22; and Powell, *People of the Sacred Mountain*, 2:1327–28 n. 10. See also the thoughtful evaluation in Barnett, *Touched by Fire*, 194–97.

15. Harvey, "Campaigning with Sheridan," 88; General Sheridan to Sherman, Dec. 7, 1868, Sheridan Papers, Roll 13. In another missive of the same date, Sheridan wrote Sherman, "I judge from your instructions to me, that it is not intended to make peace and feed these Indians, without holding them responsible for the murders and thefts they have committed." Ibid., Roll 76.

16. Particulars of the role of the Nineteenth Kansas Infantry in the campaign are summarized in White, "Winter Campaigning with Sheridan and Custer," 101–13. See also Hadley, "Nineteenth Kansas Cavalry," 443–58.

17. Keim, *Sheridan's Troopers*, 137.

18. The officers who comprised the party were General Sheridan; Colonel Custer; Major James W. Forsyth; Captains J. Schuyler Crosby, Andrew J. McGonnigle, Samuel Robbins (promoted vice Hamilton, Nov. 27, 1868), and George W. Yates; Assistant Surgeon Morris J. Asch; First Lieutenants William W. Cooke, Charles Brewster, Owen Hale, Myles Moylan, and Thomas W. Custer; and Second Lieutenant John F. Weston. *New York Herald*, Jan. 4, 1869.

19. Custer to AAAG, Department of the Missouri, Dec. 22, 1868, in Senate, *Letter of the Secretary of War*, 3.

20. Keim, *Sheridan's Troopers*, 143–44; Custer to AAAG, Department of the Missouri, Dec. 22, 1868, in Senate, *Letter of the Secretary of War*, 3; George B. Jenness, "History of the 19th Kansas Cavalry," n.d., Manuscripts Division, Kansas State Historical Society, Topeka.

21. Mutilation of dead enemies was common among the Cheyennes and other plains tribes, its purpose to wreak ultimate revenge, assuring that the dead entered the next world thusly incapacitated. It was often practiced in the aftermath of combat by women and children. Scalping commonly occurred incidentally and was not as significant a part of the Cheyennes' war honors tradition as was the practice of counting coup, or touching an enemy. Most scalps taken by warriors and others were regarded merely as souvenirs. On the matter of mutilation and scalping among Plains societies, see Moore, *The Cheyenne*, 124–25; McGinnis, *Counting Coup and Cutting Horses*, 28–29; and

George B. Grinnell, "Coup and Scalp among the Plains Indians," in Owen, Deetz, and Fisher, *North American Indians,* 520 ff.

22. Custer to AAAG, Department of the Missouri, Dec. 22, 1868, in Senate, *Letter of the Secretary of War,* 4. Custer likely was alluding to a statement by Black Eagle of the Kiowas, one of the earliest Indian recollections of the Washita, which was sent from Fort Cobb within six days of the encounter. Philip McCusker to Murphy, Dec. 3, 1868, in Hazen, "Some Corrections of *Life on the Plains,"* in Custer, *My Life on the Plains,* 398–400. Hazen transmitted a copy to the army hierarchy, noting that it represented one of "not less than fifty accounts of the battle of Washita, from different individuals belonging to every tribe in that country." Ibid., 400.

23. *New York Herald,* Dec. 24, 1868; Keim, *Sheridan's Troopers,* 150. A thorough account of the Blinn episode, which includes the complete text of Blinn's letter, is Justus, "Saga of Clara H. Blinn," 11–20, 31.

24. Elliott's mother requested that her son's body be returned for burial in Centreville, Indiana. AAG, Division of the Missouri, to General Sheridan, Dec. 5, 1868 (containing request for shipment of remains), Entry 2538, Vol. 1, RG 393, Pt. 1; Sherman to Mary Elliott, Dec. 5, 1868, ibid.; Sherman to General Sheridan, Dec. 5, 1868, ibid. Sherman shortly wrote Elliott's mother: "it may be some time before I hear of the remains of Major Elliott being started. You shall have earliest notice." Sherman to Mary Elliott, Dec. 12, 1868, ibid. Elliott, meantime, was buried temporarily at Fort Cobb. AAG, Division of the Missouri, to Mary Elliott, Jan. 11, 1869, ibid. Apparently, the Blinns were likewise buried there temporarily. Jenness, "History of the 19th Kansas Cavalry." When Fort Cobb closed, Elliott's body was removed to Fort Arbuckle, presumably along with those of the Blinns. Following the abandonment of Fort Arbuckle in 1870, all three bodies were disinterred and reburied at Fort Gibson, where they lie today in Fort Gibson National Cemetery.

25. Custer to AAAG, Department of the Missouri, Dec. 22, 1868, in Senate, *Letter of the Secretary of War,* 4–5. Also reproduced in Custer, *My Life on the Plains,* 288–89. The three unknowns listed above, together with one other man not accounted for in Custer's list, were Private John George, Company H; Private John McClernan, Company E; Sergeant Erwin Vanousky, Company M; and Private Frederick Stobascus, Company M. See appendix A. Obviously, certain particularly sensitive material was excised from the descriptions of the mutilations. In a special report on the condition of Elliott's body, Dr. Lippincott recorded: "Two bullet holes in head, one in left cheek, right hand cut off, left hand almost cut off, penis cut off, deep gash in right groin, deep gash in calves of both legs, little finger of left hand cut off, and throat cut." (Note the significant differences in this description from the published version.) Medical Records, Fort Cobb, File D, Box 4, RG 94, Records of the Adjutant General's Office, NA. Major George B. Jenness of the Kansas troops also stated that Elliott's right hand had been severed. "History of the 19th Kansas Cavalry." Captain Benteen wrote a friend, "nearly all had been horribly mangled in a way delicacy forbids me to mention," a statement that strongly suggests that most of the soldiers' genitalia had been cut off or otherwise defiled. *Missouri Democrat,* Feb. 9, 1869. Years later Ben Clark gave this account of the bodies:

"Every body except Elliott's had been mutilated. Skulls were crushed in with war clubs, ears and noses and legs had been cut off, scalps torn away and the bodies pierced with bullets and arrows. Elliott had been greatly admired by the Indians for his bravery long before the fight. They remembered this when he was dead and treated him as a valorous foe by severing his right hand at the wrist and his left foot at the ankle, leaving each attached by a tendon. The body bore no other marks save the death wounds." *New York Sun*, May 14, 1899. Similarly, Major Jenness remarked that "all [the bodies] but that of Elliott [had been] horribly mutilated." "History of the 19th Kansas Cavalry." On this point, see also Thomas Shanley account, *The Daily Oklahoman*, Aug. 2, 1925.

26. The precise location of the burial of Elliott's men has not been determined. Ben Clark recalled that the burials were made "just above or west of our camp" and that the army camp was on the north side of the Washita "where it bends the farthest north, some six miles or so below the Black Kettle camp." Clark to Barde, May 1, 1903, Fred S. Barde Collection, Archives and Manuscripts Division, Oklahoma Historical Society, Oklahoma City. The remains of the seventeen soldiers presumably lie there yet.

27. Spotts, *Campaigning with Custer*, 76; W. R. Smith (formerly of Company F, Nineteenth Kansas Volunteer Cavalry) letter, *National Tribune*, Mar. 26, 1925; Harvey, "Campaigning with Sheridan," 89. While the Kiowas played no immediate role in the Washita action affecting the village, it is possible that some of their warriors took part in the subsequent long-range dueling between the cavalrymen and the Indians from the downriver camps. As previously indicated, there exists substantial evidence that some Kiowas participated in the killing of Elliott's command. Colonel Hazen, however, presented records that showed that most of that tribe were camped within twenty miles of Fort Cobb on the night of November 26 and that some of the leaders, notably Satanta, Satank, Timber Mountain, and Lone Wolf, remained at the agency the following morning—the very time of the attack on Black Kettle's village—and therefore could not have been involved in the fighting. But Philip McCusker, an interpreter at Fort Cobb, recalled that about thirty lodges of Kiowas under Big Bow and To-hau-son that had never been to Fort Cobb were indeed set up near the Washita camps of the Cheyennes and Arapahos and participated in the fighting. Hazen, "Some Corrections of 'Life on the Plains,'" *Chronicles of Oklahoma*, 307, 314, 318.

28. Hazen stated that the Blinns had been captured by Arapahos and had been killed by them, "the Kiowas never having been in any way responsible in this case. . . . I was on the point of rescuing her [Clara Blinn] and in correspondence with her, when the battle took place." Hazen, "Some Corrections of 'Life on the Plains,'" *Chronicles of Oklahoma*, 305. But two of Captain Alvord's scouting reports, dated November 22 and 26, 1868, expressly state that the Blinns were held in one of the Cheyenne camps. Alvord noted on the twenty-second, "at the Cheyenne camp there is a white woman and her child, understood to have been captured on the Santa Fe road in September [sic] last." On the twenty-sixth he wrote: "The white woman held as a captive at that [Cheyenne and Arapaho] camp is Clara Blinn—her son Willie, two years old, is with her." "Reports of Officers in the West and Southwest, 1874–75 [sic]," Military Division of the Missouri Papers. And Clara Blinn herself stated in her

letter of November 7, "we are with the Cheyenne[s]." Justus, "Saga of Clara H. Blinn," 13.

29. Custer, *My Life on the Plains*, 293; General Sheridan to AAG, Division of the Missouri, Dec. 24, 1868, Sheridan Papers, Roll 76.

30. Evans's expedition is delineated in *Army and Navy Journal*, Mar. 13, 1869; and General Sheridan to AAG, Department of the Missouri, Dec. 31, 1868, in *Army and Navy Journal*, Jan. 30, 1869. For his lengthy and detailed report, see Evans to AAAG, Headquarters, District of New Mexico, Jan. 23, 1869, Sheridan Papers, Roll 76. For Carr's expedition, see Carr to General Sheridan, Dec. 20, 1868, Jan. 18, 20, 1869, "Reports of Officers in the West and Southwest, 1874–75 [sic]," Military Division of the Missouri Papers; Carr to AAG, Department of the Missouri, Apr. 7, 1869, Sheridan Papers, Roll 76; Leckie, *Military Conquest of the Southern Plains*, 114–19; and, especially, Taylor, "Carr-Penrose Expedition," 159–76. For the role of the Tenth Cavalry in the operations of 1868–69, see Leckie, *Buffalo Soldiers*, 26–44.

31. General Sheridan to AAG, Division of the Missouri, Jan. 1, 1869, in *Army and Navy Journal*, Jan. 23, 1869; Spotts, *Campaigning with Custer*, 82; Harvey, "Campaigning with Sheridan," 91. For Camp Wichita and Fort Sill, see Frazer, *Forts of the West*, 124; and, especially, Nye, *Carbine and Lance*. By March 1869, Camp Wichita, commanded by Colonel Benjamin Grierson (who also commanded the District of the Indian Territory), was garrisoned by four companies of the Tenth Cavalry and two companies of the Sixth Infantry. "About 4,000 Indians are in the vicinity of the post, on the reservation. They are the following named bands: Three bands of Comanches—Pennetacos, 250 strong, chiefs Tosheway, Asahabit and Essatoyet; Noconees, 320 strong, chief Ta-ha-yer-qua-hip (Horse Buck); Yamparicos, 360 strong, chiefs Ten Bear, Iron Mountain, Howear and Little Crow; Kiowas, about 790 strong, chiefs Satanta, Lone Wolf, Black Eagle and Kicking Eagle; [Kiowa-]Apaches, about 290 strong, chiefs Wolf Sleeve and Soomsetah; Arapahoes, about 370 strong, chiefs Little Raven, yellow Bear and Storm; Caddoes, about 450 strong, chiefs Warloopi and George Washington." *Army and Navy Journal*, Apr. 24, 1869.

32. At Fort Sill, Colonel Hazen would help inaugurate procedures that would come to represent President Grant's Peace Policy, wherein members of various church denominations were invited to run the Indian agencies. When the Bureau of Indian Affairs assumed control of the Fort Sill agency, the Quakers took over, introducing the tribesmen to the tenets of severalty and husbandry. Pratt, *Battlefield and Classroom*, 36 n. 14.

33. Alvord to Grierson, Feb. 5, 1869, Benjamin H. Grierson Papers, Newberry Library, Chicago, Rolls 1–2 (transcribed excerpts, Library, Fort Davis National Historical Site, Oklahoma City); Powell, *People of the Sacred Mountain*, 2:703–4; Spotts, *Campaigning with Custer*, 103.

34. Custer, *My Life on the Plains*, 343. Custer claimed that "one of the objects of the expedition" was to find and secure the release of two white women alleged to have been taken by the Cheyennes and supposedly still in their custody. Ibid., 353.

35. Custer to General Sheridan, Mar. 21, 1869, "Reports of Officers in the West and Southwest, 1874–75 [sic]," Military Division of the Missouri Papers (also in Sheridan Papers, Roll 76); Spotts, *Campaigning with Custer*, 140–41.

In his memoir, *My Life on the Plains*, Custer does not mention the departure for the Washita field depot of a large part of his command. Private Harvey was one of those who accompanied Myers's column. On the day after his arrival at the Washita depot, he toured the encounter site, erroneously commenting, "the bones of our dead lay all over the ground; the wolves dug them up and ate all the flesh off of them." Obviously, he saw Indian remains, not army dead. In his entry of March 17, Harvey corrected himself, reporting, "on our old battle ground, nothing to be seen but some old skull bones of dead Indians, killed in the fight." Harvey, "Campaigning with Sheridan," 101–2. See also John Murphy, "Reminiscences of the Washita Campaign and of the Darlington Indian Agency," *Chronicles of Oklahoma* 1 (Sept. 1923): 267; and "A. L. Runyon's Letters," 72–74. David L. Spotts, who had been with the Kansas troops, stated that the depot stood one mile below the encounter site, thus presumably east from where Black Kettle's village had been located. Spotts to E. C. Searcy, Jan. 20, 1933, Folder 7, Box S-23, E. C. Searcy Collection, Western History Collections, University of Oklahoma Library, Norman.

36. Custer to General Sheridan, Mar. 21, 1869, "Reports of Officers in the West and Southwest, 1874–75 [sic]," Military Division of the Missouri Papers; Custer, *My Life on the Plains*, 354. Efforts to find the exact site of the camp in the 1930s are explained in Spotts to Searcy, Jan. 20, Feb. 9, 1933, Folder 7, Box S-23, Searcy Collection; and Spotts to Thoburn, Feb. 16, 1933, 86.01, File 11, Box 33, WA-2, Thoburn Papers.

37. The lodge in which the parley took place held the *Maahotse*, the Four Sacred Arrows that with the Sacred Buffalo Hat comprised the cornerstones of Cheyenne religion and society. According to Cheyenne oral history, the Indians purposefully seated Custer directly beneath the Sacred Arrows. Chief Medicine Arrows told Custer, "if you are acting treachery toward us, sometime you and your whole command will be killed." George Bent to George E. Hyde, Sept. 1905, George Bent Manuscripts, Colorado Historical Society, Denver, as cited in Berthrong, *Southern Cheyennes*, 337. According to the Cheyennes, this incident forecasted the deaths of Custer and his immediate command at the Little Bighorn River in Montana Territory on June 25, 1876. George Bent described the event: Custer sat "right under the sacred arrows, which were hanging from a forked stick made for that purpose. Lighting his pipe, Rock Forehead [Medicine Arrows (Stone Forehead), keeper of the arrows] held it while Custer smoked, telling Custer at the same time, in Cheyenne, that if he was acting treacherously he and all his command would soon be killed. When Custer had smoked, Rock Forehead took the pipe stick and loosened the ashes, then poured them on Custer's toes to give him bad luck." Hyde, *Life of George Bent*, 325. The most detailed account of the episode from the Cheyenne perspective is in Powell, *People of the Sacred Mountain*, 2:708–11. For the sequel, see ibid., 1030; and Powell, *Sweet Medicine*, 1:120–23. For variant aspects, see Stands in Timber and Liberty, *Cheyenne Memories*, 82–83.

38. Cheyennes from Little Robe's village who turned themselves in at Camp Wichita on April 9, 1869, reported that the hostages seized at the Sweetwater were Lean Man, Little Bear, and Big Head, all of which names are identical to, or can be construed closely from, those given above. Grierson to AAG, Department of the Missouri, Apr. 10, 1869, Sheridan Papers, Roll 76.

The mixed-blood George Bent, who was not present, identified the three as Lean Face, Fat Bear, and Curly Hair. Northern Cheyenne tribal historian John Stands in Timber in 1960 identified an 1869 photo of the men as Little Bear, Hairless Bear, and Island. A niece of Island claimed that the picture was of Younger Bear, Chief Comes in Sight, and Island. For Bent's account of the incident, as obtained from participants, see Hyde, *Life of George Bent*, 325–26.

39. Custer, *My Life on the Plains*, 370; George W. Brown, "Reminiscences of a Scout," *Sturm's Oklahoma Magazine* 11 (Dec. 1910): 56. Sarah White later became a schoolteacher and married a farmer, H. C. Brooks, with whom she had seven children. She died in 1939 in Concordia, Kansas. Her colleague in captivity, Mrs. Morgan, rejoined her husband, who had been wounded in the attack on their farm. They raised a family, but Mrs. Morgan eventually entered an asylum in Topeka, where she died in 1902. Spotts, *Campaigning with Custer*, 207–15; *Kansas City Times*, May 31, 1939.

40. Spotts to Thoburn, Feb. 13, 16, 18, Mar. 6, 1933, 86.01, File 11, Box 33, WA-2, Thoburn Papers; Custer to General Sheridan, Mar. 21, 1869, "Reports of Officers in the West and Southwest, 1874–75 [sic]," Military Division of the Missouri Papers. For personal recollections of the incidents at Medicine Arrows's village, see Custer to General Sheridan, Mar. 21, 1869; Custer, *My Life on the Plains*, 353–76; Custer, *Following the Guidon*, 56–57; Spotts, *Campaigning with Custer*, 153–60; Ryan, *Ten Years*, 70–73; "Narrative by Josephus Bingaman," Eli S. Ricker Collection, Manuscript Division, Nebraska State Historical Society, Lincoln; Moore, "Nineteenth Kansas Cavalry in the Washita Campaign," 361–64 (which closely details the release of the women); and Brown, "Life and Adventures," 107–9. An able synthesis of Indian and non-Indian accounts is Powell, *People of the Sacred Mountain*, 2:707–18. But see also the comprehensive presentations in Dixon, "Custer and the Sweetwater Hostages," 82–108; and White, "White Women Captives of the Southern Cheyennes," 335–42. The three chiefs were initially incarcerated in the Fort Hays stockade with the Washita prisoners. When the commanding officer attempted to transfer them to the guardhouse without interpreting to them a reason, the Indians believed that they were to be executed. They rushed the guards with knives, and two—Fat Bear and Dull Knife—died in the struggle. Berthrong, *Southern Cheyennes*, 338.

41. The new Cheyenne and Arapaho reservation touched on the Cimarron River to the northeast and the North Fork of the Red River to the southwest and included the Washita country, embracing Fort Cobb, the Antelope Hills, and the scene of the army attack of November 27, 1868. For technical boundaries, see Charles C. Royce, comp., "Indian Land Cessions in the United States," in *Eighteenth Annual Report of the Bureau of American Ethnology, 1896–97*, 2 pts. (Washington, D.C.: Government Printing Office, 1899), 2: 852–53.

42. In addition to materials specifically cited above, this account of the post-Washita phase of Sheridan's campaign is drawn from the following sources: Sheridan's report, Nov. 1, 1869, in *Report of the Secretary of War, 1869*, 48–51; Custer to General Sheridan, Mar. 21, 1869, "Reports of Officers in the West and Southwest, 1874–75 [sic]," Military Division of the Missouri Papers; Letter, *St. Louis Republican*, reprinted in *New York Times*, May 3,

1869, and in *Army and Navy Journal*, May 8, 1869; Sheridan, *Personal Memoirs*, 2:323–47; Crawford, *Kansas in the Sixties*, 325–35; Godfrey's account, clipping from unidentified newspaper, [ca. 1897–98], File 16, Box 24, William J. Ghent Papers, LC; Moore, "Nineteenth Kansas Cavalry in the Washita Campaign," 360–64; Hadley, "Nineteenth Kansas Cavalry," 443–56; Berthrong, *Southern Cheyennes*, 329–39, 344; Leckie, *Military Conquest of the Southern Plains*, 106–13, 119–26; Hutton, *Phil Sheridan and His Army*, 75–110; and Brill, *Conquest of the Southern Plains*, 183–248. For succeeding events leading to the 1874 Red River War involving the Cheyennes and other tribes, and for the war itself, see Leckie, *Military Conquest of the Southern Plains*, 133–235; Haley, *Buffalo War*; and Monnett, *Massacre at Cheyenne Hole*.

CHAPTER 9. CONTROVERSIES

1. The post-engagement experiences of the Black Kettle village refugees must have been similar to those following the Sand Creek Massacre, though the physical magnitude of Chivington's strike greatly outweighed that at the Washita. George Bent expressed little about the direct Washita aftermath among the Cheyennes, perhaps because he had not been there. Hyde, *Life of George Bent*, 324 ff. Neither Powell, *People of the Sacred Mountain*, nor Berthrong, *Southern Cheyennes*, contains much information regarding the post-Washita experience, suggesting that this phase of Southern Cheyenne history was never adequately recorded. That the people's immediate condition was poor is indicated in the following missive in which scouts had expressed that the Cheyennes were "in mourning for their losses, their people starving, their ponies dying, their dogs all eaten up, and no buffalo. . . . They are in a bad fix." Sheridan to AAG, Division of the Missouri, Jan. 1, 1869, Philip H. Sheridan Papers, LC, Roll 76.

2. Custer's report, Nov. 28, 1868, reproduced in Senate, *Letter of the Secretary of the Interior*, 25, 29. See Sheridan to Sherman, Dec. 2, 1868, in ibid., 40; and Sheridan's report, Nov. 1, 1869, in *Report of the Secretary of War, 1869*, 48 (in which the general justifies the Washita attack). See also Custer, *My Life on the Plains*, 241–71; and Sheridan, *Personal Memoirs*, 2:313–31. Yet Keim's book, published in 1885, still contains mention of the two white boys and the murder of the woman and child. *Sheridan's Troopers*, 119. And Elizabeth B. Custer, in quoting her husband's 1868 report of the Washita engagement, included the references in her 1890 publication, *Following the Guidon*, 40.

3. See, for example, Spotts, *Campaigning with Custer*, 75–76; Mathey, "Washita Campaign," 40; Ryan, *Ten Years*, 56; and Keim, *Sheridan's Troopers*, 119.

4. *Kansas City Star*, Dec. 4, 1904. See also Clark's account, *New York Sun*, May 14, 1899 (in which he recounted the incident, stating that "the sharpshooters mistook the child for a white captive"). Clark's interview with Walter M. Camp took place on October 22, 1910, and is presented, along with the *Star* account, in Foley, "Walter Camp & Ben Clark," 21, 23. Beyond the notation included in his report of November 28, 1868, for Custer's description of the incident, see *My Life on the Plains*, 243–44.

5. This perception seems to have been most common among the Kansas volunteers, perhaps because they were not present and thus did not precisely comprehend the configuration of the Washita action. See, for example, George B. Jenness, "History of the 19th Kansas Cavalry," n.d., Manuscripts Division, Kansas State Historical Society, Topeka; Moore, "Nineteenth Kansas Cavalry in the Washita Campaign," 358; Moore's account, *Kansas City Times*, May 31, 1939; Crawford, *Kansas in the Sixties*, 325; Hadley, "Nineteenth Kansas Cavalry," 444–45; and W. R. Smith, letter, *The National Tribune*, Mar. 26, 1925.

6. *New York Herald*, Jan. 4, 1869 (reprinted in Keim, *Sheridan's Troopers*, 150); Custer, *My Life on the Plains*, 290; Sheridan, *Personal Memoirs*, 2:330–31. Ben Clark believed the Blinns were found at the site of the former Arapaho camp. Clark to Barde, May 1, 1903, Fred S. Barde Collection, Archives and Manuscripts Division, Oklahoma Historical Society, Oklahoma City; Foley, "Walter Camp & Ben Clark," 21.

7. Justus, "Saga of Clara H. Blinn," 13; "Semi-Weekly Report No. 1. Summary of information relating to Indians," Nov. 22, 1868, "Reports of Officers in the West and Southwest, 1874–75 [sic]," Military Division of the Missouri Papers, Manuscript Division, U.S. Army Military History Institute, Army War College, Carlisle Barracks, Pa.; "Semi-Weekly Report No. 2. Summary of Information regarding hostile Indians," Nov. 26, 1868, ibid. Blinn did not refer to White and Morgan in her letter, suggesting that these women were kept together in another village.

8. Sheridan to Sherman, Jan. 1, 1869, in U.S. House, *Difficulties with Indian Tribes*, 41st Cong., 2d sess., 1869, H. Exec. Doc. 240, 242; *Report of the Secretary of War*, 1869, 48; Barnett, *Touched by Fire*, 163–64. The disposition and present location of the ledger book, if it still exists, has not been determined.

9. *(St. Louis) Missouri Democrat*, Feb. 9, 1869. The sarcasm-laden letter is reproduced in Graham, *Custer Myth*, 212–13. The Custer-Benteen confrontation is described by Benteen in Carroll, *Benteen-Goldin Letters*, 266–27. See also Bates, *Custer's Indian Battles*, 15–16. Ben Clark claimed that Benteen had approached him within days of the engagement, when it was believed that Elliott and his followers had been killed, "and asked me if I would be willing to make the statement that Custer knowingly let Elliott go to his doom without trying to save him. I refused to have anything to do with the matter." *New York Sun*, May 14, 1899.

10. Custer did not discuss aspects of the loss of Elliott and his men in his report of Nov. 28, 1868. See Senate, *Letter of the Secretary of the Interior*, 26. His brief account of Elliott's disappearance and presumed demise is in Custer, *My Life on the Plains*, 246–47, 257–58. His quoted remarks from Sheridan's report respecting Elliott's fight are in ibid., 286–89. Sheridan wrote that Custer's theory was "that Elliott and his men had strayed off on account of having no guide, and would ultimately come in all right to Camp Supply or make their way back to Fort Dodge." *Personal Memoirs*, 2:320. Ben Clark, who was present at the Washita, stated years later: "the charge was made against Custer in after years that he gave the order which led Elliott to his death and then abandoned him to his fate. This accusation was false. Custer knew nothing of Elliott's going. Half an hour after Elliott and his men rode away Custer came up and asked me what had become of Elliott." *New York Sun*, May 14, 1899.

11. On this divisive issue, see Utley, *Cavalier in Buckskin*, 75–76; and Barnett, *Touched by Fire*, 160–63. This controversy, along with others stemming from the Washita action, is discussed at length in Watson and Russell, "Battle of the Washita," passim.

12. *Webster's New Collegiate Dictionary, Based on Webster's New International Dictionary*, 2d ed. (Springfield, Mass.: G. and C. Merriam, 1959), 74; Wilhelm, *Military Dictionary*, 52. Further exposition of the concept of "offensive battle" appears in Farrow, *Military Encyclopedia*, 2:432–33.

13. *The American Heritage College Dictionary*, 3d ed. (New York: Houghton Mifflin, 2000), 835; Wilhelm, *Military Dictionary*, 310. "Indiscriminate" means "not discriminate; showing lack of discrimination or distinction." Synonyms include "wholesale" and "sweeping," meaning "including all within the range of choice or operation." *Webster's New Collegiate Dictionary*, 425.

14. Quoted in Keim, *Sheridan's Troopers*, 103.

15. For discussion of the convergence, or encirclement, tactic, see Jamieson, *Crossing the Deadly Ground*, 44–46. Beyond Washita, the army used similar tactics (with varying elements as well as levels of success) in attacking Indian villages at Blue Water Creek, Neb., September 3, 1855; Summit Springs, Colo., July 11, 1869; McClellan Creek, Tex., September 29, 1872; Snake Mountain, Wyo. Terr., July 4, 1874; Powder River, Wyo. Terr., March 17, 1876; Slim Buttes, Dak. Terr., September 9, 1876; Red Fork of Powder River, Wyo. Terr., November 25, 1876; Muddy Creek, Mont. Terr., May 7, 1877; Big Hole, Mont. Terr., August 9, 1877; and Bear's Paw Mountains, Mont. Terr., September 30, 1877. It is likely too that the tactics were to have been employed at the Little Bighorn on June 25, 1876.

16. Custer's report, Nov. 28, 1868, in Senate, *Letter of the Secretary of the Interior*, 26; Edward S. Godfrey, interview by Walter M. Camp, Mar. 3, 1917, Box 3, Walter M. Camp Papers, BYU, microfilm; Custer, *My Life on the Plains*, 244; *New York Sun*, May 14, 1899; *Kansas City Star*, Dec. 4, 1904; Clark letter, *Overland Monthly*, Nov. 1909; Foley, "Walter Camp & Ben Clark," 22; Brill, *Conquest of the Southern Plains*, 156–57. Clark told Walter Camp: "No women were killed by soldiers in cold blood. Some were killed unavoidably. The Osage Indians killed some before they were stopped." Foley, "Walter Camp & Ben Clark," 20. Custer claimed to have admonished his men against killing noncombatants, with the caveat that in hand-to-hand fighting, women and youths might present as formidable adversaries as the warriors. *My Life on the Plains*, 241. In describing Romero's mission, Custer wrote, "it was difficult to convince the squaws and children that they had anything but death to expect at our hands." Custer, *My Life on the Plains*, 244. The order against killing noncombatants apparently was common knowledge in the weeks after the assault. Private Spotts noted in his diary that he had learned that "many of the squaws and children escaped during the fight because the orders were to spare the women and children." *Campaigning with Custer*, 75.

In addition, the number of fatalities at the Washita has never been authoritatively determined. While Custer claimed that his command had killed 103 warriors (later revised, reportedly according to information acquired from the Indians, to 140 total Indians killed), the Cheyennes themselves, in fact, offered figures that were mere fractions of the army's number, registering, on average,

12 men killed and 20 women and children killed, a total fatality figure of about 32 people from among approximately 250 present when the attack commenced. Adding in the 53 prisoners, it appears that about 165 villagers, many doubtless wounded or otherwise injured, managed to escape the onslaught and flee to the downriver camps. (The calculation of fatalities is based on casualty figures presented in chapter 7. See appendix B for a presentation accounting for at least 58 Cheyennes killed.)

17. For scalping on the part of the Osages, see Custer's report, Nov. 28, 1868, in Senate, *Letter of the Secretary of the Interior*, 25 (charging the Osages with taking the scalp of Black Kettle). See also *New York Herald*, Dec. 24, 1868; Custer, *My Life on the Plains*, 256; and *New York Sun*, May 14, 1899. For the whipping of women fleeing the village, see Brill, *Conquest of the Southern Plains*, 156–57; and Powell, *People of the Sacred Mountain*, 1:606. For instances of army scalping, see Custer, *My Life on the Plains*, 256–57; and Ryan, *Ten Years*, 53–54.

18. A modern study that analyzes Sand Creek and Washita relative to the existing Laws of War (promulgated throughout the army in General Orders No. 100, as issued in April 1863) concludes that the former affair was indeed a violation of those principles but that, within the context of its time, the Washita attack was justified. See Veggeberg, "Laws of War on the American Frontier." For Darwinian views regarding Indians, see Fritz, *Movement for Indian Assimilation*, 114, 123–24.

19. Several true massacres occurred during the course of army-Indian relations in the trans-Mississippi West and influenced the course of Indian-white relations on the frontier during the last half of the nineteenth century. One, of course, was Sand Creek, a clearly premeditated and indisputable human catastrophe in which at least 150 Cheyennes and Arapahos were killed. The others were the premeditated Bear River Massacre of Northwestern Shoshone Indians on January 19, 1863, in which at least 250 tribesmen perished; the Marias River Massacre (the so-called Baker Battle) of January 23, 1870, wherein troops assailed a camp of Piegan Indians in northwestern Montana Territory, leaving 173 people dead; and the Wounded Knee Massacre of December 29, 1890, resulting from an escalating confrontation between troops and Lakotas on the Pine Ridge Reservation in South Dakota in which Indian fatalities numbered at least 250. Fatality figures for these encounters are from *Bear River Massacre Site*, 16; *Reconnaissance Survey of Indian–U.S. Army Battlefields*, 85; and Jensen, Paul, and Carter, *Eyewitness at Wounded Knee*, 20.

20. Custer's purposeful application at Little Bighorn of tactics employed at the Washita seems to have dominated the contemporary (1876) opinion among officers of the regiment in the immediate wake of that disaster. See, for example, Garlington, *Narrative*, 9.

21. Marquis, *She Watched Custer's Last Battle*, 8.

Appendix A

1. H. C. Hackbusch, survey field notes, June 1873, Survey Record Books, Roger Mills County Courthouse, Cheyenne, Okla.; 1873 survey map, Oklahoma

Department of Libraries, Oklahoma City; Berthrong, *Cheyenne and Arapaho Ordeal*, 91–181.

2. The pile was rebuilt once by a Seventh Cavalry officer, Second Lieutenant Allyn K. Capron, whose sudden death in combat as a "Rough Rider" under Colonel Theodore Roosevelt during the Santiago Campaign in 1898 drew widespread media attention.

3. Thoburn to Scott, Apr. 3, 1918, 86.01, File 11, Box 33, WA-3, Joseph B. Thoburn Papers, Archives and Manuscripts Division, Oklahoma Historical Society, Oklahoma City. For a view of the slab, sans surrounding stones and skulls, as relocated on the hill, see *Kansas City Star*, Dec. 4, 1904.

4. *The Cheyenne Star*, Dec. 5, 1930, July 21, 1932, Jan. 19, 1933. See also Casady, *Once Every Five Years*, 70. Late in 1930 Congressman James V. McClintic introduced a bill in the House of Representatives seeking an appropriation of ten thousand dollars to erect a monument "to honor Chief Black Kettle and all American soldiers who died in the battle." *The Cheyenne Star*, Dec. 11, 1930.

5. *The Cheyenne Star*, Oct. 21, 1965; Casady, *Once Every Five Years*, 136; Thetford, "Battle of the Washita Centennial," 360. See the account of Lawrence Hart, a Cheyenne tribal participant in the centennial observance, in Warde, "Final Report on Cooperative Agreement 1443CA125098002 Modification 1, Conduct Oral History Research for Washita Historical Site, Sept. 30, 1999," 9–11. This overview of monument construction is drawn from the following sources: *New York Sun*, May 14, 1899; Hornbeck, "Battle of the Washita," 30, 31, 34; Scott, *Some Memories of a Soldier*, 153; Barnitz to Thoburn, Nov. 16, 1910, 86.01, File 11, Box 33, WA-2, Thoburn Papers; Scott to Walter M. Camp, Dec. 4, 1910, Folder 15, Box 1, Walter M. Camp Papers, BYU; W. Scott Samuel to Colonel Campbell, Feb. 8, 1918, 86.01, File 11, Box 33, WA-2, Thoburn Papers; Thoburn to Godfrey, Sept. 20, 1918, ibid.; Godfrey to Thoburn, Sept. 24, 1918, ibid.; *The Daily Oklahoman*, July 27, 1930; clipping from an unidentified newspaper, Nov. 26, 1930, Lee Harkins Collection, Archives and Manuscripts Division, Oklahoma Historical Society, Oklahoma City; Van Zandt, "Battle of the Washita, Revisited," 57–65; and *The (Woodward, Okla.) Daily Press*, Nov. 13, 1968. The National Park Service tract comprises the north half of Section 12, Township 13 North, Range 23 West, Indian Prime Meridian.

6. Public Law 104-333, 104th Cong., 2d sess. (Nov. 12, 1996).

7. *New York Sun*, May 14, 1899; *Kansas City Star*, Dec. 4, 1904.

8. Barde map, [ca. 1900], 82.80, Box 42, "No. 3" (oversized), Fred S. Barde Collection, Archives and Manuscripts Division, Oklahoma Historical Society, Oklahoma City. This map, superimposed on a section map, shows successively refined pencil drawings of the loop where the village was situated, together with other encounter-related landscape features as they existed around 1900.

9. Camp to Barnitz, n.d. [ca. Oct.–Nov. 1910], quoted in Barnitz to Thoburn, Nov. 16, 1910, BA. I.C. .948 File Box 86.01, Thoburn Papers; Ben Clark, interview notes, 1910, Walter M. Camp Manuscripts, Lilly Library, Indiana University, Bloomington. See Ben Clark map, 1897, Hugh L. Scott Papers, LC. See Cowley, *Cultural Landscape Inventory*, 60; and Haynes, "Late Quaternary Geology of the Washita Battlefield," 3.

10. Rush, "What Indian Tongues Could Tell," 13 (map) [hereafter cited as Rush map]; Brill, *Conquest of the Southern Plains,* 132.

11. *Kansas City Star,* Dec. 4, 1904; Rush map.

12. *Kansas City Star,* Dec. 4, 1904; Clark, interview notes.

13. Godfrey, "Reminiscences, Including the Washita Battle," 490; *New York Sun,* May 14, 1899; *Kansas City Star,* Dec. 4, 1904; Ben Clark, interview by Walter M. Camp, Oct. 22, 1910, Camp Manuscripts; Clark map, 1897; Rush map; sketch map, enclosed in Clark to Mr. Burnett, July 7, 1913, Hist 129, Box 1, Manuscripts Division, Kansas State Historical Society, Topeka; Lees et al., "Archaeology of the Washita Battlefield National Historic Site," 18–19.

14. *New York Sun,* May 14, 1899; Foley, "Walter Camp & Ben Clark," 22–23; Barnitz and Barnitz, *Life in Custer's Cavalry,* 219. For a map drawn by Captain Barnitz showing part of what must be a speculative route for Thompson's approach, see ibid., 217.

15. *Kansas City Star,* Dec. 4, 1904; Foley, "Walter Camp & Ben Clark," 23; Barnitz and Barnitz, *Life in Custer's Cavalry,* 219.

16. Foley, "Walter Camp & Ben Clark," 22; Albert Barnitz, interview by Walter M. Camp, Dec. 5, 1910, Camp Manuscripts; Barnitz and Barnitz, *Life in Custer's Cavalry,* 219–20, 223–25 (map, 217).

17. Camp to Barnitz, n.d., [ca. Oct.–Nov. 1910], quoted in Barnitz to Thoburn, Nov. 16, 1910, Thoburn Papers; Barnitz interview, Dec. 5, 1910; Lees et al., "Archaeology of the Washita Battlefield National Historic Site," 18. Clark took compass readings from a position on Custer's command knoll and reported that Sugar Loaf was fifteen degrees west of north. Barnitz interview, Dec. 5, 1910. See also Barnitz and Barnitz, *Life in Custer's Cavalry,* 217 (map).

18. Clark stated that Custer "rode straight to a little knoll that overlooks the village on the south, and from that point issued many of his orders. On this knoll stands the brown sandstone marker which Captain [sic] Scott of Fort Sill erected several years ago." *Kansas City Star,* Dec. 4, 1904; Clark interview, Oct. 22, 1910; Clark map, 1897 (showing presumed location of command knoll); Barde map, [ca. 1900]; Lees et al., "Archaeology of the Washita Battlefield National Historic Site," 19, citing Betty Wesner, interview by Bob Duke, Cheyenne, Okla., spring 1996. Barde's map indicates that Custer occupied a point beneath the high embankment in the northwest quarter of Section 12 as his headquarters.

19. Barnitz to Walter M. Camp, Nov. 29, 1910, Folder 14, Box 1, Camp Papers, Roll 1; Edward S. Godfrey, "Notes on Chapter XXII of Colonel Homer Wheeler's 'Buffalo Days,'" Accounts Written or Annotated by E. S. Godfrey Sr., Box 16, Godfrey Family Papers Indian Wars, Manuscript Division, U.S. Army Military History Institute, Army War College, Carlisle Barracks, Pa. Ben Clark, however, perhaps mistakenly, placed Hamilton much closer to Barnitz's and Elliott's position. Clark map, 1897; *Kansas City Star,* Dec. 4, 1904.

20. Lees et al., "Archaeology of the Washita Battlefield National Historic Site," 20–21.

21. Clark map, 1897; *Kansas City Star,* Dec. 4, 1904.

22. Rush map; Brill, *Conquest of the Southern Plains,* 161–63, 303–5; Powell, *People of the Sacred Mountain,* 1:606–7.

23. *Kansas City Star*, Dec. 4, 1904; Rush map; Foley, "Walter Camp & Ben Clark," 20; Rush map.

24. Godfrey, "Reminiscences, Including the Washita Battle," 492; Lees et al., "Archaeology of the Washita Battlefield National Historic Site," 21–22.

25. Clark map, 1897; *New York Sun*, May 14, 1899; Foley, "Walter Camp & Ben Clark," 20.

26. See Lees et al., "Archaeology of the Washita Battlefield National Historic Site," 48–49; Lees, "Archaeological Evidence," 36–37, 39.

27. Clark map, 1897; *Kansas City Star*, Dec. 4, 1904; Foley, "Walter Camp & Ben Clark," 20.

28. Bell to Camp, July 28, 1911, Folder 19, Box 1, Camp Papers, Roll 1; Barnitz to Joseph B. Thoburn, Oct. 29, 1910, BA-1B Thoburn, 947, 86.01, Thoburn Papers; Edward S. Godfrey, interview by Walter M. Camp, Mar. 3, 1917, Box 3, Camp Papers, microfilm; Camp to Godfrey, Nov. 13, 1919, Edward S. Godfrey Collection, LC; Lees et al., "Archaeology of the Washita Battlefield National Historic Site," 21.

29. Keim, *Sheridan's Troopers*, 144; Clark map, 1897; Clark interview, Oct. 22, 1910, Camp Manuscripts; *New York Sun*, May 14, 1899; Custer, *My Life on the Plains*, 249; Barde map, [ca. 1900]; Lees et al., "Archaeology of the Washita Battlefield National Historic Site," 48–49. Ben Clark pointed out that the "Bluff where shot ponies right near and NE of Mr. W. T. Bonner's house. It rises at south edge of that piece of land on which village stood. . . . To bluff where horses shot 105 degrees W. Of N. Or 74 degrees W. Of S. To center of village." Clark interview. Although many horse bones had previously been removed from the site, in 1933 there were still "bones of every description. Skulls, legs, vertebrae, every kind of bone known to a horse was present." Van Zandt, "Battle of the Washita, Revisited," 65.

30. Rush map; Lees et al., "Archaeology of the Washita Battlefield National Historic Site," 24–25. Barde map, [ca. 1900], contains the notation that Elliott's men were killed in the southeast quarter of Section 7, an unlikely place given that these soldiers had crossed east of Sergeant Major Creek. It is possible that Barde meant the designated place to be that where Kennedy had been killed, an altogether feasible location.

31. Rush map.

32. For descriptions and/or plattings of the areas where the deaths of Elliott's party took place, see Barde map, [ca. 1900], sheet 2; Rush map; Lees, et al., "Archaeology of the Washita Battlefield National Historic Site," 24–25. See also note 29 above. Ben Clark placed the site of Elliott's demise in the southeast quarter of Section 5, which is actually north of the Washita. Foley, "Walter Camp & Ben Clark," 22. A Spencer cartridge casing was found on the east side of Sergeant Major Creek approximately a quarter mile south of the site specified in the Indian accounts. Lees et al., "Archaeology of the Washita Battlefield National Historic Site," 48.

33. *Kansas City Star*, Dec. 4, 1904. A bold mark in the southeastern part of the river loop on Ben Clark's 1897 map possibly represents the location of Scott's monument.

BIBLIOGRAPHY

MANUSCRIPTS

1930s Federal Writers' Project. Archives and Manuscripts Division. Oklahoma Historical Society. Oklahoma City.

Barde, Fred S. Collection. Archives and Manuscripts Division. Oklahoma Historical Society. Oklahoma City.

Barnitz, Albert. Papers. Archives and Manuscripts Division. Oklahoma Historical Society. Oklahoma City.

Bent, George. Manuscripts. Samuel Tappan Papers. Colorado Historical Society, Denver.

Bent-Hyde Correspondence. Charles F. Bates Papers. Coe Collection. Beinecke Rare Book and Manuscript Library. Yale University, New Haven, Connecticut.

Camp, Walter M. Manuscripts. Manuscripts Department, Lilly Library. Indiana University, Bloomington.

———. Papers. Brigham Young University Library, Provo, Utah.

Campbell, Walter S. Collection. Western History Collections. University of Oklahoma Library, Norman.

Clark, Ben. Collection. Western History Collections. University of Oklahoma Library, Norman.

Duke, Doris. Oral History Collection. University of Oklahoma Indian Institute, Norman.

Ghent, William J. Papers. Manuscripts Division. Library of Congress, Washington, D.C.

Godfrey, Edward S. Papers. Manuscripts Division. Library of Congress, Washington, D.C.

Godfrey Family Papers Indian Wars. Military Division of the Missouri Papers. Manuscript Division, Army War College. U.S. Army Military History Institute, Carlisle, Pennsylvania.

Grinnell, George Bird. Papers. Braun Research Library. Southwest Museum, Los Angeles, California.

Hackbusch, H. C. Survey field notes, June 1873. Survey Record Books. Roger Mills County Courthouse, Cheyenne, Oklahoma.

Jenness, George B. "History of the 19th Kansas Cavalry," n.d. Manuscripts Division. Kansas State Historical Society, Topeka.

Myrick, Herbert. Collection. The Huntington Library. San Marino, California.

Page, John H. "Reminiscences of Indian Wars in Kansas and Indian Territory, 1866 and 1871," ca. 1895–98. Old Guard Museum, Fort Myer, Virginia.

Record Group 77. Records of the Office of the Chief of Engineers. National Archives, Washington, D.C.

Record Group 92. Records of the Office of the Quartermaster General. National Archives, Washington, D.C.

Record Group 94. Records of the Adjutant General's Office. National Archives, Washington, D.C.

Record Group 112. Records of the Office of the Surgeon General. National Archives, Washington, D.C.

Record Group 393. Records of U.S. Army Continental Commands. National Archives, Washington, D.C.

Regimental Returns of the Seventh Cavalry. Kenneth Hammer Collection. Little Bighorn Battlefield National Monument, Crow Agency, Montana. Microfilm.

Ricker, Eli S. Collection. Manuscript Division. Nebraska State Historical Society, Lincoln.

Searcy, E. C. Collection. Western History Collections. University of Oklahoma Library, Norman.

Scott, Hugh L. Papers. Manuscripts Division. Library of Congress, Washington, D.C.

Sheridan, Philip H. Papers. Manuscripts Division. Library of Congress, Washington, D.C.

Sherman, William T. Papers. Manuscripts Division. Library of Congress, Washington, D.C.

Sipes, John L. Collection. Archives and Manuscripts Division. Oklahoma Historical Society. Oklahoma City.

Taylor, J. E. File. National Anthropological Archives. Smithsonian Institution, Washington, D.C.

Thoburn, Joseph B. Papers. Archives and Manuscripts Division. Oklahoma Historical Society. Oklahoma City.

GOVERNMENT PUBLICATIONS

Bear River Massacre Site: Final Special Resource Study and Environmental Assessment. Denver: National Park Service, 1996.

Cowley, Jill. *Cultural Landscape Inventory, Level Two, Washita Battlefield National Historic Site*. Santa Fe: National Park Service Intermountain Region, Santa Fe Support Office, 1999.

Kappler, Charles J., comp. and ed. *Indian Affairs. Laws and Treaties*. 2 vols. Washington, D.C.: Government Printing Office, 1904.

Office of the Surgeon General. *Circular No. 3*. Washington, D.C.: Government Printing Office, 1871.

Reconnaissance Survey of Indian–U.S. Army Battlefields of the Northern Plains. Denver: National Park Service, 1998.

Report of the Commissioner of Indian Affairs, 1849–50. Washington, D.C.: Government Printing Office, 1850.

Report of the Commissioner of Indian Affairs, 1865. Washington, D.C.: Government Printing Office, 1865.

Report of the Commissioner of Indian Affairs, 1866. Washington, D.C.: Government Printing Office, 1866.

Report of the Secretary of the Interior, 1869. Washington, D.C.: Government Printing Office, 1869.

Report of the Secretary of War, 1868. Washington, D.C.: Government Printing Office, 1869.

Report of the Secretary of War, 1869. Washington, D.C.: Government Printing Office, 1869.

Roll of the Officers and Enlisted Men of the Third, Fourth, Eighteenth, and Nineteenth Kansas Volunteers, 1861. Topeka: W. Y. Morgan, State Printer, 1902.

Thian, Raphael P., comp. *Notes Illustrating the Military Geography of the United States, 1813–1880*. Washington, D.C.: Government Printing Office, 1881. Reprint, Austin: University of Texas Press, 1979.

U.S. Senate. *Letter of the Secretary of the Interior, Communicating, in Compliance with the Resolution of the Senate of the 14th ultimo, Information in Relation to the Late Battle of the Washita River*. 40th Cong., 3d sess., 1869. S. Exec. Doc. 13.

————. *Letter of the Secretary of War, Communicating Copies of Reports upon Indian Affairs in the Military Division of the Missouri*. 40th Cong., 3d sess, 1869. S. Exec. Doc. 40.

————. *Report of the Joint Committee on the Conduct of the War, Massacre of the Cheyenne Indians*. 38th Cong., 2d sess., 1865. S. Rept. 142.

————. *Report of the Joint Special Committee. Condition of the Indian Tribes with Appendix (The Chivington Massacre)*. 39th Cong., 2d sess., 1867. S. Rept. 156.

————. *Report of the Secretary of War, Communicating . . . a Copy of the Evidence Taken at Denver and Fort Lyon, Colorado Territory by a Military Commission Ordered to Inquire into the Sand Creek Massacre, November 29, 1864*. 39th Cong., 2d sess., 1867. S. Exec. Doc. 26.

U.S. War Department. *The War of the Rebellion: A Compilation of the Official Records of the Union and Confederate Armies*. 73 vols. in 128 pts. Washington, D.C.: Government Printing Office, 1880–1901.

NEWSPAPERS

Army and Navy Journal. 1868. 1869.
Cheyenne Star. 1930. 1965.
Custer County Post-Dispatch. 1915–35.
Daily Oklahoman. 1914. 1925. 1929. 1930.
Harpers Weekly. 1869.
Kankakee Sunday Journal. 1952.
Kansas City Star. 1904.
Kansas City Times. 1908. 1939.
Mariposa Gazette. 1869.
Missouri Democrat. 1869.
National Tribune. 1901. 1925.
New York Daily Tribune. 1868.
New York Herald. 1868.
New York Sun. 1899.
New York Times. 1868. 1869.
New York Tribune. 1877.
St. Francis Herald. 1990.
St. Louis Republic. 1911.
St. Louis Democrat. 1869.
Sayre Record. Unknown date.
Watonga Republican. 1997.
Winners of the West. 1925.
(Woodward, Okla.) Daily Press. 1968.

BOOKS

Afton, Jean; David F. Halaas; Andrew E. Masich; and Richard N. Ellis. *Cheyenne Dog Soldiers: A Ledgerbook History of Coups and Combats.* Boulder: University Press of Colorado, 1997.
The American Annual Cyclopaedia and Register of Important Events of the Year 1868. New York: D. Appleton, 1870.
The American Heritage College Dictionary. 3d ed. New York: Houghton Mifflin, 2000.
Athearn, Robert G. *William Tecumseh Sherman and the Settlement of the West.* Norman: University of Oklahoma Press, 1956.
Barnard, Sandy. *Custer's First Sergeant John Ryan.* Terre Haute, Ind.: AST, 1996.
Barnett, Louise. *Touched by Fire: The Life, Death, and Mythic Afterlife of George Armstrong Custer.* New York: Henry Holt, 1996.
Barnitz, Albert, and Jennie Barnitz. *Life in Custer's Cavalry: Diaries and Letters of Albert and Jennie Barnitz, 1867–1868.* Edited by Robert M. Utley. New Haven: Yale University Press, 1977.
Bates, Charles Francis. *Custer's Indian Battles.* Bronxville, N.Y.: Privately published, 1936.
Baughman, Robert W. *Kansas in Maps.* Topeka: Kansas State Historical Society, 1961.

Beck, Warren A., and Ynez D. Haase. *Historical Atlas of the American West.* Norman: University of Oklahoma Press, 1989.

Berthrong, Donald J. *The Cheyenne and Arapaho Ordeal.* Norman: University of Oklahoma Press, 1976.

———. *The Southern Cheyennes.* Norman: University of Oklahoma Press, 1963.

Brady, Cyrus Townsend. *Indian Fights and Fighters.* New York: Doubleday, Page, 1904.

Brill, Charles J. *Conquest of the Southern Plains.* Oklahoma City: Golden Saga, 1938.

Burkey, Blaine. *Custer, Come at Once! The Fort Hays Years of George and Elizabeth Custer, 1867–1870.* Hays, Kans.: Society of Friends of Historic Fort Hays, 1976.

Burns, Louis F. *A History of the Osage People.* Fallbrook, Calif.: Ciga, 1989.

Carriker, Robert C. *Fort Supply, Indian Territory: Frontier Outpost on the Plains.* Norman: University of Oklahoma Press, 1970.

Carroll, John M., comp. *The Sand Creek Massacre: A Documentary History.* New York: Sol Lewis, 1973.

———, comp. *Washita!* Bryan, Tex.: Privately printed, 1978.

———, ed. *The Benteen-Goldin Letters on Custer and His Last Battle.* New York: Liveright, 1974.

Carroll, John M., and Byron Price, comps. *Roll Call on the Little Big Horn, 28 June 1876.* Fort Collins, Colo.: Old Army, 1974.

Casady, Kline E. *Once Every Five Years.* Oklahoma City, 1974.

Chalfant, William Y. *Cheyennes and Horse Soldiers: The 1857 Expedition and the Battle of Solomon's Fork.* Norman: University of Oklahoma Press, 1989.

Chandler, Melbourne C., comp. *Of Garry Owen in Glory: The History of the Seventh United States Cavalry Regiment.* Annandale, Va.: Turnpike, 1960.

Coffman, Edward M. *The Old Army: A Portrait of the American Army in Peacetime, 1784–1898.* New York: Oxford University Press, 1986.

Crawford, Samuel J. *Kansas in the Sixties.* Chicago: A. C. McClurg, 1911.

Custer, George A. *My Life on the Plains; or, Personal Experiences with Indians.* Norman: University of Oklahoma Press, 1963.

Custer, Elizabeth B. *Following the Guidon.* New York: Harper and Brothers, 1890.

Dixon, David. *Hero of Beecher Island: The Life and Military Career of George A. Forsyth.* Lincoln: University of Nebraska Press, 1994.

Farrow, Edward S. *Farrow's Military Encyclopedia: A Dictionary of Military Knowledge.* Rev. ed. 3 vols. New York: Military-Naval, 1895.

Fenneman, Nevin M. *Physiography of Western United States.* New York: McGraw-Hill, 1931.

Foner, Jack D. *The United States Soldier between Two Wars: Army Life and Reforms, 1865–1898.* New York: Humanities, 1970.

Fritz, Henry E. *The Movement for Indian Assimilation, 1860–1890.* Philadelphia: University of Pennsylvania Press, 1963.

Frost, Lawrence A. *The Court-Martial of General George Armstrong Custer.* Norman: University of Oklahoma Press, 1968.

Garlington, Ernest A. *The Lieutenant E. A. Garlington Narrative: Part I.* Edited by John M. Carroll. Bryan, Tex.: Privately printed, 1978.

Garretson, Martin S. *The American Bison.* New York: New York Zoological Society, 1938.

Graham, William A., ed. *The Custer Myth: A Source Book of Custeriana.* Harrisburg, Pa.: Stackpole, 1953.

Grinnell, George Bird. *The Cheyenne Indians.* 2 vols. New York: Cooper Square, 1923.

———. *The Fighting Cheyennes.* New York: Charles Scribner's Sons, 1915.

Haley, James L. *The Buffalo War: The History of the Red River Indian Uprising of 1874.* New York: Doubleday, 1976.

Hammer, Kenneth. *Biographies of the 7th Cavalry, June 25th 1876.* Fort Collins, Colo.: Old Army, 1972.

Heitman, Francis B., comp. *Historical Register and Dictionary of the United States Army, from Its Organization, September 29, 1789, to March 2, 1903.* 2 vols. Washington, D.C.: Government Printing Office, 1903.

Henry, Guy V. *Military Record of Civilian Appointments in the United States Army.* 2 vols. New York: Carleton, 1869.

Hoebel, E. Adamson. *The Cheyennes: Indians of the Great Plains.* New York: Holt, Rinehart, and Winston, 1960.

Hoig, Stan. *The Battle of the Washita: The Sheridan-Custer Indian Campaign of 1867–69.* Garden City, N.Y.: Doubleday, 1976.

———. *The Peace Chiefs of the Cheyennes.* Norman: University of Oklahoma Press, 1980.

———. *The Sand Creek Massacre.* Norman: University of Oklahoma Press, 1961.

———. *Tribal Wars of the Southern Plains.* Norman: University of Oklahoma Press, 1993.

Hornaday, William T. *The Extermination of the American Bison.* New York: New York Zoological Society, 1938.

Hoxie, Frederick E., ed. *Encyclopedia of North American Indians: Native American History, Culture, and Life from Paleo-Indians to the Present.* Boston: Houghton Mifflin, 1996.

Hunt, Charles B. *Natural Regions of the United States and Canada.* San Francisco: W. H. Freeman, 1974.

Hutton, Paul A. *Phil Sheridan and His Army.* Lincoln: University of Nebraska Press, 1985.

Hyde, George. *Life of George Bent Written from His Letters.* Edited by Savoie Lottinville. Norman: University of Oklahoma Press, 1968.

Jamieson, Perry D. *Crossing the Deadly Ground: United States Army Tactics, 1865–1899.* Tuscaloosa: University of Alabama Press, 1994.

Jensen, Richard E.; R. Eli Paul; and John E. Carter. *Eyewitness at Wounded Knee.* Lincoln: University of Nebraska Press, 1991.

Jones, Douglas C. *The Treaty of Medicine Lodge.* Norman: University of Oklahoma Press, 1966.

Josephy, Alvin M. *The Civil War in the American West.* New York: Alfred A. Knopf, 1991.

Keim, DeB. Randolph. *Sheridan's Troopers on the Borders: A Winter Campaign on the Plains*. 1870. Reprint, Williamstown, Mass.: Corner House, 1973.

Kraenzel, Carl Frederick. *The Great Plains in Transition*. Norman: University of Oklahoma Press, 1955.

Kraft, Louis. *Custer and the Cheyenne: George Armstrong Custer's Winter Campaign on the Southern Plains*. El Segundo, Calif.: Upton and Sons, 1995.

Kroeker, Marvin. *Great Plains Command: William B. Hazen in the Frontier West*. Norman: University of Oklahoma Press, 1976.

Leckie, Shirley A. *Elizabeth Bacon Custer and the Making of a Myth*. Norman: University of Oklahoma Press, 1993.

Leckie, William H. *The Buffalo Soldiers: A Narrative of the Negro Cavalry in the West*. Norman: University of Oklahoma Press, 1967.

———. *The Military Conquest of the Southern Plains*. Norman: University of Oklahoma Press, 1963.

Liddic, Bruce R., and Paul Harbaugh, eds. *Camp on Custer: Transcribing the Custer Myth*. Spokane, Wash.: Arthur H. Clark, 1995.

Marquis, Thomas B. *She Watched Custer's Last Battle: Her Story, Interpreted in 1927*. Hardin, Mont.: Privately published, 1933.

Marshall, J. T. *The Miles Expedition of 1874–1875: An Eyewitness Account of the Red River War*. Edited by Lonnie J. White. Austin, Tex.: Encino, 1971.

Mathews, John Joseph. *The Osages: Children of the Middle Waters*. Norman: University of Oklahoma Press, 1961.

McChristian, Douglas C. *The U.S. Army in the West, 1870–1880: Uniforms, Weapons, and Equipment*. Norman: University of Oklahoma Press, 1995.

McGinnis, Anthony. *Counting Coup and Cutting Horses: Intertribal Warfare on the Northern Great Plains, 1738–1889*. Evergreen, Colo.: Cordillera, 1990.

McHugh, Tom. *The Time of the Buffalo*. New York: Alfred A. Knopf, 1972.

Mills, Charles K. *Harvest of Barren Regrets: The Army Career of Frederick William Benteen, 1834–1898*. Glendale, Calif.: Arthur H. Clark, 1985.

———, comp. *Rosters from 7th U.S. Cavalry Campaigns, 1866–1896*. Mattituck, N.J. and Bryan, Tex.: J. M. Carroll, 1983.

Milner, Joe E., and Earle R. Forrest. *California Joe, Noted Scout and Indian Fighter*. Caldwell, Idaho: Caxton, 1935.

Monaghan, Jay. *Custer: The Life of General George Armstrong Custer*. Boston: Houghton Mifflin, 1959.

Monnett, John H. *Massacre at Cheyenne Hole: Lieutenant Austin Henely and the Sappa Creek Controversy*. Niwot: University Press of Colorado, 1999.

———. *The Battle of Beecher Island and the Indian War of 1867–1869*. Niwot: University Press of Colorado, 1992.

Moore, John H. *The Cheyenne*. Cambridge, Mass.: Blackwell, 1996.

———. *The Cheyenne Nation: A Social and Demographic History*. Lincoln: University of Nebraska Press, 1987.

Nye, Wilbur S. *Carbine and Lance: The Story of Old Fort Sill*. 3d ed. rev. Norman: University of Oklahoma Press, 1969.

Owen, Roger C.; James J. F. Deetz; and Anthony D. Fisher, eds. *The North American Indians: A Sourcebook*. New York: Macmillan, 1967.

Portrait and Biographical Record of Oklahoma. Chicago: Chapman, 1901.

Powell, Peter J. *People of the Sacred Mountain: A History of the Northern Cheyenne Chiefs and Warrior Societies, 1830–1879, with an Epilogue, 1969–1974.* 2 vols. San Francisco: Harper and Row, 1981.

—————. *Sweet Medicine: The Continuing Role of the Sacred Arrows, the Sun Dance, and the Sacred Buffalo Hat in Northern Cheyenne History.* 2 vols. Norman: University of Oklahoma Press, 1969.

Pratt, Richard Henry. *Battlefield and Classroom: Four Decades with the American Indian, 1867–1904.* Edited by Robert M. Utley. New Haven: Yale University Press, 1964.

Proceedings of the Great Peace Commission of 1867–1868. Washington, D.C.: Institute for the Development of Indian Law, 1975.

Puckett, James L., and Ellen Puckett. *History of Oklahoma and Indian Territory and Homeseekers' Guide.* Vinita, Okla.: Chieftain, 1906.

Records of Living Officers of the United States Army. Philadelphia: L. R. Hamersly, 1884.

Rickey, Don, Jr. *Forty Miles a Day on Beans and Hay: The Enlisted Soldier Fighting the Indian Wars.* Norman: University of Oklahoma Press, 1963.

Rister, Carl Coke. *Border Command: General Phil Sheridan in the West.* Norman: University of Oklahoma Press, 1944.

Ryan, John M. *Ten Years with General Custer Among the American Indians.* Edited by John M. Carroll. Bryan, Tex.: Privately printed, n.d.

Scott, Hugh Lennox. *Some Memories of a Soldier.* New York: Century, 1928.

Sheridan, Philip H. *Personal Memoirs of P. H. Sheridan. General United States Army.* 2 vols. New York: Charles L. Webster, 1888.

Spotts, David L. *Campaigning with Custer and the Nineteenth Kansas Volunteer Cavalry on the Washita Campaign, 1868–1869.* Edited by Earl A. Brininstool. Los Angeles: Wetzel, 1928.

Stands in Timber, John, and Margot Liberty. *Cheyenne Memories.* New Haven: Yale University Press, 1967.

Sully, Langdon. *No Tears for the General: The Life of Alfred Sully, 1821–1879.* Palo Alto, Calif.: American West, 1974.

Thoburn, Joseph B. *Standard History of Oklahoma.* 2 vols. Chicago: American Historical Society, 1916.

Thornbury, William D. *Regional Geomorphology of the United States.* New York: John Wiley and Sons, 1965.

Thrapp, Dan L. *Encyclopedia of Frontier Biography.* 3 vols. Lincoln: University of Nebraska Press, 1988.

Trenholm, Virginia Cole. *The Arapahoes, Our People.* Norman: University of Oklahoma Press, 1970.

U.S. Army Gallantry and Meritorious Conduct, 1866–1891. Alexandria, Va.: Planchet, 1986.

Urwin, Gregory J. W. *Custer Victorious: The Civil War Battles of General George Armstrong Custer.* Rutherford, N.J.: Fairleigh Dickinson University Press, 1983.

—————. *The United States Cavalry: An Illustrated History.* Poole, Dorset, U.K.: Blandford, 1983.

Utley, Robert M. *Cavalier in Buckskin: George Armstrong Custer and the Western Military Frontier.* Norman: University of Oklahoma Press, 1988.

———. *Frontier Regulars: The United States Army and the Indian, 1866–1891.* New York: Macmillan, 1973.

———. *Frontiersmen in Blue: The United States Army and the Indian, 1848–1865.* New York: Macmillan, 1967.

Ware, Eugene F. *The Indian War of 1864.* New York: St. Martin's, 1960.

Warner, Ezra J. *Generals in Blue: Lives of the Union Commanders.* Baton Rouge: Louisiana State University Press, 1992.

Webb, Walter Prescott. *The Great Plains.* Boston: Ginn, 1931.

Webster's New Collegiate Dictionary, Based on Webster's New International Dictionary. 2d ed. Springfield, Mass.: G. and C. Merriam, 1959.

Wedel, Waldo R. *Prehistoric Man on the Great Plains.* Norman: University of Oklahoma Press, 1961.

Wert, Jeffry D. *Custer: The Controversial Life of George Armstrong Custer.* New York: Simon and Schuster, 1996.

Weslager, C. A. *The Delaware Indians: A History.* New Brunswick, N.J.: Rutgers University Press, 1972.

West, Elliott. *The Contested Plains: Indians, Goldseekers, and the Rush to Colorado.* Lawrence: University Press of Kansas, 1998.

Wilhelm, Thomas. *A Military Dictionary and Gazetteer.* Rev. ed. Philadelphia: L. R. Hamersly, 1881.

William, Thomas Benton. *The Soul of the Red Man.* Privately published, 1937.

Wooster, Robert. *The Military and United States Indian Policy, 1865–1903.* New Haven: Yale University Press, 1988.

Wynkoop, Edward W. *The Tall Chief: The Unfinished Autobiography of Edward W. Wynkoop, 1856–1866.* Edited by Christopher B. Gerboth. Denver: Colorado Historical Society, 1993.

ARTICLES

"A. L. Runyon's Letters from the 19th Kansas." *Kansas Historical Quarterly* 9 (February 1940): 58–75.

Brown, George W. "Life and Adventures of George W. Brown." Edited by William E. Connelley. *Collections of the Kansas State Historical Society* 17 (1928): 98–113.

Clark, Ben. Letter. *Overland Monthly*, November 1909, 532.

Despain, S. Matthew. "Captain Albert Barnitz and the Battle of the Washita: New Documents, New Insights." *Journal of the Indian Wars* 1 (spring 1999): 135–44.

Dixon, David. "Custer and the Sweetwater Hostages." In *Custer and His Times: Book Three,* edited by Gregory J. W. Urwin and Roberta Fagan, 82–108. Conway: University of Central Arkansas Press, 1987.

Drum, Richard C. "Reminiscences of the Indian Fight at Ash Hollow, 1855." *Collections of the Nebraska State Historical Society* 16 (1911): 143–51.

Ediger, Theodore A., and Vinnie Hoffman. "Some Reminiscences of the Battle of the Washita." *The Chronicles of Oklahoma* 33 (summer 1955): 137–41.

Foley, James R. "Walter Camp & Ben Clark." *Research Review: The Journal of the Little Big Horn Associates* 10 (January 1996): 17–27.

Gage, Duane. "Black Kettle: A Noble Savage?" *The Chronicles of Oklahoma* 45 (autumn 1967): 244–51.

Godfrey, Edward S. "Some Reminiscences, Including an Account of General Sully's Expedition against the Southern Plains Indians, 1868." *The Cavalry Journal* 36 (July 1927): 421–25.

———. "Some Reminiscences, Including the Washita Battle, November 27, 1868." *The Cavalry Journal* 37 (October 1928): 481–500.

Hadley, James A. "The Nineteenth Kansas Cavalry and the Conquest of the Plains Indians." *Transactions of the Kansas State Historical Society* 10 (1907–8): 428–56.

Harrison, Peter. "The Eyes of the Sleepers: Cheyenne Accounts of the Washita Attack." *The English Westerners' Society Brand Book* 31 (summer 1997): 1–24.

Harvey, Winfield Scott. "Campaigning with Sheridan: A Farrier's Diary." Edited by George H. Shirk. *The Chronicles of Oklahoma* 37 (spring 1959): 68–105.

Hazen, William B. "Some Corrections of 'Life on the Plains.'" *Chronicles of Oklahoma* 3 (December 1925): 295–318.

———. "Some Corrections of Life on the Plains." In *My Life on the Plains*, by George Armstrong Custer, 383–407. Norman: University of Oklahoma Press, 1962.

Hornbeck, Lewis N. "The Battle of the Washita." *Sturm's Oklahoma Magazine* 5 (January 1908): 30–34.

Hunt, Fred A. "The Subjugation of Black Kettle." *Overland Monthly*, n.s., 54 (July 1909): 104–7.

"In Memoriam: Brevet Major Louis McLane Hamilton Captain 7th U.S. Cavalry." *The Chronicles of Oklahoma* 46 (winter 1968–69): 362–86.

Isern, Thomas D. "The Controversial Career of Edward W. Wynkoop." *Colorado Magazine* 56 (winter–spring 1979): 1–18.

Jenness, George B. "Lost in the Snow at Old Camp Supply." *Sturm's Oklahoma Magazine* 5, no. 4 (n.d.): 52–57.

Justus, Judith P. "The Saga of Clara H. Blinn at the Battle of the Washita." *Research Review: The Journal of the Little Big Horn Associates* 14 (winter 2000): 11–20, 31.

Lees, William B. "Archaeological Evidence: The Attack on Black Kettle's Village on the Washita River." *Journal of the Indian Wars* 1 (spring 1999): 33–41.

Markantes, Charles G. "James E. Taylor, Artist & Correspondent." *Research Review: The Journal of the Little Big Horn Associates* 12 (winter 1998): 2–13.

Montgomery, Mrs. Frank C. "Fort Wallace and Its Relation to the Frontier." *Kansas Historical Collections* 17 (1926–28): 189–283.

Moore, Horace L. "The Nineteenth Kansas Cavalry in the Washita Campaign." *The Chronicles of Oklahoma* 2 (December 1924): 350–65.

Moore, John H.; Margot P. Liberty; and A. Terry Straus. "Cheyenne." In *Handbook of North American Indians*, edited by Raymond J. DeMallie. Vol. 13, *Plains*, 863–85. Washington, D.C.: Smithsonian Institution, 2001.

Munsall, C. S. "The 7th U.S. Cavalry at the Battle on the Washita." *Nebraska History* 7 (October–December 1924): 123–24.

Murphy, John. "Reminiscences of the Washita Campaign and of the Darlington Indian Agency." *Chronicles of Oklahoma* 1 (September 1923): 259–79.

Powers, Ramon. "The Northern Cheyenne Trek through Western Kansas in 1878: Frontiersmen, Indians, and Cultural Conflict." *The Trail Guide* 17 (September, December 1972): 1–35.

Rea, Bob. "The Washita Trail: The Seventh U.S. Cavalry's Route of March to and from the Battle of the Washita." *The Chronicles of Oklahoma* 76 (fall 1998): 244–61.

Rush, Frank. "What Indian Tongues Could Tell: The Red Man's Story of the Conquest of the Western Plains." *Wilds and Waters* 2 (December 1930): 11–13, 27, 34; 3 (January 1931): 11–13, 27, 34.

Shirk, George H. "The Journal of Private Johnson: A Fragment." *The Chronicles of Oklahoma* 44 (winter 1971): 437–50.

Shoemaker, Arthur. "Osage Scouts Helped George Armstrong Custer Track down Cheyenne Raiders on the Washita." *Wild West* 5 (June 1992): 10, 11, 71–73.

Tahan (Joseph K. Griffis). "The Battle of the Washita." *The Chronicles of Oklahoma* 8 (September 1930): 272–81.

Taylor, Morris F. "The Carr-Penrose Expedition: General Sheridan's Winter Campaign, 1868–1869." *The Chronicles of Oklahoma* 51 (summer 1973): 159–76.

Thetford, Francis. "Battle of the Washita Centennial, 1968." *The Chronicles of Oklahoma* 46 (winter 1968–69): 358–61.

Thoburn, Joseph B. "Names of Oklahoma Streams." *Sturm's Oklahoma Magazine* 11 (December 1910): 57–60.

Van Zandt, Howard F. "The Battle of the Washita, Revisited: A Journey to a Historic Site in 1933." *The Chronicles of Oklahoma* 62 (spring 1984): 56–69.

Watson, Elmo Scott, and Don Russell. "The Battle of the Washita, or Custer's Massacre?" *Chicago Westerners Brand Book* 5 (November 1948): 49–56; (December 1948): 1–4.

Wedel, Waldo R. "The Great Plains." In *Prehistoric Man in the New World*, edited by Jesse D. Jennings and Edward Norbeck, 193–220. Chicago: University of Chicago Press, 1964.

White, Lonnie J. "The Cheyenne Barrier on the Kansas Frontier, 1868–1869." *Arizona and the West* 4 (spring 1962): 51–64.

———. "General Sully's Expedition of the North Canadian, 1868." *Journal of the West* 11 (January 1972): 75–98.

———. "White Women Captives of the Southern Plains Indians, 1866–1875." *Journal of the West* 8 (July 1969): 327–54.

———. "Winter Campaigning with Sheridan and Custer: The Expedition of the Nineteenth Kansas Volunteer Cavalry." In *Hostiles and Horse Soldiers: Indian Battles and Campaigns in the West*, by Lonnie J. White, 89–118. Boulder, Col.: Pruett, 1972.

Wright, Robert M. "Reminiscences of Dodge." *Kansas Historical Collections* 9 (1905–6): 66–72.

OTHER SOURCES

Haynes, C. Vance. "Late Quaternary Geology of the Washita Battlefield: A Tentative Assessment." Report for Washita Battlefield National Historic Site, November 8, 1995.

Hal K. Rothman and Associates. "Historic Landscape Conditions and Use Study, Washita Battlefield National Historic Site." Draft report, 1999. Washita Battlefield National Historic Site, Cheyenne, Okla.

Lees, William B.; Douglas D. Scott; Bob Rea; and C. Vance Haynes. "Archeology of the Washita Battlefield National Historic Site." Draft document, October 31, 1997. Oklahoma Historical Society, Oklahoma City.

Mangum, Neil C., comp. "Inside Black Kettle's Village, Washita River, Nov. 27, 1868." National Park Service information sheet, n.d.

———. "Muster Roll 7th Cavalry, Washita Battle." Typescript, ca. 1995.

Rea, Bob. "Research: Original Stockade Location." Fort Supply Historic Site, Oklahoma, n.d.

Roberts, Gary L. "Sand Creek: Tragedy and Symbol." Ph.D. diss., University of Oklahoma, 1984.

Scott, Douglas D. "Firearms Identification of the Cartridge Cases from the Washita Battlefield." Report prepared for National Park Service Midwest Archeological Center, Lincoln, Neb., 1996.

Veggeberg, Vernon T. "Laws of War on the American Frontier: General Orders 100 and the Cheyenne-White Conflict." Master's thesis, Colorado State University, 1999.

Warde, Mary Jane. "Final Report on Cooperative Agreement 1443CA1250 98002 Modification 1, Conduct Oral History Research for Washita Historical Site." Report prepared for the National Park Service, 1999. Oklahoma Historical Society, Oklahoma City.

"Washita Battlefield." National Register of Historic Places Inventory Nomination Form. Washita Battlefield National Historic Site, Cheyenne, Okla., 1976.

INDEX